SHOULDER-BELT PLATES
AND BUTTONS

SHOULDER-BELT

PLATES

AND BUTTONS

MAJOR H. G. PARKYN, O.B.E.

The Naval & Military Press Ltd

Published by

The Naval & Military Press Ltd
Unit 10 Ridgewood Industrial Park,
Uckfield, East Sussex,
TN22 5QE England

Tel: +44 (0) 1825 749494
Fax: +44 (0) 1825 765701

www.naval-military-press.com
www.military-genealogy.com

In reprinting in facsimile from the original, any imperfections are inevitably reproduced and the quality may fall short of modern type and cartographic standards.

CONTENTS

	PAGE
INTRODUCTION	ix
THE SHOULDER-BELT PLATE	1
BUTTONS	3
THE HOUSEHOLD CAVALRY	7
1ST KING'S DRAGOON GUARDS	10
THE QUEEN'S BAYS (2ND DRAGOON GUARDS)	12
3RD CARABINIERS (PRINCE OF WALES'S DRAGOON GUARDS)	13
4TH/7TH ROYAL DRAGOON GUARDS	16
5TH ROYAL INNISKILLING DRAGOON GUARDS	19
1ST THE ROYAL DRAGOONS	22
THE ROYAL SCOTS GREYS (2ND DRAGOONS)	24
3RD THE KING'S OWN HUSSARS	27
4TH QUEEN'S OWN HUSSARS	29
7TH QUEEN'S OWN HUSSARS	31
8TH KING'S ROYAL IRISH HUSSARS	33
9TH QUEEN'S ROYAL LANCERS	34
10TH ROYAL HUSSARS (PRINCE OF WALES'S OWN)	36
11TH HUSSARS (PRINCE ALBERT'S OWN)	38
12TH ROYAL LANCERS (PRINCE OF WALES'S)	39
13TH/18TH ROYAL HUSSARS (QUEEN MARY'S OWN)	40
14TH/20TH KING'S HUSSARS	42
15TH/19TH THE KING'S ROYAL HUSSARS	45
16TH/5TH THE QUEEN'S ROYAL LANCERS	48
17TH/21ST LANCERS	51
THE ROYAL REGIMENT OF ARTILLERY	54
THE CORPS OF ROYAL ENGINEERS	58
GRENADIER GUARDS	60
COLDSTREAM GUARDS	63
SCOTS GUARDS	66
THE ROYAL SCOTS (THE ROYAL REGIMENT)	69
THE QUEEN'S ROYAL REGIMENT (WEST SURREY)	73
THE BUFFS (ROYAL EAST KENT REGIMENT)	77
THE KING'S OWN ROYAL REGIMENT (LANCASTER)	80
THE ROYAL NORTHUMBERLAND FUSILIERS	84
THE ROYAL WARWICKSHIRE REGIMENT	88
THE ROYAL FUSILIERS (CITY OF LONDON REGIMENT)	91
THE KING'S REGIMENT (LIVERPOOL)	94
THE ROYAL NORFOLK REGIMENT	97
THE ROYAL LINCOLNSHIRE REGIMENT	101

The Devonshire Regiment	104
The Suffolk Regiment	107
The Somerset Light Infantry (Prince Albert's)	110
The West Yorkshire Regiment (The Prince of Wales's Own)	113
The East Yorkshire Regiment (The Duke of York's Own)	116
The Bedfordshire and Hertfordshire Regiment	119
The Royal Leicestershire Regiment	122
The Royal Irish Regiment	125
The Green Howards (Alexandra, Princess of Wales's Own Yorkshire Regiment)	128
The Lancashire Fusiliers	131
The Royal Scots Fusiliers	134
The Cheshire Regiment	137
The Royal Welch Fusiliers	140
The South Wales Borderers	143
The King's Own Scottish Borderers	146
The Cameronians (Scottish Rifles)	149
The Royal Inniskilling Fusiliers	153
The Gloucestershire Regiment	157
The Worcestershire Regiment	161
The East Lancashire Regiment	166
The East Surrey Regiment	170
The Duke of Cornwall's Light Infantry	174
The Duke of Wellington's Regiment (West Riding)	178
The Border Regiment	182
The Royal Sussex Regiment	186
The Royal Hampshire Regiment	189
The South Staffordshire Regiment	193
The Dorset Regiment	197
The South Lancashire Regiment (The Prince of Wales's Volunteers)	201
The Welch Regiment	205
The Black Watch (Royal Highland Regiment)	209
The Oxfordshire and Buckinghamshire Light Infantry	215
The Essex Regiment	220
The Sherwood Foresters (Nottinghamshire and Derbyshire Regiment)	224
The Loyal Regiment (North Lancashire)	228
The Northamptonshire Regiment	232
The Royal Berkshire Regiment (Princess Charlotte of Wales's) ...	236
The Royal Marines	240
The Queen's Own Royal West Kent Regiment	243
The King's Own Yorkshire Light Infantry	247
The King's Shropshire Light Infantry	251
The Middlesex Regiment (Duke of Cambridge's Own)	255
The King's Royal Rifle Corps	259
The Wiltshire Regiment (The Duke of Edinburgh's)	263
The Manchester Regiment	267
The North Staffordshire Regiment (The Prince of Wales's)	272
The York and Lancaster Regiment	276
The Durham Light Infantry	280
The Highland Light Infantry (City of Glasgow Regiment)	283

SEAFORTH HIGHLANDERS (ROSS-SHIRE BUFFS, THE DUKE OF ALBANY'S)	... ...	288
THE GORDON HIGHLANDERS	... ...	292
THE QUEEN'S OWN CAMERON HIGHLANDERS	... ...	296
THE ROYAL ULSTER RIFLES	... ...	299
THE ROYAL IRISH FUSILIERS (PRINCESS VICTORIA'S)	... ...	302
THE CONNAUGHT RANGERS	... ...	307
THE ARGYLL AND SUTHERLAND HIGHLANDERS (PRINCESS LOUISE'S) ...	... ...	311
THE PRINCE OF WALES'S LEINSTER REGIMENT (ROYAL CANADIANS) ...	... ...	316
THE ROYAL MUNSTER FUSILIERS	... ...	319
THE ROYAL DUBLIN FUSILIERS	... ...	323
THE RIFLE BRIGADE (PRINCE CONSORT'S OWN)	... ...	327
THE ROYAL ARMY SERVICE CORPS	... ...	332
THE ROYAL ARMY MEDICAL CORPS	... ...	335
THE ROYAL ARMY ORDNANCE CORPS	... ...	337
APPENDIX. THE STANLEY COMMITTEE	... ...	339
BIBLIOGRAPHY	... ...	341

INTRODUCTION

THIS BOOK is an endeavour to place on record some of the many changes in the design of the shoulder-belt plates and buttons worn by the British Regular Army, but does not include badges and designs which have been shown only on standards and colours. The author well knows that it is not a complete list, and it is doubtful if it is possible to compile one. Nor is it possible in many cases to give actual dates on which the various plates and buttons came into use.

This work has only been made possible by the help and ready co-operation of a number of historians of British military uniform and of collectors of army badges; among the former must be mentioned the late Mr. P. W. Reynolds and the late Rev. P. Sumner, who helped very considerably during their lifetime.

Mr. L. E. Buckell is still doing research work of immense value and has always been willing to help with advice and information.

Among the many collectors who have helped with photographs or descriptions of items in their collection are Mr. A. R. Cattley, Mr. H. Y. Usher, who has made a special study of the north country regiments, Mr. W. F. Hughes, Mr. R. Tilling and Mr. C. C. P. Lawson.

The *Journal of the Society for Army Historical Research* has been a veritable mine of information; and thanks to the care taken over articles by the Honorary Editor, Mr. W. Y. Baldry, and the Honorary Secretary, Mr. A. S. White, the information could be relied on as being accurate.

Mr. A. S. White, the Chief Librarian at the War Office, has given me invaluable help, advice and encouragement in my effort. Not only has he allowed me to do research work in the War Office Library, but he has helped with his great knowledge on all points of British Army history.

Major Pereira, the curator of the Scottish United Services Museum, and his predecessor, the late Major I. Mackay Scobie, have given me much help with Scottish units. Major Pereira has also helped considerably by the *Journal of the Badge Collectors' Society*, of which he is Honorary Editor.

Valuable help and information has also been received from The Marquess of Cambridge; Mr. J. W. Firmin; Mr. A. W. Wheen, Keeper of Books at the Victoria and Albert Museum Library; Major D. A. Campbell, late R.A.;

Lieutenant-Colonel P. H. M. May, D.L.I.; Lieutenant-Colonel E. C. Phillipson-Stow and Major Salusbury Trelawny of the D.C.L.I.; Lieutenant-Colonel M. B. Savage, Lieutenant-Colonel P. Young, Colonel R. M. Grazebrook, Mr. R. Jones and the Library Staff of the R.U.S.I. and the Royal Irish Fusiliers.

The author also had the benefit of a long period of correspondeoce with the late Mr. William Calver, of New York, who gave him invaluable information concerning buttons which had been discovered in the old British camps in America.

Finally I must record my thanks to Mr. A. L. Kipling and Mr. N. Britton of the staff of Messrs. Gale and Polden for all their help, advice and patience in compiling this book.

THE SHOULDER-BELT PLATE

THERE DOES NOT APPEAR to be any actual order for the wearing of shoulder-belt plates. The custom of officers of Infantry Regiments wearing the sword belt over the right shoulder instead of round the waist came in during or a little before the American War of Independence; for other ranks it appears to have been a little later. It has been suggested that the custom originated from its being easier and quicker to sling the belt over the shoulder than round the waist under the waistcoat and coat. Inspection Reports of the 1st Foot dated 1777 state that men wore waist belts over the shoulder, while that of 1774 for the 3rd Buffs reads: "Clothing according to regulation except an additional shoulder strap on right shoulder for convenience of carrying the Waist Belt." At first the belt was worn with its original waist-belt clasp, but this was replaced by a plate of special design worn first as a clasp or buckle, but which soon became an ornament.

At the time of the introduction of shoulder-belt plates, few regiments had distinctive badges of their own, and even those that had did not always display them except on the Regimental Colour. The great majority of infantry regiments' plates had only the regimental number, which had been given to them in 1751, in conjunction with a wreath or spray of leaves which was frequently surmounted by a crown.

When in 1782 county titles were given to the infantry regiments, the title was often added to the plate, and in the case of the 48th Regiment with the design of the County arms.

In 1768 Horse and Light Dragoons were ordered to wear their sword belts over the right shoulder, but Dragoon Guards and Dragoons continued to wear them round the waist.

Comparatively few cavalry regiments seem to have had shoulder-belt plates and information about them is even harder to obtain than in the case of the infantry.

As a rule the actual plate was of metal of the same colour as the officers' lace, but as usual in the British Army there were exceptions.

The shape of the early plates was, generally, in a form of oval, a small oblong, or elliptical, but in most cases these were soon replaced by plates slightly larger and more oval in shape, which in turn gave way to slightly larger oblong plates with rounded corners. There is no actual date for these changes, but this last mentioned design of plate seems to have disappeared almost entirely by 1825 and to have been replaced by larger plates often with square-cut corners, which appear to have been used until about 1840. These plates gradually became larger and more decorative until, when finally abolished in 1855, they were in many cases of very fine workmanship and most elaborate in design, having in many cases been used as a means of displaying the various battle honours awarded to regiments after the conclusion of the Peninsular and Waterloo campaigns, a fact which caused many regiments to adopt larger plates.

In 1830 it was ordered that all Regular regiments were to have gold lace and not silver. This meant new plates for a number of regiments, although in several cases the old silver ones were retained in use for several years longer.

The beaded star which became popular in military badges was introduced about the same time.

The illustrations of the shoulder-belt plates and buttons have not been drawn to any standard scale: the object has been to show as many designs as possible of each regiment.

It would appear to be impossible to give any actual date for the various changes in the size of the officers' shoulder-belt plates; it was certainly regulated to a certain degree by the width of the belt, but the fancy of the makers entered into the production as well.

In the author's collection he has one hall-marked 1784, the size of which is $3 \times 2\frac{1}{4}$ inches, but three others of the same period vary from under $2 \times 2\frac{1}{2}$ inches, $2\frac{1}{4} \times 1\frac{1}{2}$ inches and $2\frac{3}{4} \times 2$ inches. During the Peninsular period the plates seem to have stabilized at $3\frac{1}{4} \times 2\frac{3}{4}$ inches, but there were no doubt variations. Many of the early plates were of copper with silver or gilt faces.

To compile a complete record of the various changes of the designs worn is impossible, and the following are only recorded owing to the generous help of army historians, regiments and the many collectors mentioned in the author's preface.

Much useful information is to be obtained from portraits of officers if executed by reliable artists, but in some cases it would appear that the officer concerned is shown wearing a plate not in current use at the time of the painting. Officers may well have purchased their belts and shoulder-belt plates from the effects of some officer killed in action or who had left the Service, or even to have worn plates formerly used by relations in their regiments.

To add to the difficulty of dating plates is the fact that some regiments in the early nineteenth century had different designs for their various battalions, while the actual makers of badges nearly always had some small difference in the design they turned out and frequently in the actual size.

Prints also give information, although in the majority of cases they do not show sufficient detail.

Comparatively few Regimental Histories have reliable chapters on the uniform and even less so in the case of the badges of the regiments concerned. This is especially the case in the older publications and much valuable information must have been lost by this omission. To mention special histories is invidious, but that of the Royal Scots stands out as a work of reference.

BUTTONS

BEFORE THE ORDER of the 21st September, 1767, the officers' buttons were, in most cases, made of thin gilt or silver metal, usually of the colour of the lace on the coat, laid on bone or wooden backs, over the rim of which the metal was turned. The face of the button, generally, had an artistic design of a non-regimental nature and was secured to the back by a paste or cement, and the button fastened to the coat by four strands of catgut; the face of the buttons was made from a die.

The men's buttons were as a rule plain, of pewter or lead, and were of a large size with long iron shanks let into a boss of similar metal at the back.

On the 21st September, 1767, it was ordered that regimental numbers which had been given to regiments of infantry in 1751 were to be placed on the buttons of officers and other ranks. The order, addressed to Thomas Farquier, Secretary to the Clothing Board, read as follows:

WAR OFFICE,
21st September, 1767

SIR,
His Majesty having been pleased to direct that the Number of each Regiment of Dragoon Guards, Dragoons and Foot (including the Regiment of Invalids), shall be respectively mark'd on the Buttons, at the next cloathing, as likewise on the uniforms of the Officers, when they shall make new ones. I am therefore to acquaint with the same, for the information and direction of the General Officers composing the Cloathing Board.

I am, Sir,
BARRINGTON.

This order does not appear to have been pleasing to Dragoon Guards, and an order dated 25th December, 1767, directed that the three regiments of Dragoon Guards should have their initial on their buttons instead of numbers.

After 1767 for a time the size of the men's buttons remained the same with the addition of the number and, as a rule, some artistic design round it. But gradually the trend was for the buttons to become smaller in size. Numbered buttons had been adopted in the French Army as early as 1762. A popular design for their buttons was the number of the regiment displayed within a broken circle with a dot at the opening; this was all enclosed by a thin single-line circle.

It is quite likely that the original order of 21st September, 1767, was in reality the official recognition of a growing custom in the British Army; many of the early pewter buttons having a similar design to those of the French, of a broken circle with or without a dot at the opening, and which is still popularly known as a French circle and dot.

The officers' bone-backed button remained in use with the addition of the regimental number on its face for some years, but there was also at this time another type of officers' button consisting of a thin, gilt or silver metal face ornamented by the regimental design, with the edge turned over a thin metal back. The button was fastened to the garment by a small metal shank. These were soon replaced by a flat, single-piece flat metal button with a longer and stronger metal shank, which continued in use for some years.

It was not until about 1800 that button-makers began to put the names of their firms on the back of the buttons. Buttons have naturally been made by many firms in this country, but the chief makers of military buttons are the two old firms of Firmin's and Jennens.

The dates of the various changes of title in these two firms are: 1677, Thomas Firming; 1770, Firmin; 1771-1780, Samuel Firmin; 1797, Firmin & Westall; 1812, Philip Firmin; 1815, Firmin & Langdale; 1824, Firmin & Sons; 1826, Robert Firmin; 1839, Firmin & King; 1841, Philip & Samuel Firmin; now Firmin & Sons Ltd.

Messrs. Jennens & Co., 1800-1832; Charles Jennens, 1832-1912; Jennens & Co. London, 1912-1924; Jennens & Co. Ltd. In 1924 the firm was amalgamated with Messrs. Gaunt & Son of Birmingham and London.

Messrs. Jennens have stated that it was not until 1860 that their firm began to stamp the back of the buttons they made with the design of the Prince of Wales's coronet and feathers.

About 1800 most of the men's pewter buttons were made by Messrs. Nutting, of London. The firm combined with that of Sherlock in 1840 and finally disappeared in 1912.

Among many other firms to make buttons were those of Sir Edward Thomason, in business about 1800-1850; Sherlock & Co, Kings Street, Covent Garden, about 1780-1880; and W. Twigg & Co. Ltd., .established 1840.

About 1900 a number of the older design of officers' buttons were restruck, probably for collectors and regimental collections.

All the designs worn by other ranks, 1855-1871, on their tunic buttons have also been restruck. At first these had the name of the firm on the back, but later had the words "special made" or plain backs.

Many other firms also made military buttons and there were many slight differences in rendering the approved design.

The flat single-piece officers' buttons were gradually replaced by a convex or open-backed button with a longer shank, but later this gave way to a convex one with a closed back. The tend was for the button to become more and more convex until 1855, when with the introduction of the tunic a new size button was introduced, slightly larger than before and, except for a few exceptions, with a rim.

Even as late as 1855 officers of a few regiments had retained the flat, single-piece button, while the author knows of a case in which an officer who did not like the change to the larger tunic rimmed buttons introduced in 1855 had a special set made for himself without the rim.

The men's pewter buttons were abolished in 1855 and replaced by brass of a regimental design.

The 1855-1871 buttons for other ranks were mostly made by Smith & Wright of Birmingham.

In 1871 the regimental button for other ranks was abolished and replaced by one with the Royal arms except in the case of Household Cavalry, Cavalry of the Line, R.A., R.E., Foot Guards, Rifles and certain Departmental Corps. Hussars wore plain ball buttons. About the same time it became the custom for N.C.Os. in certain regiments to wear regimental buttons.

The buttons worn on the shell jacket about 1855 by other ranks had in most cases the simple design of the regimental number below a crown within a raised single circle. The design was in relief and the buttons, which were of the same size as the old coatee pewter buttons, had closed backs.

There were also two other types of buttons which, as they were of almost a private design of the regiment and not official, have not been recorded under their respective regiments. They were

(a) The officers' mufti button worn on the blue frock coat of the 1840-1850 period. These buttons were of coatee size and as a rule had the design of the initials of the regiment in cypher below a crown; the design mounted. The buttons were very well made.

(b) Officers' mess waiters' buttons. These came into use about 1835. The buttons were flat single piece and with the design in relief. They were the equivalent to the circular livery button, and of the same size. Many were of very attractive design.

In 1902 it was ordered that all buttons other than for mess dress and cap were to be die struck, but as usual there were exceptions in those worn.

In 1928 the regimental buttons for other ranks were reintroduced. In some regiments the small buttons worn on the cap or in mess uniform were of a different design to the full-size button.

THE HOUSEHOLD CAVALRY

TITLES

1660-1685	The 1st or His Majesty's Own Troop of Guards.
1685-1788	The 1st Troop of Life Guards of Horse.
1788-1922	The 1st Life Guards.
1660-1670	The 3rd or the Duke of Albemarle's Troop of Guards.
1670-1685	The 2nd or Queen's Troop of Guards.
1685-1788	The 2nd Troop of Life Guards of Horse. (The 3rd and 4th Troops were disbanded 1746.)
1788-1922	2nd Life Guards.
1661-1687	The Royal Regiment of Horse.
1687-1750	The Royal Regiment of Horse Guards.
1750-1819	Royal Horse Guards. Blue.
1819-	Royal Horse Guards (The Blues).
1922	The Life Guards.
	Royal Horse Guards (The Blues).

BADGES

The Royal Arms.
The Royal Crest.
The Star of the Order of the Garter.

BATTLE HONOURS (*Dates authorized from 1815 to 1855*)

PENINSULA, 29th March, 1815.
WATERLOO, 23rd November, 1815.

SHOULDER-BELT PLATES

The 1st and 2nd Life Guards originate from two troops of Horse composed chiefly of Cavaliers who had served under Charles II.

Soon after the union with Scotland, a Scotch troop was added, making a total of four.

In 1678 a troop of Horse Grenadier Guards was formed and divided into four divisions, one to each troop, while soon after 1684 a 2nd or Scotch troop of Horse Grenadier Guards was formed.

In 1788 the 2nd or Queen's Troop of Life Guards and the 2nd Scots Horse Guards became the 2nd Regiment of Life Guards.

Fig. 1 is a very fine plate sold some years ago at Messrs. Glendining's. The star silver. The lettering within the Garter gold on red enamelled ground. The Garter gilt with pierced letters on blue enamelled ground. The crown gilt with red cap.

The badge would appear to be that of the 2nd (Scots) Troop Horse Grenadier Guards, *circa* 1780.

Plates of uniforms of the two regiments of Life Guards in the British Military Library show the 1st as wearing oblong silver plates with cut corners, crown and 'GR'. This plate is shown in a portrait of Lieutenant-Colonel Herbert, 1797-1812. Those for the 2nd were oval of gilt with the design of crown and 'GR'. The design and rim in silver. Mr. P. W. Reynolds records a brass plate oblong with cut corners and the design of '1' surmounted by a crown worn by other ranks of the 1st Life Guards.

Almack's book* illustrates an oval badge with the Royal arms.

1

BUTTONS

Little appears to be known of the early buttons of the three regiments. In an account of clothing issued by the Great Wardrobe which appeared in the autumn, 1941, issue of the *Journal of the Society for Army Historical Research* it records that in 1690 eight and a half dozen pewter buttons at 7d. per dozen were issued to the Horse Grenadier Guards for hautbois and drummers.

About 1830 the officers' buttons of the 2nd Life Guards were single sheet, open-backed and slightly convex; they had the design of the number '2' surmounted by the letters 'LG', all within a crowned garter inscribed *Honi soit qui mal y pense*. The only difference in the design for the 2nd Life Guards from those of the 1st about 1850 was the number '2' replaced the number '1'.

The buttons of the 1st Life Guards, *circa* 1850, had scalloped edges and the design of 'LG' surmounted by a crown and below the letters the number '1'. This design was replaced by one which lasted for a number of years. It was the

---

* "Regimental Badges worn in the British Army one hundred years ago."

letters 'LG' reversed and intertwined surmounted by an eight-looped crown and with the number '1' between the crown and the letters.

About 1860 the design for the 2nd became the Royal crest between the letters 'L' and 'G', with the number '2' below the crown. The scalloped edge was retained.

The Royal Horse Guards button, with the exception of the change in the shape of the crown, has remained practically unchanged, the design being the letters 'RHG' surmounted by a crown. Mr. P. W. Reynolds states that this design was displayed engraved on the buttons in 1798.

In 1922, after the amalgamation of the two regiments of Life Guards, the design was the letters 'LG' reversed and intertwined, surmounted by the Royal crest. The mess jacket buttons of the Life Guards had the design as worn on the tunic mounted. The Royal Horse Guards had the design mounted on the mess waistcoat button.

1st KING'S DRAGOON GUARDS

TITLES
  1685-1714   The Queen's (or 2nd) Regiment of Horse.
  1714-1746   The King's Own Regiment of Horse.
  1746-1920   1st (King's) Dragoon Guards.
  1920-   1st King's Dragoon Guards.

BADGES
  The Royal Cypher within the Garter.
  The Royal Warrant, 1751, states that the King's Cypher within the Garter and crown was displayed on the housings, holster caps and standards of the regiment.
  The Double-Headed Eagle of Austria, adopted as a badge in 1896 as a mark of respect for H.I.M. the Emperor Joseph, who was gazetted Colonel-in-Chief of the regiment in that year. The badge was discontinued soon after the outbreak of the First World War and the design of the letters 'K' over 'DG' within a crowned garter and star was worn. The garter was inscribed *Honi soit qui mal y pense*. In 1938 the double-headed eagle was readopted.
  The Star of the Order of the Garter.

BATTLE HONOURS (*Dates authorized from 1815 to 1855*)
  WATERLOO, 8th December, 1815.
  SEVASTOPOL, 16th October, 1855.

SHOULDER-BELT PLATES

Circa 1800 the officers wore an oval shoulder-belt plate; silver, with the design engraved as shown in Fig. 2.

2

BUTTONS

The officers' buttons *circa* 1800 were flat single sheet, with the design of the letters 'K' over 'DG' in relief within a crowned garter inscribed *Honi soit qui mal y pense*, the lettering engraved, all on a sunk star.

3

The coatee button 1840-1855 had the same design, and it was retained on the subsequent tunic buttons with the difference that the initials 'KDG' were in Old English capital letters. The officers' buttons had the design mounted, other ranks' stamped.

THE QUEEN'S BAYS
(2nd DRAGOON GUARDS)

TITLES
1685-1688 Colonel the Earl of Peterborough's Regiment of Horse.
1688-1715 The Third Regiment of Horse; also by its Colonel's name.
1715-1727 The Princess of Wales's Own Royal Regiment of Horse.
1727-1746 The Queen's Own Royal Regiment of Horse.
1746-1872 The 2nd The Queen's Dragoon Guards.
1872-1920 2nd Dragoon Guards (Queen's Bays).
1920-   The Queen's Bays (2nd Dragoon Guards).

BADGES
The Royal Cypher within the Garter.
The word 'Bays' in Old English lettering within a crowned wreath of bay leaves.
The Royal Warrant of 1751 states that the badge on the housings, holster caps and standards was the Queen's Cypher within the Garter.
In 1909 the Cypher of Queen Caroline within the Garter was authorized in place of the Royal Cypher within the Garter.
Motto: *Pro Rege et Patria*, authorized in 1909.
The Star of the Order of the Garter.

BUTTONS
The officers' coatee button of about 1830 had the design shown in Fig. 4, the letters 'Qs' over 'D.G' being incised within a raised single line ring, all within a sunk star.

4

About 1880 the design was the number '2' above the cypher 'VR' intertwined and reversed, the whole surmounted by a crown. This was replaced by a button with the design of the word 'Bays' in Old English lettering within a crowned garter and star, the garter inscribed *Honi soit qui mal y pense*.
The mess waistcoat button had the design as worn on the tunic but mounted.

3rd CARABINIERS
(PRINCE OF WALES'S DRAGOON GUARDS)

TITLES
3RD DRAGOON GUARDS
- 1685-1687   Colonel The Earl of Plymouth's Regiment of Horse.
- 1687-1746   The 4th Regiment of Horse; also by the Colonel's name.
- 1746-1765   The 3rd Regiment of Dragoon Guards.
- 1765-1920   3rd (Prince of Wales's) Dragoon Guards.
- 1920-   3rd Dragoon Guards (Prince of Wales's).

CARABINIERS (6TH DRAGOON GUARDS)
- 1685-1690   The Queen's Dowager's Regiment of Horse.
- 1690-1692   The 8th (or 9th) Regiment of Horse; also by the Colonel's name.
- 1692-1745   The King's Carabiniers.
- 1745-1788   The 3rd Irish Horse.
- 1788-1920   The 6th Dragoon Guards (Carabiniers).
- 1920-   Carabiniers (6th Dragoon Guards).

- 1920-1928   3rd/6th Dragoon Guards.
- 1928-   3rd Carabiniers (Prince of Wales's Dragoon Guards).

BADGES
The Royal Warrant of 1751 gives the badges on the holster caps and standards of the 3rd Dragoon Guards as 'III DG' and those of the 3rd Irish Horse as 'III H'.

The Prince of Wales's Coronet, Plume and motto. Conferred on the 3rd Prince of Wales's Dragoon Guards in 1765 with the title.

The Rising Sun. Conferred on the 3rd (Prince of Wales's) Dragoon Guards in 1765 with the title.

The Red Dragon. Conferred on the 3rd (Prince of Wales's) Dragoon Guards in 1765 with the title 'Prince of Wales's.'

Crossed Carbines. An old badge of the Carabiniers (6th Dragoon Guards).

BATTLE HONOURS (*Dates authorized from 1815 to 1855*)
3RD DRAGOON GUARDS
- PENINSULA, 6th April, 1815.
- TALAVERA, 9th May, 1826.
- VITTORIA, 9th May, 1826.
- ALBUHERA, 5th April, 1837.

CARABINIERS (6TH DRAGOON GUARDS)
- SEVASTOPOL, 16th October, 1855.

SHOULDER-BELT PLATES

3RD DRAGOON GUARDS

The plate was copper gilt with a deep beaded edge. On this was mounted a silver star of eight points, in the centre of which, within a garter inscribed with the title, was the Prince of Wales's coronet, plume and motto. The title '3rd or Prince of Wales's Dragoon Gds' in cut-out letters over a blue enamel backing (Fig. 5).

5

BUTTONS

3RD DRAGOON GUARDS

An Inspection Report of 1769 gives the buttons as gold, numbered.

The design on both officers' coatee and tunic buttons and on the pewter buttons of the other ranks has been the same: the Prince of Wales's coronet, plume and motto with the letters 'DG' on either side and all within a garter inscribed *Honi soit qui mal y pense* for a number of years (Fig. 6).

In 1900 the cap button had the design as for the tunic but without the garter and mounted in silver.

6

Carabiniers (6th Dragoon Guards)

An Inspection Report dated 23rd May, 1768, states that the buttons were not yet numbered, and it is not until 1771 that they are noted as numbered.

The officers' coatee button *circa* 1820 was as shown in Fig. 7. Below the shield was engraved the design of two crossed carbines.

Fig. 8 is the button worn by both officers and other ranks at the time of the Crimean War. It is interesting to note the design of leaves turned inwards round the edge of the button. This was the last time the design appeared on a cavalry regiment's buttons.

7   8

The button worn 1870-1881 had the design of a sunk shield with a star of eight points. Above the star the number 'VI' and above this a scroll inscribed 'Carabineers'. Below the star the letters 'DG' and at the base of the shield two crossed carbines.

After 1881 the design became 'VI DG' within a crowned circle inscribed 'Carabiniers' in Old English capitals. The title was spelt Carabineers until 1920.

In 1928 after the two regiments were joined the design became crossed carbines with the Prince of Wales's coronet, plume and motto superimposed thereon, and a scroll below inscribed '3rd Carabiniers'.

In the 1934 Dress Regulations the mess dress button is described as having the design mounted in silver.

The cap button had the design as for the tunic button stamped, while the mess jacket had the design mounted.

4th/7th ROYAL DRAGOON GUARDS

TITLES

4TH ROYAL IRISH DRAGOON GUARDS

1685-1690   Colonel the Earl of Arran's Regiment of Horse; also as 6th Horse.
1690-1746   The Fifth Horse; also by the Colonel's name.
1746-1788   The 1st Irish Horse or The Blue Horse.
1788-1920   The 4th Royal Irish Regiment of Dragoon Guards; The 4th Royal Irish Dragoon Guards.
1920-   The 4th Royal Irish Dragoon Guards.

7TH DRAGOON GUARDS (PRINCESS ROYAL'S)

1688-1690   Colonel the Earl of Devonshire's Regiment of Horse; also as 10th Horse.
1690-1691   Schomberg's Horse.
1691-1720   The Eighth Horse; also by the Colonel's name.
1720-1749   Colonel (afterwards Earl) Ligonier's (the Eighth) Horse.
1749-1788   The 4th (or Black) Irish Horse.
1788-1920   7th (the Princess Royal's) Dragoon Guards.
1920-   7th Dragoon Guards (Princess Royal's).

1922-1936   4th/7th Dragoon Guards.
1936-   4th/7th Royal Dragoon Guards.

BADGES

4TH ROYAL IRISH DRAGOON GUARDS

The Royal Warrant of 1751 gives the badge on the housings, holster caps and standards of the 1st Irish Horse as 'I H'.
The Harp and Crown. Conferred on the regiment in 1838 by Queen Victoria.
The Star and motto of the Order of St. Patrick. Adopted as a badge by the 1st Irish Horse in 1783 when the order was instituted.
The White Horse. Was worn on the King's Standard of the regiment in 1788.

7TH DRAGOON GUARDS (PRINCESS ROYAL'S)

The Royal Warrant of 1751 gives the badge on the housings, holster caps and standards of the 4th (or Black) Irish Horse as 'IV H'.
The Crest and motto (*Quo Fata Vocant*) of Earl Ligonier. Sanctioned in 1898 as above for the 7th (Princess Royal's) Dragoon Guards. Earl Ligonier was Colonel of the regiment for twenty-nine years.
The Coronet of H.M. the Empress of Germany as Princess Royal of Great Britain and Ireland: approved in 1899 for 7th Dragoon Guards.

BATTLE HONOURS (*Dates authorized from 1815 to 1855*)
4TH ROYAL IRISH DRAGOON GUARDS
PENINSULA, 29th March, 1815.
BALACLAVA, 16th October, 1855.
SEVASTOPOL, 16th October, 1855.

SHOULDER-BELT PLATES

4TH ROYAL IRISH DRAGOON GUARDS
Fig. 9 is in Mr. Hughes' collection. The plate is gilt with the design in white metal. Size $3\frac{7}{10} \times 2\frac{1}{8}$ inches.

7TH DRAGOON GUARDS (PRINCESS ROYAL'S)
Fig. 10 is a gilt metal plate with the design incised, probably worn about 1800 or earlier. The size is $3\frac{1}{8} \times 2\frac{3}{16}$ inches.

A miniature of Cornet Richardson of Ligonier's Horse in the possession of Colonel H. Richardson shows an oval gilt plate, but unfortunately no design is discernible.

9 10

BUTTONS

4TH ROYAL IRISH DRAGOON GUARDS
The Inspection Report of May, 1768, states white metal buttons, not numbered.
The following year they are reported as having silver buttons, numbered.
The coatee button had the design of the Star of St. Patrick incised within the circle, above the shamrock was the number 'IV', the whole incised.

The tunic buttons at first had the design incised of the Star of the Order of St. Patrick, the circle inscribed 'RIDG Quis Separabit'. In 1904 the button had the star design, but the title '4th Royal Irish Dragoon Guards' was placed round the edge of the button outside the star. The design was incised.

7TH DRAGOON GUARDS (PRINCESS ROYAL'S)
The 1768 Inspection Report states buttons yellow metal, numbered. The officers' button about 1810 was gilt, open-backed, convex, with the design shown in Fig. 11, in low relief.

11

The tunic buttons until 1920 had the design of the cypher 'PRDG' below the coronet of the Princess Royal.

The design of the crest and motto of Earl Ligonier engraved was worn on the mess waistcoat buttons.

After the uniting of the two regiments the design has been 'IV-VII' surmounted by the coronet of the Princess Royal.

5th ROYAL INNISKILLING DRAGOON GUARDS

TITLES
5TH DRAGOON GUARDS
- 1685-1687   Colonel the Duke of Shrewsbury's Regiment of Horse.
- 1687-1717   The Sixth (or Seventh) Regiment of Horse; also by the Colonel's name.
- 1717-1788   The 2nd (or Green) Irish Horse.
- 1788-1804   The Fifth Dragoon Guards.
- 1804-1920   The 5th (Princess Charlotte of Wales's) Dragoon Guards.
- 1920-   5th Dragoon Guards (Princess Charlotte of Wales's).

THE INNISKILLINGS (6TH DRAGOONS)
- 1689-1751   By the Colonel's name.
- 1751-1920   6th (Inniskilling) Dragoons.
- 1920-   The Inniskillings (6th Dragoons).

- 1922-1927   5th/6th Dragoons.
- 1927-1935   5th Inniskilling Dragoon Guards.
- 1935-   5th Royal Inniskilling Dragoon Guards.

BADGES
The Royal Warrant of 1751 gives the badge on the housings and holster caps, and guidons when carried, of the Second Horse as 'IInd' and that of the 6th Inniskilling Dragoons as having the Castle of Inniskilling within a wreath.

The White Horse of Hanover. Granted to the 5th Princess Charlotte of Wales's Dragoon Guards by King George III.

The motto *Vestigia nulla retrorsum* is mentioned in the Royal Warrant of 1751 as being borne on the guidons of the 2nd (or Green) Irish Horse.

BATTLE HONOURS (*Dates authorized from 1814 to 1855*)
5TH DRAGOON GUARDS
- SALAMANCA, 26th October, 1814.
- PENINSULA, 6th April, 1815.
- VITTORIA, 14th February, 1820.
- TOULOUSE, 14th February, 1820.
- BALACLAVA, 16th October, 1855.
- SEVASTOPOL, 16th October, 1855.

6TH INNISKILLING DRAGOONS
- WATERLOO, 8th December, 1815.
- BALACLAVA, 16th October, 1855.
- SEVASTOPOL, 16th October, 1855.

SHOULDER-BELT PLATES

Figs. 12 and 13 are from a plate which appeared in the Spring, 1949, number of the *Journal of the Society for Army Historical Research*. The period they were worn must be about 1775-1780. They are in a local museum being formed at Carlow.

Fig. 12 is described as an elliptical brass plate, $2 \times 1\frac{1}{2}$ inches flat, and with two eye lugs at the back. Fig. 13 is of bronze gilt and is slightly more than 3 inches long by $2\frac{3}{10}$ inches broad, and has four studs at the back. Both are almost certainly officers' plates.

12

13

BUTTONS

5TH DRAGOON GUARDS

The early bone-backed officers' buttons had the design of 'II' above the word 'Horse'; round the edge of the buttons was a design of leaves turned inwards. The whole in relief on gilt surface.

The Regimental History describes the buttons on an undress jacket worn by Captain H. Moore, who served in the regiment 1796-1799, as white metal with 'V DG' Roman numeral placed in the middle above the block letters, encircled by a garter round which was printed in block letters the regimental motto *Vestigia nulla retrorsum*.

The design on the officers' coatee buttons 1840-1855 had the design of 'V' above the letters 'DG' in relief on a ribbed ground within a crowned garter inscribed *Vestigia nulla retrorsum*, the whole on a sunk cut star. The tunic button, 1855-1922, had the same design except that the Roman 'V' was replaced by an Arabic one.

6TH INNISKILLING DRAGOONS

The officers' buttons about 1820 were flat silver with the design engraved of the castle. By some curious mistake the flag displayed above the castle was the Union Jack instead of St. George's Cross. This mistake occurs again in quite recent issues of buttons. The buttons since 1855 had the castle above the number 'VI' and the button had a deep scalloped rim. Other ranks' pewter buttons *circa* 1800 had the same design as officers'.

After 1935 the design on the buttons was the Castle of Inniskilling with St. George's Colour flying. Above the castle the number 'V' and on either side of the castle the letters 'D' 'G', the whole within a single-line circle. Between the circle and the edge of the button is inscribed the motto.

The 1904 and 1911 Dress Regulations gives the mess waistcoat as having the design of the castle in silver.

The 1934 Dress Regulations gives the mess dress button as having the design of the Castle of Inniskilling with the monogram 'V DG' beneath engraved on a flat gilt button.

1st THE ROYAL DRAGOONS

TITLES
1661-1683   The Tangiers Horse.
1683-1690   The King's Own Royal Regiment of Dragoons.
1690-1751   The Royal Regiment of Dragoons.
1751-1920   1st (Royal) Dragoons.
1920-   1st The Royal Dragoons.

BADGES
The 1751. Crest first appears as a regimental badge in the Clothing Warrant of Royal

An Eagle commemorates the capture of the Eagle of the 105th French Regiment at Waterloo. Authorized 30th April, 1838.

Motto: *Spectemur agendo*. Authorized to retain, 15th December, 1856. It had appeared in the Queen's Regulations in 1844.

BATTLE HONOURS (*Dates authorized from 1815 to 1855*)
PENINSULA, 6th April, 1815.
WATERLOO, 8th December, 1815.
BALACLAVA, 16th October, 1855.
SEVASTOPOL, 16th October, 1855.

SHOULDER-BELT PLATES
In the "Milne" Sale, 1913, a small oblong gilt plate attributed to the regiment was sold. In the centre was the Royal crest within a crowned garter inscribed *Honi soit qui mal y pense*. The corners of the plate were cut, and round the edge was an engraved border of leaves.

BUTTONS
In the advertisement for a deserter from the regiment in 1780 he is said to have on his buttons "the number of the Regiment within a semi-circle of a horse-shoe".

In the Zeughaus Museum, Berlin, there was before the war a uniform of the regiment, *circa* 1787. The buttons were of two designs, both gilt, and the design in relief:

(a) A horse-shoe enclosing the letters 'I' over 'D'. The button had a plain edge.

(b) A horse-shoe enclosing the letters 'I' over 'D'. A wreath of laurel around. The button had a roped edge (Fig. 14). The button had a gilt face on a metal back.

14

About 1850 the design was the Lion of England without a crown, within a crowned garter inscribed 'Royal Dragoons'. The design was retained for many years, but with the lion displayed crowned.

In 1904 the design was as before, but the garter was inscribed *Honi soit qui mal y pense*, and a scroll with the title 'Royal Dragoons' was added below the garter.

The design on the officers' tunic button was mounted.

THE ROYAL SCOTS GREYS (2nd DRAGOONS)

TITLES
1668-1707   The Royal Regiment of Scots Dragoons.
1707-1751   The Royal Regiment of North British Dragoons.
1751-1866   2nd or Royal North British Dragoons.
1866-1877   2nd Royal North British Dragoons (Scots Greys).
1877-1920   2nd Dragoons (Royal Scots Greys).
1920-   The Royal Scots Greys (2nd Dragoons).

BADGES
The Thistle within the circle and motto of St. Andrew is given in the Royal Warrant of 1751 as being worn on the housings, holster caps and guidons when carried.

The White Horse and motto *Nec aspera terrent* was worn on the flap of the Grenadier cap. A water-colour painting by C. Hamilton Smith, *circa* 1813, shows the badge on the back of the bearskin and on the guidon in 1751. It was still worn in silver or white metal at the back of the bearskin cap in full dress until 1914.

An Eagle. Commemorates the capture of the Eagle of the 45th French Regiment at Waterloo. Authorized 13th March, 1838.

Motto: *Second to None*, supposed to have been adopted in 1715. Authorized 29th July, 1839.

Royal Arms on the Grenade of the Plume socket.

BATTLE HONOURS (*Dates authorized from 1815 to 1855*)
WATERLOO, 8th December, 1815.
BALACLAVA, 16th October, 1855.
SEVASTOPOL, 16th October, 1855.

SHOULDER-BELT PLATES

In the "British Military Library" is a print of an officer of the regiment, *circa* 1799. He is shown wearing an oval gilt plate.

Fig. 15 is of the officers' shoulder-belt plate worn about 1802. The plate is gilt with the design mounted in the same metal, with a red cloth background to the design in the centre of the Garter.

15

BUTTONS

The late Rev. P. Sumner writes in an article in the *Journal of the Society for Army Historical Research*, Vols. XV, XVI, dealing with the uniform of the 2nd Dragoons that in January, 1704, an officer of the regiment wrote asking for a set of the "best style double gilt buttons of the newest fashion".

The early officers' buttons had the design shown in Fig. 16, and were gilt plated.

The other ranks' pewter button prior to 1810 had the design of the letter 'D' below the number '2' within a circle of leaves turned inwards.

About 1800 the officers' buttons were flat, gilt, single piece, with the design engraved of '2' within a spray of thistle (Fig. 17).

After 1835 the eagle was placed on the buttons (Fig. 18). The button had a scalloped rim and for the officers was of dead gilt and flat. The pewter button worn by other ranks was of the same design.

16 17 18

The late Rev. P. Sumner, in the above-mentioned articles, recorded a button shown on a sergeant's coatee (*circa* 1825) in a waxwork exhibition held at Glasgow in 1896. The button is stated to be "gilt with a crown at top,

'Waterloo' in the centre and thistle at bottom". There does not appear to be any other evidence as to whether this design was ever worn, and I doubt if it can be accepted as reliable.

When in 1877 the title was changed to Royal Scots Greys the letters below the eagle were changed from 'RNBD' to 'RSG'.

The 1904, 1911 and 1934 Dress Regulations give the mess dress button as plain gilt, burnished, with the eagle mounted in silver.

3rd THE KING'S OWN HUSSARS

TITLES
1685-1689   The Queen Consort's Own Regiment of Dragoons.
1689-1692   Known by the Colonel's name.
1692-1714   Queen's Dragoons.
1714-1751   The King's Own Regiment of Dragoons.
1751-1818   The 3rd (King's Own) Dragoons.
1818-1861   The 3rd (King's Own) Light Dragoons.
1861-1920   The 3rd (King's Own) Hussars.
1920-   3rd The King's Own Hussars.

BADGES
The White Horse of Hanover. Borne on the housings and holster caps, and on the guidons when carried, within the Garter, in 1751.
Motto: *Nec aspera terrent*. Borne on the guidons when carried, 1751. Authorized from 1814.

BATTLE HONOURS (*Dates authorized from 1814 to 1855*)
SALAMANCA, 26th October, 1814.
PENINSULA, 6th April, 1815.
VITTORIA, 7th September, 1821.
TOULOUSE, 7th September, 1821.
CABOOL, 22nd June, 1842.
MOODKEE, 8th June, 1847.
FEROZESHAH, 8th June, 1847.
SOBRAON, 8th June, 1847.
PUNJAUB, 14th December, 1852.
CHILLIANWALLAH, 14th December, 1852.
GOOJERAT, 14th December, 1852.

SHOULDER-BELT PLATES
Fig. 19 shows the very unusual design of plate worn by the regiment *circa* 1780. The plate was brass with the design engraved; the centre of the plate was belled out and the four corners flattened.

19

BUTTONS

The officers' bone-backed buttons had the design (Fig. 20) in relief; the other ranks' pewter buttons had the same design.

The officers' buttons *circa* 1800 were flat, gilt, single sheet, with the design of '3' over 'D' within a narrow ornamental circle. Round the edge of the button a circle of similar design, all engraved (Fig. 21).

20

21

The officers' buttons *circa* 1820 were gilt with the design of 'LD' below the number '3' and superimposed by a crown in relief. About 1840 the design was of the White Horse within a crowned garter inscribed '3rd or King's Own' in relief.

The 1934 Dress Regulations gives the officers' mess vest button as flat, engraved with 'KOH' in monogram.

4th QUEEN'S OWN HUSSARS

TITLES
- 1685-1702 The Princess Anne of Denmark's Dragoons.
- 1702-1751 By its Colonel's name.
- 1751-1788 The 4th Dragoons.
- 1788-1818 The 4th or Queen's Own Dragoons.
- 1818-1861 The 4th (Queen's Own) Light Dragoons.
- 1861-1920 The 4th (Queen's Own) Hussars.
- 1920-   4th Queen's Own Hussars.

BADGES
The 1751 Royal Warrant records the regimental badge on the housings and holster caps and on the guidons when carried, as being 'IV D'.
Motto: *Mente et Manu*. Authorized 1906.

BATTLE HONOURS (*Dates authorized from 1814 to 1855*)
SALAMANCA, 26th October, 1814.
PENINSULA, 6th April, 1815.
TALAVERA, 6th April, 1819.
ALBUHERA, 6th April, 1819.
VITTORIA, 6th April, 1819.
TOULOUSE, 6th April, 1819.
AFFGHANISTAN, 18th July, 1840.
GHUZNEE, 18th July, 1840.
ALMA, 16th October, 1855.
BALACLAVA, 16th October, 1855.
INKERMAN, 16th October, 1855.
SEVASTOPOL, 16th October, 1855.

BUTTONS

The officers' buttons *circa* 1800 were silver, flat, with the design engraved of 'IV' surmounted by a crown and with the title 'Queen's Own' below the number (Fig. 22).

22   23

After becoming Light Dragoons the button in 1830 was half ball with the design engraved of the letters 'LD' with 'IV' above (Fig. 23).

Soon after 1830 the buttons had the design of the cypher 'AR' in relief on a lined ground within a crowned garter and star. The crown and star sunk, the garter raised and engraved 'IV Queen's Own LD'.

7th QUEEN'S OWN HUSSARS

TITLES

    1690-1715   By its Colonel's name.
    1715-1727   The Princess of Wales's Own Royal Dragoons.
    1727-1751   The Queen's Own Dragoons.
    1751-1784   7th or Queen's Own Dragoons.
    1784-1807   The 7th or Queen's Own Light Dragoons.
    1807-1861   7th (Queen's Own) Light Dragoons Hussars.
    1861-1866   7th The Queen's Own Hussars.
    1866-   7th Queen's Own Hussars.

BADGES

    The letters 'QO' interlaced within the Garter.

    The Royal Warrant, 1751, states the Queen's Cypher was borne on the housings and holster caps, and on the guidons when carried, of the regiment.

    Mr. L. E. Buckell, in an article on "Light Cavalry Helmets" which appeared in Vol. XX of the *Journal of the Society for Army Historical Research*, writes: "The double 'CR' cypher was worn generally by regiments styled 'Queen's' prior to 1830."

    The late Rev. P. Sumner, in Vol. XXI of the *Journal of the Society for Army Historical Research*, writes: "On accession of William IV in 1830 the Regiments of Light Cavalry that bore the designation 'Queen's' mostly adopted the 'AR' cypher of the new Queen (Adelaide), but the 7th Hussars either then or shortly afterwards adopted a monogram 'QO' (Queen's Own) instead of the personal cypher, and so it has remained ever since."

BATTLE HONOURS (*Dates authorized from 1815 to 1855*)

    PENINSULA, 6th April, 1815.
    WATERLOO, 8th December, 1815.

SHOULDER-BELT PLATES

The officers' shoulder-belt plate *circa* 1794 had the design shown in Fig. 24. The plate was oblong, of silver, and is described in the Regimental History by C. R. B. Barrett.

24

BUTTONS

Fig. 25 is the officers' gilt button *circa* 1860; the design was in relief, the button having a scalloped edge.

The 1934 Dress Regulations gives the mess vest buttons as flat, gilt, having the design engraved of 'QO' reversed and intertwined.

25

8th KING'S ROYAL IRISH HUSSARS

TITLES
1693-1751	By its Colonel's name Regiment of Dragoons.
1751-1775	The 8th Dragoons.
1775-1777	The 8th Light Dragoons.
1777-1822	The 8th The (King's Royal Irish) Light Dragoons.
1822-1861	8th The King's Royal Irish (Light) Dragoons (Hussars).
1861-1920	8th (King's Royal Irish) Hussars.
1920-	8th King's Royal Irish Hussars.

BADGES
The Royal Warrant of 1751 gives the badge on the housings and holster caps, and on the guidons when carried, as 'VIII D'.

The Harp and Crown. A General Order dated 14th March, 1825, directed that the Harp and Crown badge and the regimental motto should be retained on its standards. These had originally been authorized in 1777.

Motto: *Pristinæ virtutis memores*. Authorized to retain, 14th March, 1825, originally authorized 1777.

BATTLE HONOURS (*Dates authorized from 1825 to 1855*)
HINDOOSTAN, 14th March, 1825.
LESWARREE, 14th March, 1825.
ALMA, 16th October, 1855.
BALACLAVA, 16th October, 1855.
INKERMAN, 16th October, 1855.
SEVASTOPOL, 16th October, 1855.

BUTTONS

The Inspection Report dated May, 1768, gives the buttons as silver, not numbered. The report for the following year records them as numbered, and that for 1784 says of the buttons: "Silver, with a lion, harp and crown and number of the regiment."

Fig. 26 is of the silver ball button worn about 1810.

26

The 1934 Dress Regulations states that the service dress and mess vest buttons were burnished gilt with 'KRIH' above the number 'VIII', surmounted by a crown.

9th QUEEN'S ROYAL LANCERS

TITLES
- 1715-1751   By its Colonel's name Regiment of Dragoons.
- 1751-1783   The 9th Dragoons.
- 1783-1816   The 9th Light Dragoons.
- 1816-1830   The 9th Regiment of Light Dragoons (Lancers).
- 1830-1861   9th or (Queen's Royal) Light Dragoons (Lancers).
- 1861-1920   9th (Queen's Royal) Lancers.
- 1920-   9th Queen's Royal Lancers.

BADGES

The Royal Warrant of 1751 gives the badge on the housings and holster caps, and guidons when carried, as 'IX D'.

The Royal Arms of Her late Majesty Queen Adelaide, which was composed of two shields; the dexter containing the arms of Great Britain and Ireland quartering Hanover on an escutcheon of pretence, the whole surrounded by the Garter; the sinister the fifteen quarterings of Mecklenberg Strelitz surrounded by a chaplet of rue leaves, a special mark of the House of Saxony. The badge was worn on the full-dress Lancer cap plate.

The double cypher 'AR' given to the regiment with the title 'Queen's', 22nd July, 1830.

In an article by Mr. L. E. Buckell which appeared in No. 78, Vol. XX, of the *Journal of the Society for Army Historical Research*, he states that the 9th Light Dragoons about 1807 or 1808 had on their helmets the design of a spray of Rose, Thistle and Shamrock surmounted by a crown.

BATTLE HONOURS (*Dates authorized from 1815 to 1855*)
- PENINSULA, 6th April, 1815.
- PUNNIAR, 22nd June, 1844.
- SOBRAON, 8th June, 1847.
- PUNJAUB, 14th December, 1852.
- CHILLIANWALLAH, 14th December, 1852.
- GOOJERAT, 14th December, 1852.

BUTTONS

The Inspection Report of May, 1768, states "Officers' buttons not yet numbered", but this had been done by the following year.

The officers' lead-backed buttons had the design in relief on a silver face of 'IX' above the letters 'Ds' (Fig. 27). One of these buttons was in the National Museum of Ireland.

About 1835 the officers' buttons had the design of the cypher 'AR' intertwined and reversed, resting on crossed lances with the pennons flying; a crown above and 'IX' below. The same design has been retained, but the number is shown in Arabic and not Roman characters. A peculiarity of the design was the showing of the pennons, which were inclined upwards. This has been retained on the present button (Fig. 28).

27   28

The cap button has the design as for the tunic, but die struck.

10th ROYAL HUSSARS
(PRINCE OF WALES'S OWN)

TITLES

1715-1751	By its Colonel's name Regiment of Dragoons.
1751-1783	The 10th Dragoons.
1783-1806	The 10th, or Prince of Wales's Own Light Dragoons.
1806-1811	The 10th, or Prince of Wales's Own Hussars.
1811-1861	10th (The Prince of Wales's Own Royal) Light Dragoons (Hussars).
1861-1920	10th (The Prince of Wales's Own Royal Regiment of Light Dragoons) Hussars.
1920-	10th Royal Hussars (Prince of Wales's Own).

BADGES

The Royal Warrant of 1751 states that on the housings and holster caps, and on the guidons when carried, the design of 'XD' was displayed.

The Prince of Wales's Coronet, Plume and motto. Worn since 1783 when the title 'Prince of Wales's Own' was given.

The Rising Sun. Worn since 1783 when the title 'Prince of Wales's' was given.

The Red Dragon. Worn since 1783 when the title 'Prince of Wales's' was given.

The White Horse of Hanover.

BATTLE HONOURS (*Dates authorized from 1815 to 1855*)

PENINSULA, 6th April, 1815.
WATERLOO, 8th December, 1815.
SEVASTOPOL, 16th October, 1855.

SHOULDER-BELT PLATES

No. 93, Vol. XXIII, of the *Journal of the Society for Army Historical Research* reproduces a portrait of an officer of the 10th Light Dragoons, 1795. He wears an oval silver pouch-belt plate which is described by the late Rev. P. Sumner as having the design of "A gilt crown surmounting a blue garter, with a silver centre, bearing the plume of feathers with a scroll underneath on which is probably the motto 'Ich Dien' and a border of gilt laurel leaves outside." The same pattern seems to be suggested in the Windsor miniatures. In Almack's book is illustrated the plate shown in Fig. 29. The date would be about 1800. The plate was polished silver with the design mounted in the same metal.

29

BUTTONS

The pewter buttons *circa* 1783 had the design of the Prince of Wales's coronet and plume, with the letters 'X LD'. The button had a roped rim (Fig. 30).

30

About 1830 the officers' ball buttons had the design of 'X RH' below the plume, coronet and motto of the Prince of Wales.

The 1934 Dress Regulations gives for large ball buttons, gilt burnished, with the Prince of Wales's plumes over 'X RH'. The mess vest buttons were flat with the Prince of Wales's plume over 'X RH' and a crown above.

11th HUSSARS (PRINCE ALBERT'S OWN)

TITLES
    1715-1751 By its Colonel's name Regiment of Dragoons.
    1751-1783 The 11th Dragoons.
    1783-1840 The 11th Light Dragoons.
    1840-1920 The 11th (Prince Albert's Own) Hussars.
    1920-   11th Hussars (Prince Albert's Own).

BADGES
    The Royal Warrant, 1751, states the badge on the housings and holster caps, and on the guidons when carried, was 'XI D'.
    The Sphinx superscribed 'Egypt'. Commemorates the services of the regiment in Egypt, 1801. Authorized 6th July, 1802.
    The Crest and motto *Treu und Fest* of the late Prince Consort. Authorized 17th November, 1876.

BATTLE HONOURS (*Dates authorized from 1802 to 1855*)
    EGYPT AND THE SPHINX, 6th July, 1802.
    PENINSULA, 6th April, 1815.
    WATERLOO, 8th December, 1815.
    BHURTPORE, 6th December, 1826.
    SALAMANCA, 26th July, 1838.
    ALMA, 16th October, 1855.
    BALACLAVA, 16th October, 1855.
    INKERMAN, 16th October, 1855.
    SEVASTOPOL, 16th October, 1855.

BUTTONS

Circa 1790 the design of 'XI D' was displayed in relief on the buttons. About 1830 the buttons were of gilt with the design in relief shown in Fig. 31.

31

    The writer has in his collection what appears to be an officers' mess waiter button; the design is the Sphinx inscribed 'Egypt' within a crowned garter inscribed *Motus componere*. Below the Sphinx the number 'XI' and the letters 'LD'. There is no record of this motto being officially granted.
    The 1934 Dress Regulations gives the service dress and mess vest buttons as flat, gilt, engraved with 'PAO' in monogram surmounted by a crown.

12th ROYAL LANCERS (PRINCE OF WALES'S)

TITLES
1715-1751 By its Colonel's name Regiment of Dragoons.
1751-1768 The 12th Dragoons.
1768-1816 The 12th (the Prince of Wales's) Light Dragoons.
1816-1817 The 12th (the Prince of Wales's) Lancers.
1817-1920 The 12th (Prince of Wales's Royal) Lancers.
1920-   12th Royal Lancers (Prince of Wales's).

BADGES
The Royal Warrant of 1751 gives the badge on the housings and holster caps, and on the guidons when carried, as 'XII D'. In the Warrant for 1768, by which time the regiment had become Light Dragoons, the badge was described as the feathers issuing out of the coronet on the housings and holster caps. On the guidon when carried the feathers coming out of the coronet and also having the badges of the Red Dragon, Rising Sun, and motto *Ich Dien*.

The Sphinx superscribed 'Egypt'. Commemorates the services of the regiment in Egypt, 1801. Authorized 6th July, 1802.

BATTLE HONOURS (*Dates authorized from 1802 to 1855*)
EGYPT AND THE SPHINX, 6th July, 1802.
PENINSULA, 6th April, 1815.
WATERLOO, 8th December, 1815.
SEVASTOPOL, 16th October, 1855.

BUTTONS
Fig. 32 is the design of the officers' ball button *circa* 1810; the design was engraved. That shown in Fig. 33 was worn later. The design in relief.

32   33

About 1855 the design was the number '12' superimposed on crossed lances, with a crown above. The button had a scalloped rim. This design is still worn.

The cap button had the design die struck as on the tunic button, and the mess waistcoat the same mounted.

13th/18th ROYAL HUSSARS
(QUEEN MARY'S OWN)

TITLES

13TH HUSSARS

1715-1751   By its Colonel's name Regiment of Dragoons.
1751-1783   The 13th Dragoons.
1783-1861   13th Light Dragoons.
1861-1920   13th Hussars.

18TH HUSSARS

1759-1763   The 19th Light Dragoons.
1763-18C7   The 18th Light Dragoons (or 4th Light Dragoons, 1766-1769).
1807-1821   The 18th King's. Disbanded.
1858-1861   18th Light Dragoons (Hussars).
1861-1904   18th Hussars.
1904-1905   18th Princess of Wales's Hussars.
1905-1910   18th (Victoria Mary Princess of Wales's Own) Hussars.
1910-1919   18th (Queen Mary's Own) Hussars.
1919-1920   The 18th (Queen Mary's Own) Royal Hussars.
1920-   18th Royal Hussars (Queen Mary's Own).
1920-1935   13th/18th Royal Hussars.
1935-   13th/18th Royal Hussars (Queen Mary's Own).

BADGES

The Royal Warrant of 1751 states that the 13th Dragoons displayed on their housings, holster caps and guidons the device of 'XIII D'.

Motto: *Viret in Æternum*. The old motto of the 13th Hussars said to have been borne since the formation of the regiment in 1715. Probably was an allusion to the original green facings of the regiment. Authorized 12th January, 1833.

The Royal Warrant of 1768 records the design worn on the housings, holster caps and guidons of the 18th Light Dragoons as being 'XVIII LD'.

Motto: *Pro Rege, pro Lege, pro Patria conamur*. Authorized to the 18th Hussars in 1883.

BATTLE HONOURS (*Dates authorized from 1815 to 1855*)

13TH HUSSARS

PENINSULA, 6th April, 1815.
WATERLOO, 8th December, 1815.
ALMA, 16th October, 1855.
INKERMAN, 16th October, 1855.
BALACLAVA, 16th October, 1855.
SEVASTOPOL, 16th October, 1855.

18TH HUSSARS
  PENINSULA, 6th April, 1815.
  WATERLOO, 8th December, 1815.
      (*Authorized to resume*, 20th November, 1858)

BUTTONS

13TH HUSSARS

The buttons are reported as numbered in an Inspection Report dated May, 1768. About 1830 the design was 'XIII' above 'LD' engraved within a crowned star of eight points, the design incised; below the star, the motto *Viret in Æternum*, and above the honours 'Peninsula', 'Waterloo'. This design, but in relief, and with the number in Arabic figures, was worn until 1861 (Fig. 34).

18TH HUSSARS

The Inspection Report dated 3rd June, 1768, states silver buttons, numbered, were worn.

Fig. 35 is the design worn on the officers' bone-backed button *circa* 1780. The buttons had silver faces.

Fig. 36 is the design on the officers' silver ball buttons about 1807. The design, except for the leaves, was incised.

34

35

36

14th/20th KING'S HUSSARS

TITLES

14TH KING'S HUSSARS
1715-1776	By its Colonel's name.
1776-1798	The 14th Light Dragoons.
1798-1830	The 14th (or Duchess of York's Own) Light Dragoons.
1830-1861	The 14th (The King's) Light Dragoons.
1861-1920	14th (King's) Hussars.
1920-	14th King's Hussars.

20TH HUSSARS
1759-1763	The 20th Inniskilling Light Dragoons. Disbanded.
1779-1783	The 20th Light Dragoons. Disbanded.
1791-1802	The 20th Jamaica Light Dragoons.
1802-1818	The 20th Light Dragoons. Disbanded.
1858-1861	The 2nd Bengal European Light Cavalry.
1861-	20th Light Dragoons.
1861-1920	20th Hussars.
1920-1936	14th/20th Hussars.
1936-	14th/20th King's Hussars.

BADGES

14TH HUSSARS

The Royal Crest. The Royal Warrant of 1751 states that the housings, holster caps and guidons displayed the design 'XIV D'.

Originally the device worn on the regiment's appointments was the Royal Cypher and Crown. In 1798 when the title 'Duchess of York's' was given to the regiment the Prussian Eagle was adopted. The eagle is a black one, displayed crowned, sceptred, bearing an orb in the sinister talon and charged on the centre of each wing with a small plain cross.

In 1830, on the change of title, the King's Crest (Royal Crest) within the Garter was directed to be worn, and when in 1861 the regiment became Hussars, the Royal Cypher and Crown were placed on the front corners of the shabracque, while the Royal Cypher within a garter inscribed 'Fourteenth Hussars'—surmounting the garter being an eight-looped crown—and the Prussian Eagle were displayed on the hind corners.

20TH HUSSARS

The badge of an Alligator was worn on the Light Dragoon helmet in 1797, but when the regiment returned to England in 1802 it was replaced by the Garter enclosing the cypher 'GR' and surmounted by the Royal Crest.

BATTLE HONOURS (*Dates authorized from 1815 to 1855*)
14TH HUSSARS
   PENINSULA, 6th April, 1815.
   TALAVERA, 17th February, 1820.
   FUENTES D'ONOR, 17th February, 1820.
   SALAMANCA, 17th February, 1820.
   VITTORIA, 17th February, 1820.
   ORTHES, 17th February, 1820.
   DOURO, 22nd July, 1837.
   PUNJAUB, 14th December, 1852.
   CHILLIANWALLAH, 14th December, 1852.
   GOOJERAT, 14th December, 1852.

SHOULDER-BELT PLATES

In 1796 the other ranks of the 14th Hussars had oval brass plates with the design incised of 'XIV' above the letters 'LD' in script. The plate had a roped or beaded rim (Fig. 37).

37

BUTTONS

14TH KING'S HUSSARS
The buttons prior to 1861, when the regiment became Hussars, had the design of 'XIV' above the letters 'KLD'. Above the number a crown, and below the letters 'KLD' a spray of laurel. 'Peninsula' was inscribed above the crown. The button had a scalloped rim. Later the design was the same, but the number was shown '14'.

20TH HUSSARS

Fig. 38 is of the officers' ball button, *circa* 1810, of the 20th Light Dragoons. The design was engraved.

38

The mess jacket button had in silver the design of 'XX' and the letter 'H' surmounted by a crown.

After the amalgamation of the two regiments the button is given in the Dress Regulations of 1934 as flat, gilt, engraved with 'XIV' above 'XX', surmounted by a crown.

15th/19th THE KING'S ROYAL HUSSARS

TITLES

15TH KING'S HUSSARS
1759-1766 The 15th Light Dragoons.
1766-1807 The 15th (or the King's) Light Dragoons (or 1st King's Light Dragoons (1766-1769)).
1807-1861 The 15th (or the King's) Light Dragoons (Hussars).
1861-1920 15th (the King's) Hussars.

19TH ROYAL HUSSARS (QUEEN ALEXANDRA'S OWN)
1759-1763 The 19th Light Dragoons. Disbanded as 18th Hussars in 1821.
1779-1783¹ The 19th Light Dragoons. Disbanded.
1781-1786 The 23rd Light Dragoons.
1786-1817 The 19th Light Dragoons.
1817-1821 The 19th Lancers. Disbanded.
1858-1861 The Hon. East India Company's 1st Bengal European Cavalry.
1861 The 19th Light Dragoons.
1861-1885 The 19th Hussars.
1885-1902 The 19th (Princess of Wales's Own) Hussars.
1902-1908 19th Alexandra Princess of Wales's Own Hussars.
1908-1920 19th (Queen Alexandra's Own Royal) Hussars.
1920- 19th Royal Hussars (Queen Alexandra's Own).

1920-1933 15th/19th Hussars.
1933- 15th/19th King's Royal Hussars.

BADGES

15TH KING'S HUSSARS
The Royal Crest within the Garter. An old badge of the 15th. The Royal Warrant of 1768 states that it was displayed on the holster caps and on the guidons of the regiment.
Motto: *Merebimur.*
Authority to retain the motto was given in a letter dated 10th December, 1856, which states that the motto was said to have been worn on the appointments of the regiment since the battle of Emsdorf, 1760. In "The Discipline of the Light Horse, 1778", the motto is given as *Merebimur Emsdorf.*
In an article on the Morier paintings at Wilton by the late Rev. P. Sumner which appeared in No. 74, Vol. XIX, of the *Journal of the Society for Army Historical Research*, it states that the motto *The Swift, the Vigilant and Bold* was displayed on the shabracque *circa* 1760.

Special Badge for Emsdorf.—A design of crossed flags was displayed on the flap of the officers' pouches and on the sabretaches and shabracques to commemorate the gallantry of the regiment at the battle of Emsdorf in 1760, when they defeated and captured five battalions of Foot together with three Colours and nine guns. In 1769 this was commemorated by an inscription on the front of their Light Dragoon helmet.

19TH HUSSARS
The Elephant. Superscribed "Assaye". The badge of the old 19th Light Dragoons, given to commemorate the services of the regiment at the battle of Assaye, authorized 15th April, 1803. The Honours of the older regiment were authorized to be borne by the present regiment in 1874. The Dannebrog Cross worn as a collar badge in 1900.

BATTLE HONOURS (*Down to* 1855)
15TH THE KING'S HUSSARS
EMSDORF. On the standards according to the Royal Warrant of 1768.
VILLIERS EN COUCHE. First appears in Army List, 1818; since 1911 spelt Villers en Cauchies.
EGMONT-OP-ZEE, 8th April, 1828.
PENINSULA, 29th March, 1815.
SAHAGUN, 23rd February, 1832.
VITTORIA, 23rd February, 1832.
WATERLOO, 15th November, 1815.

19TH ROYAL HUSSARS
SERINGAPATAM, 28th March, 1818.
ASSAYE, 15th April, 1807.
NIAGARA, 19th May, 1815.

SHOULDER-BELT PLATES

15TH THE KING'S HUSSARS
Almack's book illustrates an officer's shoulder-belt plate of the regiment worn about 1800.
The plate was oblong, of silver, and had the design of the Royal crest within a crowned garter inscribed with the motto *Honi soit qui mal y pense*; below the garter a label inscribed 'Emsdorf'. The plate had an ornamental border (Fig. 39).

19TH ROYAL HUSSARS
Fig. 40 is of an officers' silver engraved plate of the 19th Light Dragoons which existed 1779-1783 and were then disbanded.

39   40

BUTTONS

15TH (THE KING'S) HUSSARS
In 1768 the design on the officers' silver buttons was the letter 'K' above 'LD' and '15' below.

19TH ROYAL HUSSARS
The officers' buttons *circa* 1812 had the design of the elephant surmounted by a crown, above which was the word 'Assaye'. On the left of the elephant the letter 'L' and on the right the letter 'D'. Below the number 'XIX'.
    The 1934 Dress Regulations gives the button on the mess vest and forage cap as having the Royal crest within the Garter and motto.

16th/5th THE QUEEN'S ROYAL LANCERS

TITLES

16TH THE QUEEN'S LANCERS
- 1759-1766   The 16th Light Dragoons.
- 1766-1769   The 2nd Queen's Light Dragoons.
- 1769-1816   The 16th or the Queen's Light Dragoons.
- 1816-1861   16th (The Queen's) Light Dragoons (Lancers).
- 1861-1920   16th (The Queen's) Lancers.
- 1920-   16th The Queen's Lancers.

5TH ROYAL IRISH LANCERS
- 1689-1693   By its Colonel's name.
- 1694-1704   The Irish Dragoons or by its Colonel's name.
- 1704-1751   The Royal Dragoons of Ireland.
- 1751-1799   The 5th (Royal Irish) Dragoons. Disbanded.
- 1861-1920   The 5th (Royal Irish) Lancers.
- 1920-   5th Royal Irish Lancers.
- 1922-1954   16th/5th Lancers.
- 1954   16th/5th The Queen's Royal Lancers.

BADGES

16TH THE QUEEN'S LANCERS
The Royal Warrant of 1768 states that the 16th Light Dragoons displayed on their housings, holster caps and guidons the design of the Queen's Cypher within the Garter and that the motto *Aut cursu, aut cominus armis* was displayed as well.

It was not until 1909 that the Cypher of Queen Charlotte within the Garter was officially authorized for the 16th (the Queen's) Lancers.

5TH ROYAL IRISH LANCERS
The Irish Harp and Crown. This design is given in the Royal Warrant of 1751 as being borne on the housings, holster caps and on the guidons of the 5th Royal Irish Dragoons. The design was authorized for the 5th Royal Irish Lancers in 1858.

BATTLE HONOURS (*Dates authorized from 1815 to 1855*)

16TH THE QUEEN'S LANCERS
PENINSULA, 6th April, 1815.
WATERLOO, 8th December, 1815.
TALAVERA, 16th April, 1818.
FUENTES D'ONOR, 16th April, 1818.

SALAMANCA, 16th April, 1818.
VITTORIA, 16th April, 1818.
NIVE, 16th April, 1818.
BHURTPORE, 6th December, 1826.
AFFGHANISTAN, 18th July, 1840.
GHUZNEE, 18th July, 1840.
MAHARAJPORE, 22nd June, 1844.
ALIWAL, 8th June, 1847.
SOBRAON, 8th June, 1847.

SHOULDER-BELT PLATES

16TH THE QUEEN'S LANCERS

Mr. Buckell has shown the author an excellent photograph of Captain John Walmersley, painted by Thomas Gainsborough. Mr. Buckell suggests the date as about 1773. He is shown wearing an oval breast plate with the design

41

of the letter 'C' within a crowned garter inscribed with the motto *Honi soit qui mal y pense*. The letters are shown as having a dark background, and there are signs of a design, possibly a wreath, round the garter. The plate had a raised rim.

Fig. 41 is of a silver plate with slightly rounded corners. The design is engraved, and below the plate was worn a straight silver bar.

In Mr. Tilling's collection is a plate almost identical with Fig. 41 but for slight difference in the tip of the garter, which has roped edges, and in the design of the letter 'C', which is a little larger and very slightly different.

BUTTONS

16TH THE QUEEN'S LANCERS

The officers' bone-backed buttons *circa* 1773-1783 had silver faces with the design in relief of the letter 'Q' above the letters 'LD' and the number '16' below, and a border of leaves turned inwards round the rim. The other ranks' buttons had the same design.

The same design was retained on the flat silver buttons *circa* 1800 (Fig. 43).

Mr. P. W. Reynolds records a silver officers' button, which he dates as 1788. It had the design of a crown, 'LD' and '16'.

The officers' buttons *circa* 1820 were silver with the design of a crown resting on two crossed lances at the point of their crossing. Below the crown 'XVI', at the top edge of the button the word 'Waterloo', and the bottom 'Peninsula'; on either side a spray of laurel. On the left of the crown the letters 'Qs' and on the right the letter 'L'. The whole design in low relief. About 1860 the design was the same but in much higher relief, and the buttons were gilt (Fig. 44).

In 1881 the design was a crown above the letters 'QL' with '16' below.

5TH ROYAL IRISH LANCERS

The officers' buttons of the old 5th Royal Irish Dragoons were flat, silver, with the design engraved (Fig. 42).

When re-raised the buttons had the design of the Irish Harp within a crowned circle inscribed 'Fifth Royal Irish', behind the circle crossed lances with pennons, and below the circle a spray of shamrocks.

42   43   44

17th/21st LANCERS

TITLES

17TH LANCERS (DUKE OF CAMBRIDGE'S OWN)
 1759-1763   The 18th Light Dragoons.
 1763-1822   17th Light Dragoons (or 3rd Light Dragoons 1766-1769).
 1822-1861   17th Light Dragoons (Lancers).
 1861-1876   The 17th (Light Dragoons) Lancers.
 1876-1920   The 17th (Duke of Cambridge's Own) Lancers.
 1920-   The 17th Lancers (Duke of Cambridge's Own).

21ST LANCERS (EMPRESS OF INDIA'S)
 1759-1763   The 21st Light Dragoons or Royal Windsor Foresters. Disbanded.
 1779-1783   The 21st Light Dragoons. Disbanded.
 1794-1820   The 21st Light Dragoons. Disbanded.
 1858-1861   3rd Bengal European Light Cavalry.
 1861   21st Light Dragoons.
 1861-1897   21st Hussars.
 1897-1898   21st Lancers.
 1898-1920   21st (Empress of India's) Lancers.
 1920-   21st Lancers (Empress of India's).

 1922-   17th/21st Lancers.

BADGES

17TH LANCERS

The Death's Head and motto *Or Glory*. According to tradition, the badge was adopted to commemorate the death of Wolfe. Colonel Hale, who raised the regiment, brought back the despatches announcing the General's death at Quebec. The badge is said to have been at first worn embroidered on the left breast.

The Royal Warrant of 1768 gives the badge on the holster caps as being 'XVII LD', and on the guidons when carried, the Death's Head and motto *Or Glory*. The badge had been worn from the very early days of the regiment.

Mr. L. E. Buckell, in an article in Vol. XX of the *Journal of the Society for Army Historical Research*, writes with reference to the regimental badge on the Light Dragoon helmet: "The crossed bones appear above the skull. This is the case in all reproductions of the skull and cross bones on any article of dress or equipment used by the 17th Light Dragoons prior to about 1821, when for some fifteen years the bones were crossed and the skull mounted on the bones at the point of crossing, the present arrangement being adopted early in Queen Victoria's reign."

21ST LANCERS

The Imperial Cypher 'VRI' and Crown. The crown was of the pattern displayed in the insignia of the Order of the Star of India. It was adopted in 1898 when the title 'Empress of India's' was given to the regiment.
In No. 78, Vol. XX, of the *Journal of the Society for Army Historical Research*, Mr. L. E. Buckell records that the 21st Light Dragoons had on their helmets in 1799 the design of the Royal arms.

BATTLE HONOURS (*Dates authorized to* 1855)

17TH LANCERS
ALMA, 16th October, 1855.
BALACLAVA, 16th October, 1855.
INKERMAN, 16th October, 1855.
SEVASTOPOL, 16th October, 1855.

SHOULDER-BELT PLATES

The 1771 Inspection Report states that the officers had white sword belts with a silver clasp on which was embossed in gold and black enamel the King's cypher. It was worn across the shoulder.

BUTTONS

17TH LANCERS
The buttons were recorded as numbered in 1768 Inspection Report. Fig. 45 is the design of the officers' bone-backed button *circa* 1780; the buttons had silver faces. The figures '17' and the letters 'LD' were in relief; the star was sunk. The other ranks' pewter buttons had the same design except that the star was slightly larger.
Fig. 46 is the silver button of about 1820; the design was incised.
Fig. 47 is the silver button worn after the regiment first became Lancers; the design was in relief. The showing of the crossed bones behind the skull was the old method of displaying the badge. The same design was displayed on the other ranks' pewter buttons of the period. Since about 1870 the bones have been crossed below.

45

46

47

21ST LANCERS
In Vol. XXVIII of the *Journal of the Society for Army Historical Research* an article by Mr. C. C. P. Lawson describes the uniform of the 21st Light Dragoons (The Royal Foresters). He states that on the front of the Light Dragoon helmet was the design of the Royal Cypher ('GR'), crowned, with 'R' and 'F' in block capitals on either side of it, and below the Royal Cypher on a scroll the regimental motto *Hic et ubique*.

The officers' buttons of the 21st Yorkshire Light Dragoons were gilt with the design of 'XXI' inside a circle and star of eight points, the circle inscribed 'Yorkshire LD'. The star was sunk. The button would appear to be of the 1810-1820 period.

The 21st Lancers had buttons with scalloped rims and the design of a crown between two upright lances, below the crown and across the front of the button the number 'XXI'. The button had a scalloped edge. This design was worn until 1920, when both regiments adopted the 17th's button with the skull and cross bones.

THE ROYAL REGIMENT OF ARTILLERY

TITLES
To 1716　　　The Train of Artillery.
1716-to date　The Royal Regiment of Artillery.

BADGES
The Royal Arms and supporters with a Cannon. Granted 1832.
A Grenade. Was worn on the shoulder strap above the crescent in 1834, and was embroidered on the collar of the shell jacket in 1838.
Motto:　(1) *Ubique.* Granted 1832.
　　　　(2) *Quo Fas et Gloria ducunt.* Granted 1832.

SHOULDER-BELT PLATES

A certain amount of information concerning the dates of changes of plates worn by the Royal Artillery is to be found in MacDonald's well-known history of the uniform of the regiment, but in few cases are there any descriptions. The following extracts are from it.

1779-1790. 13th June: Officers of 1st and 3rd Battalions having requested leave to wear shoulder belts, the Master-General has consented to the same.

1793. Plate 7 in MacDonald's book shows R.H.A. officers wearing a shoulder-belt plate.

1796. G.O., 30th October: "The Master-General is extremely willing to comply with the wishes of the Colonels Commandant, and desires they will fix upon a cross belt plate for the Sword, which may be uniform with that worn by the Army." p. 41.

1797. The Gunners' crossed belt carried pickets and hammer.

1799. Mention is made of officers wearing yellow breast plates.

1799. Plate 10 shows an officer with shoulder-belt plates.

1824. A new pattern plate for the shoulder belt, often called the breast plate, was introduced.

1832. 14th September: A new pattern belt plate (breast plate) introduced.

1833. Company officers had shoulder-belt plates with the design of the Royal arms encircled by a wreath of rose, shamrock and thistle. Crown above the arms and below them the motto *Ubique*; below this a field piece, and below the gun a scroll inscribed *Quo Fas et Gloria ducunt.*

1834. Cross belts abolished for R.H.A.

The writer some years ago was sent a rough drawing of what was described as a shoulder-belt plate dug up in Canada. It was of brass, oblong, and had 'RA' in script engraved on it.

Almack's book illustrates a gilt oval plate with the design also in gilt mounted. The garter which encloses the Ordnance arms is inscribed 'Home Artillery', probably a mistake—not the only one in the book with regard to titles. In the "British Military Library" an officer is shown wearing an oval gilt plate with a star design, probably Fig. 48. A specimen of this plate is in the Scottish United Services Museum in Edinburgh Castle. The plate is gilt and enamel with beaded rim; title and star engraved; cap of crown and background to the cypher red enamel; background to garter blue enamel; a narrow white enamel between the garter and red background; the cushion and pearls of the crown in white enamel. The size of the plate approx. 2½ × 2 inches. The late Curator, Major I. Mackay Scobie, dated the plate as being worn about 1780-1820, but in view of the fact that officers' belts were widened in 1805 it is probable the plate was changed about the same time.

Another early plate is in the collection of Captain P. Abbott, R.A. It is of brass, oval, with the design of three guns surmounted by three cannon-balls and a crown. Above the crown a scroll inscribed 'Royal British' and below the guns one inscribed 'Artillery'.

This plate may have been worn by other ranks to differentiate between the British and Irish artillery which in 1801 became one regiment.

Fig. 49 is a brass other ranks' plate, with the design engraved; probably 1790-1805.

A brass oblong engraved plate was worn with the design of a gun, above which was a crown flanked by 'G III' and 'R'. On either side of the gun a rammer and a match-stick. Below the gun the number '3' and two piles of cannon-balls, and at the bottom of the badge 'Royal Artillery'. Mr. A. R. Cattley is of opinion this plate was worn 1805-1820.

Fig. 50 is a brass plate with the design engraved. The Royal Artillery Drivers existed during the time of the Peninsular War.

Major D. A. Campbell informs the author that from 1823 to 1833 the design in Fig. 51 was worn. For officers the plate was a gilt one with a frosted surface and burnished edge; the cross in the centre was in red enamel with gilt edging on a white enamel ground. The garter, crown and thunderbolts were in dead gilt, the letters of the garter being pierced with a blue enamel backing. Staff sergeants wore a plate of almost similar design, but the plate was burnished with the design mounted. Other ranks would appear to have worn the design stamped.

From 1833 to 1837 the plate was gilt with the design shown in Fig. 52, but with the addition of the Hanoverian escutcheon in the centre of the shield. The size of the plate was 3 ⅜ × 3 inches.

From 1837 to 1855 the same plate but without the Hanoverian escutcheon was worn. The plate had a frosted surface with a burnished rim (Fig. 52).

BUTTONS

The early buttons of the regiment had gilt faces on bone backs with the design in relief of a gun on a carriage, with a pile of cannon-balls below its muzzle. The button had a roped rim (Fig. 53).

53

After this the button displayed the Ordnance arms. The officers' buttons *circa* 1790 had the design on two-pieced buttons with gilt faces on bone or wooden backs. The other ranks' buttons were of pewter and had the same design as the officers' (Fig. 54).

In the author's collection is a gilt convex, open back button, with the design of a shield with the Ordnance arms surmounted by the number '3'. Presumably each battalion had its own number on its buttons. In Major D. A. Campbell's account of the buttons worn by the regiment he states that it is possible that the R.H.A. wore a button of similar design.

About 1802 a button was introduced for the R.A. with a crowned garter inscribed 'Royal Regt. of Artillery' and with the Royal cypher within. This may, Major Campbell thinks, have been worn by the R.H.A. with an altered inscription.

The R.H.A. continued to wear the crown, garter and cypher button until 1855 on the jacket, and on the greatcoat until 1912. The R.A. wore a crown over three guns from 1831 to 1840, and a button with crown and three guns over a scroll inscribed 'Ubique' and with a scalloped rim from 1840 to 1855. From then onwards both R.A. and R.H.A. wore the same design except in the case of the R.H.A. greatcoat.

In 1855 the older design of crown above three guns was reverted to and worn until 1873, when the present design with a single gun with crown above was adopted.

The ball button was worn by both R.A. and R.H.A. on certain uniforms until 1924, after which it was allocated to the R.H.A. alone (Fig. 55).

The 1911 and 1934 Dress Regulations state that three small ball buttons are to be worn on the mess jacket and four on the mess vest.

The Royal Irish Artillery, who were amalgamated with the Royal Artillery in 1801, had as far as is known during their existence two designs of button.

(a) Flat gilt with the design in relief of a shield bearing the Ordnance arms and surmounted by the harp and crown; on the left of the shield is the word 'Artillery' and on the right 'Royal Irish'. The button had a beaded rim.

(b) Flat gilt with the design of a gun surmounted by the harp and crown, on either side of the crown a cannon-ball, all in relief on a sunk shield round the edge of which was a series of dots (Fig. 56).

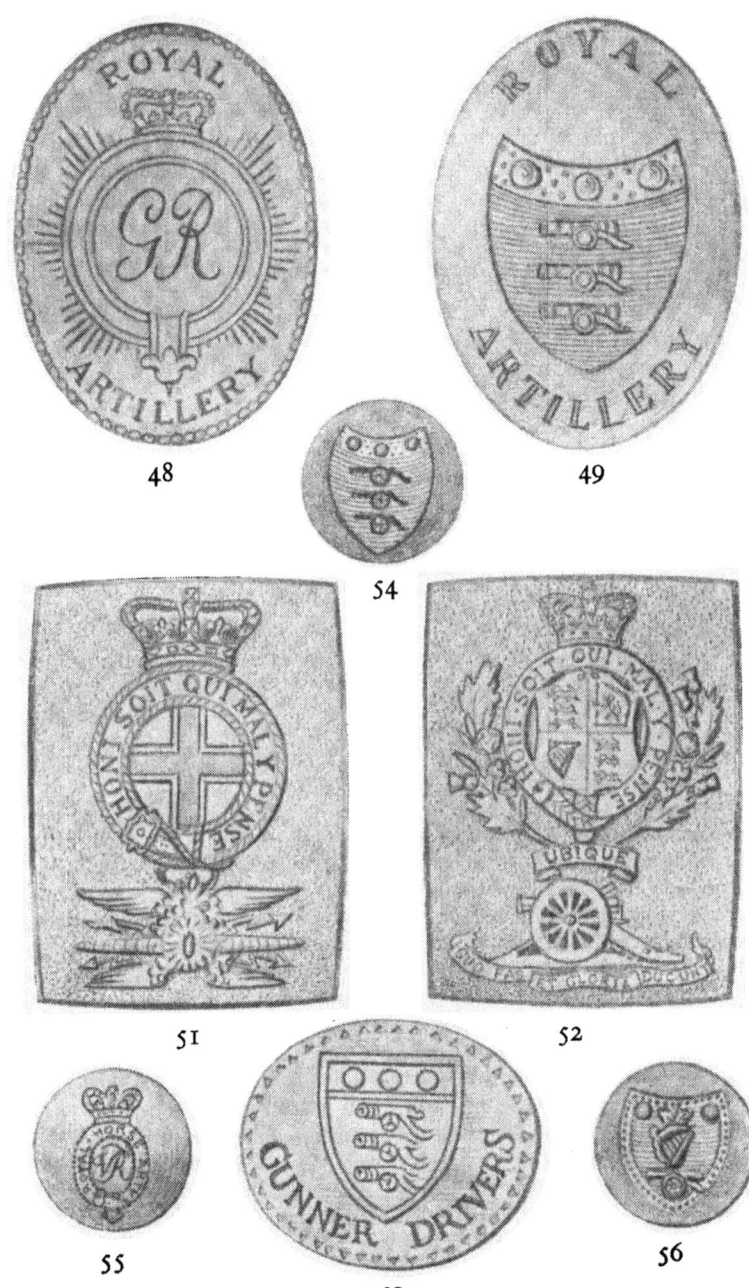

THE CORPS OF ROYAL ENGINEERS

TITLES
1757– A small number of officers were entitled Engineers in 1757.
1772–1797 The Military Company of Artificers raised at Gibraltar and amalgamated with the Royal Military Artificers in 1797.
1787–1812 The Royal Military Artificers. The officers' branch became known as Royal Engineers.
1812 The Royal Military Artificers or Sappers and Miners.
1813–1856 Royal Sappers and Miners.
1856–1949 Corps of Royal Engineers, the two branches being merged in this year.
1949– The Corps of Royal Engineers.

BADGES
(1) The Royal Arms and supporters. Authorized 1832.
(2) A Grenade was worn as a skirt ornament in 1824.
The Motto: (1) *Ubique*, authorized 1832.
(2) *Quo Fas et Gloria ducunt*, authorized 1832.

BATTLE HONOURS
WATERLOO, 15th November, 1815, to Royal Sappers and Miners.
PENINSULA, 14th February, 1816.

SHOULDER-BELT PLATES

Although the details of the dress of the Corps have been recorded in considerable detail in the Corps Journal, 1934 and 1935, by Colonel Kealy, remarkably little information is to be found about the shoulder-belt plates they wore. Connolly's "History of the Corps of Royal Engineers" states that in 1772–1786 the plates worn by the Gibraltar companies were oval with the Ordnance arms; above the cannon-balls was the word 'Gibraltar', and below this the three cannons and title 'Soldier Artificers'.

In 1796 it was directed that the officers should carry the sword "in a crossbelt (white) with an oval gilt plate, having the King's cypher with the crown over it, engraved in the centre".

Colonel Kealy's article states that the sword belt plate in 1782 was the King's cypher with the crown over it, "at some time later the cypher was surrounded by the garter, on which was placed first 'Corps of Royal Engineers' and later simply 'Royal Engineers'. It is not known when the laurel wreaths were added, but it was very probably after Waterloo when honourable awards were made to all regiments which took part in the battle, including the Royal Engineers. How the personal honours referred to in Pasley's orders were shown on the Engineer's plate is not known, possibly on separate scrolls below the Corps device." See page 196, *Journal of the Royal Engineers*, 1934.

For how long shoulder belts were worn by officers is not certain, but the General Orders of the Corps in 1817 do not mention them, although they describe a waist belt with an Engineer regulation plate, on which the badge 'Egypt', 'Peninsula', etc., may be worn by those officers who were entitled to them. From silhouettes in the R.E. Museum it appears that in 1817 other ranks were still wearing an oval plate.

Colonel Kealy states in Part III of his article dealing with other ranks: "A brass buckle had hitherto been worn on the white shoulder belt, except in the Gibraltar companies, where a plate was worn." In 1823 a universal brass plate was sanctioned carrying a device consisting of the Royal cypher surrounded by a garter bearing the name of the Corps, the whole surmounted by a crown.

In 1832 the Royal arms with supporters and the mottoes *Ubique*, *Quo Fas et Gloria ducunt* were placed on the shoulder-belt plates.

BUTTONS

The officers' buttons 1772-1786 were gilt, 1¼ inches in diameter, with the Ordnance arms, three cannon-balls, and three guns on a sunk shield. The other ranks' buttons are described in the History of the Corps as flat, brass buttons, 1¼ inches in diameter, for the red double-breasted coat.

The design on the buttons for both officers and other ranks of the Royal Sappers and Miners was the appropriate Royal cypher within a crowned garter inscribed with the title (Fig. 57).

57

When in 1856 the title was changed to that of Royal Engineers the same design with the necessary change of the Royal cypher was retained on the tunic buttons, and remained in use until 1902 when the garter was inscribed with the motto *Honi soit qui mal y pense*; below the garter the title 'Royal Engineers'.

GRENADIER GUARDS

TITLES
1660-1685   The King's Royal Regiment of Guards.
1685-1815   The First Regiment of Foot Guards.
1815-   Grenadier Guards.

BADGES
The Royal Cypher and Crown.
A Grenade. Authorized in 1815 together with the title "Grenadier" to commemorate the Regiment's defeat of the French Imperial Guards at Waterloo.

BATTLE HONOURS (*Dates authorized from 1811 to 1855*)
LINCELLES, 20th June, 1811.
CORUNNA, 9th October, 1811.
BARROSA, 9th October, 1811.
PENINSULA, 29th March, 1815.
WATERLOO, 8th December, 1815.
ALMA, 16th October, 1855.
INKERMAN, 16th October, 1855.
SEVASTOPOL, 16th October, 1855.

SHOULDER-BELT PLATES

The late P. W. Reynolds states that at the end of the eighteenth century the officers had oval gilt plates with a silver star and the Royal arms mounted on an enamel background.

Goelt's book gives for battalion officers an oval plate with the Royal arms as displayed up to 1802 (Fig. 58). The design was in low relief and the title engraved.

The Dayes plates shows plates worn by officers and N.C.Os. The officers had a gilt oval plate with star design, probably the same as shown in Fig. 59, which is from Almack's book.

The N.C.Os. had on their plates the design of a crowned garter. This design appears to have also been worn by the officers of the Light Company in 1800, as it is shown as such in a portrait of an officer by H. Edridge.

In Vol. I of the "British Military Library" an officer is shown with a gilt oval plate with design of a crowned garter; the plate had a rim.

In the portrait of Captain Duncan Campbell, 1787-1795, by Raeburn, he is shown wearing an oblong plate with the lion within a crowned garter. The garter had a blue background and the lion a crimson one. Round the edge of the plate was an ornamental border. By 1816 the plate for other ranks became oblong and had the design of the grenade.

In "Costumes of the British Army," by Gauci after Hull (1828), the officers are shown with plates of similar design to those worn by other ranks, the Royal cypher being probably displayed on the ball of the grenade.

An oil painting at Windsor Castle shows the officer in 1831 with the same plate except for the change in cypher.

Fig. 60 is the officers' plate *circa* 1815. The plate was gilt with slightly rounded corners and had the design mounted.

Fig. 61 is the officers' plate in use prior to 1855 and probably adopted in 1837.

BUTTONS

Fig. 62 is of the officers' button *circa* 1800. The button was gilt, single piece, with the design in low relief. About 1820 the design was the Royal cypher within a crowned garter (Fig. 63).

On the accession of William IV to the throne the cypher and crown were displayed within a French scroll without a dot (Fig. 64).

In 1837 the grenade was placed on the buttons below the Royal cypher and crown. This design was also worn by other ranks on their pewter buttons, but the cypher was reversed and intertwined and a grenade shown below. When the tunic was introduced the same design was retained and, except for changes in cypher necessitated by changes in Sovereigns, has remained the design for the button.

The mess jacket in the 1894 Dress Regulations is given as having a rolled collar and the waistcoat as having three regimental buttons with the design mounted.

In the 1934 Regulations the number of buttons on the waistcoat is given as four.

COLDSTREAM GUARDS

TITLES
1650-1660 Colonel Monck's Regiment of Foot.
1660-1661 The Lord General's Regiment of Foot.
1661-1670 The Lord General's Regiment of Foot Guards.
1670-1817 Coldstream Regiment of Foot Guards.
1817- Coldstream Guards.

BADGES
The Star of the Order of the Garter. A very full and extremely interesting article on the connection of the badge of the Garter star with the Coldstream Guards appeared in the *Household Brigade Magazine* for Summer, 1950, written by Lieut.-Colonel Sir Michael Adeane, K.C.V.O., C.B. The badge was granted to the Coldstream Guards by King William III in 1695. The shape of the star has varied at times from being oval to elongated, but has now been ordered to be of oval shape.
The Sphinx superscribed 'Egypt'. Commemorates the services of the Regiment in Egypt, 1801. Authorized 6th July, 1802.

BATTLE HONOURS (*Dates authorized from 1802 to 1855*)
EGYPT AND THE SPHINX, 6th July, 1802.
LINCELLES, 20th June, 1811.
TALAVERA, 12th February, 1812.
BARROSA, 12th February, 1812.
PENINSULA, 6th April, 1815.
WATERLOO, 8th December, 1815.
ALMA, 16th October, 1855.
INKERMAN, 16th October, 1855.
SEVASTOPOL, 16th October, 1855.

SHOULDER-BELT PLATES
According to illustrations in the Manual Exercise, 1795, but the drawings of which were probably executed some years before, the officers had oblong plates. The late Mr. P. W. Reynolds states that all the officers of the Grenadier Companies of the Foot Guards had oblong or rectangular plates with the design of the lion within a crowned garter. These plates would appear to be very similar to those worn for many years by the 29th Regiment. Battalion companies appear to have had oval plates with the design of the Garter star. In the case of officers the plate was gilt with a beaded rim (Fig. 65). The star was silver and the garter gilt, with the motto in pierced letters on a blue enamel ground; the cross was in red enamel. The plate for other ranks was of brass with the design incised. The plates for other ranks in the Grenadier Companies appear to have had the star with a grenade above it. Mr. Reynolds says that according to the Dayes plates in 1792 the star was surmounted by a crown.

The grenade seems to have disappeared from the plates between the years 1803 and 1812.

The Light Company appear to have had the same plates as the Battalion Companies, but to have displayed in addition a bugle-horn.

The oval plate would seem to have remained in use until about 1825, after which the star as before was displayed by the officers on a gilt matted plate (Fig. 66), size $3\frac{3}{4} \times 3$ inches. Behind the star a burnished silver gilt slip.

According to a painting of the regiment by A. J. Dubois Drahonet, 1831, colour-sergeants had plates similar to the officers.

BUTTONS

The officers' bone-backed buttons about 1780 had gilt faces with the design in relief of the letters 'Cm Gds' within a star (Fig. 67).

The pewter buttons of the other ranks had the same design; a pewter button of about 1800 had the Garter star with the garter inscribed 'Coldstream Guards'. The design was in low relief (Fig. 68).

The officers' buttons of the same period were gilt, flat, one piece, with the design of the star sunk and the garter engraved. About 1820 the design was the garter inscribed with the motto *Honi soit qui mal y pense*. The star was sunk and the motto engraved on a flat one-piece gilt button.

The coatee button, 1830-1855, had the star design as before but in relief on a convex button. The other ranks' pewter buttons had the same design as the officers on a convex button.

After the introduction of the tunic the same design was retained, the button having a rim.

The mess jacket in the 1894 Dress Regulations is given as having a rolled collar and the waistcoat as having four regimental buttons with the design mounted.

65

66

67

68

SCOTS GUARDS

TITLES
1660-1713   The Scots Regiment of Guards.
1713-1831   The 3rd Foot Guards.
1831-1877   Scots Fusilier Guards.
1877-   Scots Guards.

BADGES
The Star of the Order of the Thistle.
The Thistle.
The Sphinx superscribed 'Egypt'. Commemorates the services of the regiment in Egypt, 1801. Authorized 6th July, 1802.

BATTLE HONOURS (*Dates authorized from 1802 to 1855*)
EGYPT AND THE SPHINX, 6th July, 1802.
LINCELLES, 20th June, 1811.
TALAVERA, 11th February, 1812.
BARROSA, 11th February, 1812.
PENINSULA, 6th April, 1815.
WATERLOO, 8th December, 1815.
ALMA, 16th October, 1855.
INKERMAN, 16th October, 1855.
SEVASTOPOL, 16th October, 1855.

SHOULDER-BELT PLATES

The design of the shoulder-belt plates of the officers of the regiment appear to have always been the star of the Order of the Thistle, with slight variations in the design of the thistle and the number of its leaves.

About 1790 the plate was gilt, oval, matted surface with beaded rim. A gilt circle with the motto *Nemo me impune lacessit* engraved. The thistle gilt with the flower in red enamel and the two leaves in green enamel, outlined in gilt, all on a green enamel background. The rays of the star silver. Size $3\frac{1}{4} \times 2\frac{1}{2}$ inches.

Almack's book has a similar plate but the thistle flower having white seeds and only two leaves.

A later plate was of similar design, but the thistle shown with four leaves and the plate had a raised silver burnished rim, the thistle, letters and circle all in gilt metal (Fig. 69). The size of the plate was $3\frac{1}{2} \times 2\frac{1}{4}$ inches.

The late Rev. P. Sumner described a plate in the Cotton Museum at Waterloo. It was apparently of smaller size but otherwise of the same design, the thistle still having four leaves.

The 1792-1797 books show all ranks wearing oval badges with the star design. Size $3\frac{1}{2} \times 2\frac{1}{2}$ inches.

Another plate of similar design is given in Reynold's notes, but the circle is inscribed at the bottom '3rd Regt. Ft. Gds'.

In 1825 the oval plates were replaced by oblong ones with silver stars. In Hull's illustrations of the regiment, 1830, the plate has cut corners and there is a scroll above the star, the star having a crown.

It has been stated that in 1831, when the regiment became known as Scots Fusilier Guards, the thistle was shown with two leaves, but it was certainly shown thus some years previously.

Fig. 70 shows an officer's plate worn prior 1855, gilt frosted surface, silver star, gilt thistle with two leaves and the motto in pierced letters; a green enamel background to thistle and motto on garter, the star mounted on a burnished gilt slip. The plate has a narrow burnished edge.

BUTTONS

The officers' bone-backed buttons about 1780 had gilt faces with the design in relief shown in Fig. 71. The other ranks' pewter buttons of the period had the same design in low relief. About 1790 the design on the pewter buttons became as shown in Fig. 72, and not long after was changed to one with the star of the Order of the Thistle with a crown; this was worn on the pewter buttons until they were abolished in 1855. The officers' buttons *circa* 1800 were gilt, flat, single piece, with the design incised of the star of the Order of the Thistle. This was worn on the subsequent convex coatee button until the introduction of the tunic, since when the design has been the star of the Order of the Thistle with the appropriate crown.

The shape of the star has varied considerably, and in the size of the points.

The mess jacket in the 1894 Dress Regulations is given as having a rolled collar and the waistcoat as having three regimental buttons with the design mounted.

69

70

71

72

68

THE ROYAL SCOTS
(THE ROYAL REGIMENT)

TITLES
- 1633-1637   Hepburn's Regiment.
- 1637-1653   Le Regiment de Douglas.
- 1653-1688   The Earl of Dumbarton's Regiment of Foot.
- 1688-1751   The Royal Regiment of Foot (also known by Colonel's name until 1751).
- 1751-1812   The 1st or the Royal Regiment of Foot.
- 1812-1821   The 1st Regiment of Foot or the Royal Scots.
- 1821-1871   The 1st (the Royal) Regiment of Foot.
- 1871-1881   The 1st or the Royal Scots Regiment of Foot.
- 1881   The Lothian Regiment.
- 1881-1920   The Royal Scots (Lothian Regiment).
- 1920-   The Royal Scots (The Royal Regiment.)

BADGES
The Clothing Warrant dated 14th September, 1743, gives the King's Cypher 'GR' within the circle and motto of St. Andrew with crown over, on the front of the Grenadier caps, while on the little flap was the White Horse with the motto *Nec aspera terrent*.

The Royal Cypher within the circle of the Order of St. Andrew was painted on the drums, according to the Clothing Warrant of 1751.

The Sphinx superscribed 'Egypt' commemorates the services of the 2nd Battalion in Egypt, 1801. Authorized 6th July, 1802.

The Star of the Order of the Thistle.

BATTLE HONOURS *(Dates authorized from 1802 to 1855)*
EGYPT AND BADGE OF SPHINX, 6th July, 1802.

CORUNNA, 20th February, 1812.

PENINSULA, 29th March, 1815 (3rd Battalion, 29th March, 1815; to 1st and 2nd Battalions, 21st June, 1817).

NIAGARA, 19th May, 1815.

WATERLOO, 23rd November, 1815 (3rd Battalion, 23rd November, 1815; to 1st and 2nd Battalions, 21st June, 1817).

BUSACO, 21st June, 1817.

ST. SEBASTIAN, 21st June, 1817.

SALAMANCA, 21st June, 1817.

VITTORIA, 21st June, 1817.

NIVE, 21st June, 1817.

ST. LUCIA, 25th July, 1821.

EGMONT-OP-ZEE, 25th July, 1821.

NAGPORE, 26th February, 1823. Originally spelt Nagpoor.
MAHEIDPORE, 26th February, 1823. Originally spelt Maheidpoor.
AVA, 6th December, 1825.
ALMA, 16th October, 1855.
INKERMAN, 16th October, 1855.
SEVASTOPOL, 16th October, 1855.

SHOULDER-BELT PLATES

The Royal Scots are fortunate in having a very full and accurate record of their badges, etc., in their Regimental History, and the following notes are taken from the chapter dealing with the subject.

The early officers' shoulder-belt plates were probably oval, gilt, with the design of the star of the Order of the Thistle. Almack's book illustrates an oblong one with the title 'Loyal' on the scroll. This is obviously an error for 'Royal'. The plate was burnished gilt with the design mounted in gilt. The other ranks had the same design. In a book entitled the "British Military Library," 1799, a print shows an officer of the regiment with a gilt oval plate with design of crown, garter and thistle. This plate appears to have been worn until 1815, when Jennen's notes gave the plate worn 1816-1822 as gilt, oblong, corded circle, surmounted by a crown; in centre of circle a Union wreath, 'GR', Sphinx, and Honours (Fig. 73). The same notes describe the plate of 1822-1829 (Fig. 74) as gilt with gilt mount, 'GR' reversed in a circle inscribed with Honours and collar of St. Andrew, crown above, star of St. Andrew below.

According to the late Captain E. A. Campbell, the other ranks' brass oblong plate of the period 1812-1816 had the design struck in relief of the Royal cypher within the collar of the Order of the Thistle, with the star pendant. Above the collar a crown, and below the star a Sphinx inscribed 'Egypt'. Below this extending across the plate a scroll inscribed 'The—Scots—Royal', on either side of the star a spray of rose, shamrock and thistle. The plate had slightly rounded corners.

The plate in use 1829-1837 was as shown in Fig. 75, with the Royal cypher which varied according to the date; the plate was burnished gilt with a silver cut star and gilt rays and centre circle pierced, showing a gilt burnished back beneath. The Honours on the rays are shown upside down, the reason being to get the plain ray under the pendent badge.

From 1844 to 1855 the officers' plate was oblong, gilt, matted surface with burnished edge; in the centre a gilt St. Andrew within an oval and on a blue enamel background. At the bottom half of the oval a scroll inscribed 'The Royal Regiment'. The design all in gilt on a silver cut star.

In 1881, when the title of the regiment was for a short time changed to The Lothian Regiment; it was proposed that the full dress should be similar to that of the Highland Light Infantry.

The shoulder-belt plate proposed was an oblong silver one with the design of the star of the Order of the Thistle surmounted by a crown and with a scroll inscribed 'The Lothian Regt.' below the circle. The crown and star were in gilt metal, the thistle, circle and lettering, which were pierced, in silver on a green enamel background; the scroll with the title was also silver.

The late Major H. M. McCance writes of this badge: "The experimental one, designed when it was thought the R.S. was to wear H.L.I. kit in 1881. I have seen a photograph of an officer of that time in the kit alluded to. The plate was worn for a very short time and by few."

The plate worn since 1903, when the Scottish method of carrying the sword from a shoulder belt was resumed, was a burnished gilt one with the design mounted in silver of the star of the Order of the Thistle. In the centre on a ground of green enamel, the thistle in gilt metal, within a circle inscribed *Nemo me impune lacessit*, the circle and letters also gilt. Below the star a scroll inscribed 'The Royal Scots'.

BUTTONS

The officers' bone-backed button with gilt face and the pewter buttons for the other ranks *circa* 1780 had the design shown in Fig. 76. Later the same design was worn on officers' buttons with a closed metal back.

In the Dayes plates of uniforms, 1792-1799, a copy of which was in the Prince Consort's Library, Aldershot, the officers' buttons are shown having the design of a plain 'I'.

Major McCance described a button he had heard of as being found in Jamaica, and this may be identified as that shown in the Dayes plates. A pewter button found in Canada had the design of the thistle within a crowned garter and the title 'Royal' below. This may be the same as worn by both officers and other ranks. The thistle had the figure 'I' on the ball.

In 1829 the design on the officers' gilt convex buttons was as shown in Fig. 77. This button was replaced in 1840 by one with the star of the Order of the Thistle, with 'The Royal Regt.' at the bottom of the button. In 1859 the word 'Royal' was moved to above the star, and the word 'Regt.' remained at the bottom.

From 1860 or soon after the title was shown once more below the badge on the button (Fig. 78).

After 1881 the design was the star of the Order of the Thistle; below the badge, 'The Royal Scots'.

The 1904 Dress Regulations give the mess dress as having the star of the Order of the Thistle, but without the title of the regiment. The star was mounted in silver.

73

74

75

76

77

78

72

THE QUEEN'S ROYAL REGIMENT
(WEST SURREY)

TITLES

1661-1685   The Tangier Regiment or Queen's Own Regiment of Foot.
1685-1703   The Queen Dowager's Regiment of Foot. Also known by Colonel's names until 1751.
1703-1715   The Queen's Royal Regiment.
1715-1727   The Princess of Wales's Own Regiment of Foot.
1727-1751   The Queen's Own Regiment of Foot.
1751-1881   The 2nd (Queen's Royal) Regiment of Foot.
1881-1920   The Queen's (Royal West Surrey Regiment).
1920-   The Queen's Royal Regiment (West Surrey).

BADGES

The Paschal Lamb. The origin of the ancient badge of the Regiment is obscure. Regimental tradition associates the badge and the old sea green facings of the Regiment with Catherine of Braganza, the Consort of Charles II. But neither Burke nor other Heraldic authorities show any connection between the badge and the Royal armories and insignia of Portugal. Macaulay has suggested that the badge was adopted as appropriate to a regiment going to fight in Tangiers against infidels.

The lamb as originally displayed was not a "Paschal" one, nor had it any banner, and is shown on the Carlisle figures as having a bushy tail. The Colours in 1751 depicted three lambs on a green ground. In the Regulations for Clothing and Colours, 1747, it is referred to as "a Lamb being their ancient badge".

The Sphinx superscribed 'Egypt'. Commemorates the services of the regiment in the campaign of 1801. Authorized 6th July, 1802.

The White Horse. As in other regiments, the Royal Warrant of 1751 directed that the White Horse should be worn on the caps of the Grenadiers and Drummers, but at a later period this was changed to the "King's Crest". These badges remained in the Army List as being worn for some years after the head-dresses in question had been abolished.

Mottoes: *Pristinæ virtutis memor.*
          Vel exuviæ triumphant.

The origin of these two mottoes is not certain. Cannon, not a very reliable historian, associates the first with the defence of Tongres.

Chichester and Burges-Short, in their book "Records and Badges of the British Army", suggest that it is possible that the two mottoes may have been confused and that the second one commemorated Tongres and the first records service in Spain, as it does in the case of the 8th Royal Irish Hussars, who also have the motto.

Mr. C. T. Atkinson, in an article entitled "Names, Numbers and

Errors" which appeared in No. 45, Vol. XII, of the *Journal of the Society for Army Historical Research*, proves this origin to have been impossible.

The Cypher of Queen Catherine within the Garter. Authorized in 1909, to commemorate the regiment's connection with Catherine of Braganza, the Queen of Charles II.

A Naval Crown superscribed '1st June, 1794'. Authorized in 1909, to commemorate the regiment's services under Lord Howe at his victory on the 1st June, 1794.

BATTLE HONOURS (*Dates authorized from 1802 to 1855*)
   EGYPT AND THE SPHINX, 6th July, 1802.
   PENINSULA, 6th April, 1815.
   SALAMANCA, 9th July, 1816.
   VITTORIA, 4th August, 1819.
   PYRENEES, 4th August, 1819.
   NIVELLE, 4th August, 1819.
   TOULOUSE, 4th August, 1819.
   VIMIERA, 15th June, 1833.
   CORUNNA, 15th June, 1833.
   AFFGHANISTAN, 18th July, 1840.
   GHUZNEE, 18th July, 1840.
   KHELAT, 27th July, 1840.

SHOULDER-BELT PLATES

The late Rev. P. Sumner, in the *Journal of the Society for Army Historical Research*, page 248, Vol. XVIII, records a very small oval silver plate in the Regimental Museum at Guildford. He describes it as follows: "A crown beaten out and the letters 'CR' cut out like a stencil with the motto *Pristine virtutis memor* at the bottom, a beaded border, no hall mark." Its size was $2\frac{1}{2} \times 1\frac{11}{16}$ inches (Fig. 79).

Another plate of white-metal had the design engraved as in Fig. 80.

The late Rev. P. Sumner rather doubted whether these badges were authentic.

In the Dayes plates the officers' plate was shown as diamond shape (Fig. 81), and the brass oval plate of the other ranks a plain '2' below a crown.

Fig. 82 is a small silver plate worn about 1809 or before. This plate afterwards became oblong with rounded corners, the same design of the number within a crowned garter being retained, but a scroll was added below inscribed 'Egypt'. According to the Regimental History, the other ranks' plate had the same design.

This plate lasted for some years, but in 1830 one of the design in Fig. 83 was adopted and the lamb with halo was displayed on the officers' plate for the first time. The plate was gilt, the lamb and garter having a blue enamel ground. Other ranks wore a brass or gun-metal badge as in Fig. 84, which came into use about 1833 and was worn until 1855. Below the belt plate was worn a brass metal slide inscribed 'Queen's Royal'.

79

BUTTONS

The other ranks' pewter buttons of the period 1770 had the design of '2' within a narrow circle in relief (Fig. 85). This was replaced by one with a design which, in the case of the other ranks, was worn until 1874 (Fig. 86).

In the Dayes plates this design was shown as being worn by the officers on their silver buttons, and was continued until about 1820 when Fig. 87 was adopted and worn until about 1830, when the colour of the buttons was changed to gold, and the older design of the crown and number was readopted and retained until 1881.

An other ranks' pewter button found in Egypt, worn *circa* 1800, had the design in relief of '2' below a crown within a continuous wreath. This design does not appear to have been long in use.

After 1881 the design was of a Paschal Lamb with a banner over its right shoulder, within a crowned circle inscribed 'The Royal West Surrey Regiment'. Below the circle a scroll inscribed 'The Queen's'.

Later the date '1661' was added within the circle below the lamb.

In 1909 a completely new design was adopted. The banner was changed to a flag and the lamb placed on a twisted bar. Above the lamb a mural crown. Below the lamb the date '1661' and below this a scroll inscribed 'The Queen's Royal Regt'.

In the 1900 Dress Regulations the mess waistcoat and field cap had the design of the lamb mounted in silver. The cap button was die struck. The 1934 Regulations give the lamb on a plain dome.

THE BUFFS (ROYAL EAST KENT REGIMENT)

TITLES
1572-1689   The Holland Regiment. Its early service was in the service of Holland.
1689-1708   Prince George of Denmark's Regiment.
1708-1751   Known by names of the Colonel. First official use of the title "The Buffs" was in 1747.
1751-1782   The 3rd (or the Buffs) Regiment of Foot.
1782-1881   The 3rd (East Kent) Regiment of Foot (The Buffs).
1881-1935   The Buffs (East Kent Regiment).
1935-   The Buffs (Royal East Kent Regiment).

BADGES
The Green Dragon. Recorded in the Clothing Regulations of 1747 as the Green Dragon and in the Royal Warrant of 1751 referred to as "being the ancient badge of the Regiment."

The origin of the badge is lost in antiquity, but probably traces back to the fact that the regiment was raised from the Trained Bands of the City of London. The dragon was an old badge of the Saxons and is reputed to have been borne by Harold at the battle of Hastings and retained by the Norman kings. Queen Elizabeth had a golden dragon and Henry the VIII a red one as one of the supporters in the Royal arms. A silver dragon is still part of the arms of the City of London. The dragon of the Buffs has as far as is known always been "vert" or green, and has no cross of St. George on its wings like the one in the arms of the City of London.

There is also the golden dragon which was taken from the Mosque of St. Sophia in the Crusades and was placed in the belfry at Bruges and thence taken to Ghent.

Cannon may be right in supposing the dragon to have been placed on the Colours in 1707 when the regiment was at Ghent.

The White Horse of Kent and the motto *Invicta*. The old badge of the East Kent Militia was worn for a short time after 1881 by the whole regiment.

The Rose and Crown. This badge, like that of the dragon, is of very early date and probably derived from the Elizabethan period.

Motto: *Veteri frondescit honore*. Although not mentioned in the Royal Warrant of 1751, was displayed on the Colours of that date. It was not given in the Army List until 1890.

The White Horse of Hanover and motto. Was displayed on the flap of the Grenadier caps and the drums and bells of arms in 1747, but an application in 1872 for permission to bear the badge and motto and also the motto *Veteri frondescit honore* was refused.

BATTLE HONOURS (*Dates authorized from 1813 to 1855*)
DOURO, 10th September, 1813.
PENINSULA, 6th April, 1815.

TALAVERA, 4th January, 1823.
ALBUHERA, 4th January, 1823.
PYRENEES, 4th January, 1823.
NIVELLE, 4th January, 1823.
NIVE, 4th January, 1823.
PUNNIAR, 22nd June, 1844.
SEVASTOPOL, 16th October, 1855.

SHOULDER-BELT PLATES

The 1792-1797 Dayes book of plates shows the officer wearing an oblong silver plate with the design of the dragon, and the other ranks' plate also oblong but of brass with rounded corners.

Fig. 88 is from a plate in the Regimental Museum. The plate is silver with the design engraved. There is also a similar plate but with the design mounted. Other ranks' oval plates were brass with the design of the number '3' surmounted by a crown, and are almost identical with the plate worn at the same time by the 3rd Guernsey Militia.

A print of an officer of the Buffs in the "British Military Library", published 1799-1800, shows the officer wearing an oblong silver plate with the design of the number '3' surmounted by a crown, below the dragon surmounted by a scroll possibly inscribed with the regimental motto.

Mr. Reynolds, in his book of Uniforms, records a gilt oblong plate with silver crowned garter, scroll above and one below. This he dates as about 1826, but it would probably be after 1830, being gilt.

Prior to 1855 the officers' shoulder-belt plate was oblong, gilt burnished, with the dragon, with its tail going out almost straight, within a garter inscribed with the ancient motto of the regiment, all in gilt. Above the garter a curved scroll inscribed 'Peninsula', all on a silver star with square-cut rays, on the rays the seven Peninsular Honours, above the whole a gilt crown.

BUTTONS

The other ranks' pewter buttons *circa* 1780 had in relief the design in Fig. 89. The later pewter buttons had the dragon with a garter inscribed with the motto and the number '3' below.

The officers' flat, silver buttons about 1800 had the design of the dragon standing on ground, and around the upper edge of the button a scroll with the motto, below the dragon the number '3'.

A button of almost identical design was much later worn by the officers' mess waiters.

After 1830 the officers' buttons were gilt, single piece, flat, with the design of the dragon within a circle inscribed with the motto, and with '3' below the dragon.

The coatee buttons 1830-1855 displayed the dragon on a twisted bar with '3' below, within a circle with beaded edges and inscribed with the regimental motto (Fig. 90).

The tunic button which was introduced in 1855 had the same design.

After 1881 the dragon was displayed within a crowned circle inscribed 'The East Kent Regt.' 'The Buffs', and below the circle a scroll with the motto.

On the conferring of the title 'Royal' on the regiment in 1935 the design was retained with the title on the circle reading 'The Buffs' 'The Royal East Kent Regt.'.

In 1900 the officers' field cap and mess waistcoat had the design mounted in silver of the dragon and a scroll below inscribed 'The Buffs'. In the 1911 Regulations the cap button is given as die struck.

88

89

90

THE KING'S OWN ROYAL REGIMENT (LANCASTER)

TITLES

1680-1684	The 2nd Tangier Regiment.
1684-1685	The Duchess of York and Albany's Regiment of Foot.
1685-1702	The Queen's Own Regiment.
1702-1710	The Queen's Own Regiment of Marines.
1710-1713	The Queen's Own Regiment of Foot.
1713-1751	The King's Own Regiment of Foot.
1751-1815	The 4th or the King's Own Regiment of Foot.
1815-1881	The 4th (The King's Own) Regiment of Foot.
1881-1920	The King's Own (Royal Lancaster Regiment).
1920-	The King's Own Royal Regiment (Lancaster).

BADGES

The Lion of England. The ancient badge of the regiment, having been given to them by William III as a reward for their services after his landing in England.

The second or Regimental Colour of the 2nd Battalion of the regiment, raised in 1756 when they became the 62nd Regiment, displayed the lion crowned and static; an illustration of this Colour appears on page 246, Vol. X, of the *Journal of the Society for Army Historical Research*.

According to Colonel Cowper's History of the Regiment, the badge first appears on the shoulder-belt plates in 1774, and it was then shown without a crown and with the paw raised as in the Royal Standard. In 1822 the paw was lowered, but not quite to the ground; it was once more raised as before in 1855.

The Royal Cypher. Appears for the first time in the Army List of 1852, but is given in Queen's Regulations of 1844.

The Red Rose of Lancaster. Adopted as a badge by the Regular battalions of the Regiment in 1881 and displayed on the officers' waist-belt plates and as a collar badge for a short time, and is still displayed on the buttons. It was an old badge of the 1st Royal Lancashire Militia.

BATTLE HONOURS (*Dates authorized from* 1812 *to* 1855)

CORUNNA, 20th February, 1812.
PENINSULA, 6th April, 1815.
WATERLOO, 8th December, 1815.
BADAJOZ, 4th January, 1823.
SALAMANCA, 4th January, 1823.
VITTORIA, 4th January, 1823.

ST. SEBASTIAN, 4th January, 1823.
NIVE, 4th January, 1823.
BLADENSBURG, 31st May, 1827.
ALMA, 16th October, 1855.
INKERMAN, 16th October, 1855.
SEVASTOPOL, 16th October, 1855.

SHOULDER-BELT PLATES

In Colonel Cowper's History of the Regiment is a detailed description of the various changes in the design of the shoulder-belt plates and buttons, arranged in chronological order.

Shoulder-belt plates are recorded as follows:

1774. Officers', gilt, rectangular, lion above 'IV'. An illustration of an officer wearing this plate in 1780 appears on page 159 of Vol. XXVII, *Journal of the Society for Army Historical Research*. The plate was apparently silver. The brass plate worn by other ranks was oval with a milled edge. It had the design of the lion above a Roman 'IV' within an oval crowned garter. The design was mounted.

1780. Officers had oval, gilt plates with the design of the lion above a Roman 'IV'; the plate had a bevelled rim.
   In Mr. P. W. Reynolds' notes is recorded an oval plate with a beaded rim. In the centre the design of the lion above 'IV' within a crowned garter inscribed *Honi soit qui mal y pense*. Unfortunately, no mention is made of the colour of the metal.

1784. Other ranks', oval, brass, with the design of a lion surmounted by a crown. Above the crown the word 'King's' and below the lion the word 'Own'. The plate had a lined edge (Fig. 91).

1792. Officers', oval, gilt. According to Colonel Cowper's History, a lion above a crown but detached, round the bottom 'IV King's Own'.
   In the Dayes plates the design shows the Royal crest with the title 'IV or King's Own' round the lower edge (Fig. 92).

1800. Officers' rectangular gilt plate, with cut corners; silver mounted, oval, crowned garter, within which the lion and Roman 'IV'. The garter was inscribed 'The King's Own Regiment'. The size, according to Mr. P. W. Reynolds, was $3\frac{7}{8} \times 2\frac{11}{16}$ inches.
   Colonel Cowper also records an other ranks' plate found by an English Engineer in the Peninsula when deepening a well. The plate has the design of the lion within a garter and the title 'King's Own Infantry' on a scroll below. In Mr. Usher's collection is an other ranks' plate of the 1812-1820 period. The plate is die struck, its size $2\frac{1}{2} \times 3\frac{1}{2}$ inches (Fig. 93).

1820. Officers, gilt, square-cut corners, circular crowned garter within which lion and 'IV'. The garter inscribed 'The King's Own Regiment'. According to Mr. P. W. Reynolds this plate had cut corners.

1833. Officers' cut rectangular plate. The design mounted in gilt of a crowned garter, within which was a gilt lion and Roman 'IV'. The garter inscribed 'The King's Own Regiment'. These were surrounded by a silver spray of laurel leaves with scrolls below inscribed 'Corunna, Badajoz, Salamanca, Vittoria, San Sebastian, Nivelle,* Peninsula, Bladensburg, Waterloo'.

1840. Officers reverted to the design of 1820.

1848. Officers resumed the 1833 design, but the plate had heavier and more elaborate scrolls and the Battle Honour 'Nivelle' was replaced by 'Nive'.

BUTTONS

Buttons discovered in America show the officers' bone-backed buttons to have had silver faces with the design of the number '4' in relief; the button had a lined rim (Fig. 94).

Mr. Buckell, in describing the portrait of an officer of the 4th Foot, *circa* 1780, in Vol. XXVII of the *Journal of the Society for Army Historical Research*, 1949, gives the buttons as silver with 'IVth' on them.

The Dayes plates show the buttons having the plain design of 'IV'.

About 1800 the other ranks' pewter buttons had the design of 'IV', the button having a border of leaves turned inwards (Fig. 95).

The period of 1808 saw the officers' buttons with the design of the lion standing on a ground within a crowned garter inscribed 'King's Own Regiment'. The garter had lined edges. Below the garter was the Roman numerals 'IV' (Fig. 96).

The other ranks' pewter buttons of about 1810 had the same design, but the garter was inscribed 'King's Own Regiment'. This was replaced by a button of similar design but with the number 'IV' within the garter and below the lion. The lion was not in this case standing on any ground and the garter was inscribed 'The King's Own Regiment', which design continued until 1855.

The officers' coatee button, 1830-1855, had the same design as the other ranks' button. The first tunic buttons in 1881 retained the design except for the number being shown in Arabic characters, but soon after the title on the garter was changed to read 'The King's Own Royal Regiment'. After 1881 the design was the lion above the rose, and above the lion superimposed on a circle a crown; the circle inscribed 'The King's Own Royal Lancaster'. Since 1920 the circle has been inscribed 'The King's Own Royal Regiment'.

The 1904 Dress Regulations give the mess dress button as 'KORL' in monogram with a crown above, mounted in gilt.

The 1911 Regulations gives the design on the cap button as the Lion of England with crown above and rose below. The button was die struck.

* This must be a mistake for Nive.

THE ROYAL NORTHUMBERLAND FUSILIERS

TITLES
- 1674-1751　Known as "Holland Regiment" in the service of the Prince of Orange and by the name of the Colonel.
- 1751-1782　The 5th Regiment of Foot.
- 1782-1836　The 5th (Northumberland) Regiment of Foot.
- 1836-1881　The 5th (Northumberland) (Fusiliers) Regiment of Foot.
- 1881-1935　The Northumberland Fusiliers.
- 1935-　The Royal Northumberland Fusiliers.

BADGES
St. George and the Dragon. The "ancient badge" of the regiment, the origin of which is unknown; was displayed on the Colours in 1797.

A Red and White Plume with the red uppermost commemorates the gallantry of the regiment at the action of La Vigie in 1778, when the soldiers decorated themselves with the white plumes of the French Grenadiers. When in 1828 a white plume was ordered to be worn by all Line regiments other than Fusiliers and Light Infantry, the 5th were given a red and white one as a distinction. Authorized 17th June, 1829.

The King's Crest and the Red and White Rose. On the 27th March, 1868, permission was given for the regiment to retain the King's crest—*i.e.*, a crown surmounted by a lion instead of the Imperial crown—and the King's crest together with the red and white roses to be shown on the three corners of the Regimental Colours. Later, on 10th December, 1884, an application to wear the King's crest and the red and white rose as separate devices was refused.

The Rose slipped with the Crown over. Was directed in the Royal Warrant of 1751 to be displayed in the unoccupied corners of the second Colour. In "Records and Badges", by Chichester and Burges-Short, it is stated that "The Emblem of England—*i.e.*, the rose displayed with stalk and leaves, in contradistinction to the Tudor Rose which is without these appendages—and the crown over, was probably the distinguishing badge of the six Holland Regiments of 1673-4. So far as can be learned, it has always been borne by the two surviving corps, now the Royal Northumberland Fusiliers and the Royal Warwickshire Regiment."

Motto: *Quo fata vocant*. Authorized to resume in addition to its ancient badge, 31st March, 1831.

BATTLE HONOURS (*Dates authorized from 1815 to 1855*)
PENINSULA, 6th April, 1815.
ROLEIA,* 25th September, 1817.
CIUDAD RODRIGO, 25th September, 1817.

---

* An Army Order in 1911 directed the spelling to be "Rolica".

VITTORIA, 25th September, 1817.
SALAMANCA, 25th September, 1817
NIVELLE, 25th September, 1817
BADAJOZ, 28th May, 1818.
ORTHES, 28th May, 1818.
TOULOUSE, 28th May, 1818.
VIMIERA, 10th December, 1825.
BUSACO, 10th December, 1825.
CORUNNA, 20th December, 1825.
WILHELMSTAHL, 7th May, 1836.

SHOULDER-BELT PLATES

In a print of an officer of the regiment in the "British Military Library," 1799, the shoulder-belt plate is shown as an oval silver one engraved; this is probably the same as mentioned in Jennen's Notes, 1800-1815 (Fig. 97) as oval, silver, with the design of St. George and the Dragon. The same notes record the plate of 1822-1836 as an all silver oblong plate, garter, *Quo fata vocant* and St. George on an eight-pointed cut silver star.

Mr. Reynolds records a silver burnished plate with St. George and the Dragon with motto *Quo fata vocant* within a solid wreath with eleven Battle Honours round, a crown at top of the garter, all on a silver cut star. St. George is armed with a spear. This would have been worn prior to 1830, in which year the lace was changed from silver to gold.

Fig. 98 shows the gilt plate with silver St. George and gilt grenade adopted soon after 1836 when the regiment became Fusiliers and were given the Honour 'Wilhelmstahl'. The size of the plate was $3\frac{7}{8} \times 3\frac{1}{16}$ inches.

Fig. 99 is the plate worn prior to 1855. The plate, a gilt one, had the design mounted in dead gilt. Mr. Hughes has in his collection a similar plate, but with the design on the ball of the grenade mounted in silver.

BUTTONS

The officers' bone-backed buttons *circa* 1780 had the design shown in Fig. 100 in relief; the other ranks' pewter button had the same design, which later gave place to one with a plain Roman 'V'.

About 1790 the men's buttons had the design of an Arabic '5' within a French scroll with dot at opening, the button having a lined rim (Fig. 101). The officers' silver buttons of this period were slightly convex, single piece, with the design in relief of a Roman 'V' within a laurel wreath in the centre of an eight-pointed star (Fig. 102). This design was replaced by one with the Roman 'V' within a laurel wreath and was worn after 1830 in gilt until soon after 1836, when St. George and the Dragon with a small 'V' below but within a garter inscribed with the motto became the design for the officers' buttons.

This design with the alteration of the Roman numeral for an Arabic one was worn until 1881.

On the double-breasted tunic buttons the design was as worn on the coatee, the St. George facing inwards; when the single-breasted tunic was introduced the St. George faced to the right. After 1881 the design was retained with the omission of the regimental number and the motto in most dies on a girdle instead of a garter.

The 1900 Dress Regulations gives the design on the officers' field cap and mess dress button as for the tunic button, but the centre mounted in silver. In the 1904 Regulations it states the "Ring with motto in gilt, the Dragon, etc., in silver".

97

98

99

100

101

102

G

87

THE ROYAL WARWICKSHIRE REGIMENT

TITLES
1673-1688   A Holland Regiment.
1688-1751   Known by the Colonel's name.
1751-1782   The 6th Regiment of Foot.
1782-1832   The 6th (1st Warwickshire) Regiment of Foot.
1832-1881   The 6th (Royal First Warwickshire) Regiment of Foot.
1881-   The Royal Warwickshire Regiment.

BADGES
The Antelope. The badge of the regiment recorded in the Clothing Regulations of 1747 and referred to as its "Ancient badge".

The United Red and White Rose slipped and ensigned with the Imperial Crown. The emblem of England—*i.e.*, the rose displayed with stalk and leaves and not like the Tudor Rose, which has not these appendages. Was probably the badge of the six Holland regiments and has always been one of the badges of the two surviving Corps, the Royal Northumberland Fusiliers and the Royal Warwickshire Regiment.

The Bear and Ragged Staff. The old badge of the Warwick Militia and worn after 1881 for a time by the Regular battalions as a collar badge.

BATTLE HONOURS (*Dates authorized from* 1815 *to* 1855)
PENINSULA, 6th April, 1815.
NIAGARA, 28th September, 1816.
PYRENEES, 22nd January, 1818.
ORTHES, 22nd January, 1818.
ROLEIA,* 26th April, 1827.
VIMIERA, 26th April, 1827.
VITTORIA, 26th April, 1827.
NIVELLE, 26th April, 1827.
CORUNNA, 23rd May, 1827.

SHOULDER-BELT PLATES
In the Dayes plates the officers are shown wearing an oval silver badge with the antelope on a bar (Fig. 103). Fig. 104 shows the plate in Almack's book. The plate was polished silver with a metal gilt border, and gilt garter and crown. The garter pierced and with a blue enamel ground, the antelope in silver, the chain and ground gilt.

The Dayes plate shows the other ranks' plate (Fig. 105) as oval with the number '6' surmounted by a crown; above the crown is inscribed '1st Warwick-

---
* An Army Order in 1911 directed the spelling to be "Rolica".

shire' and at the bottom of the plate 'Regiment'. Fig. 106 is another design of other ranks' plates, probably worn by a different battalion.

The author saw a very fine plate of the 6th many years ago; it was an oval silver plate with a raised gilt rim. In the centre was a silver antelope within a gilt crowned garter pierced with the title of the regiment. Behind the antelope a blue enamel ground, above the crown a gilt scroll pierced with the word 'Peninsula' and one below inscribed 'Niagara'. This plate was probably worn for a very short time and was soon replaced by that in Fig. 107, which was in silver. This design in silver was retained on the gilt plate worn prior to 1855, the number 'VI' being shown below the wreath in mottled silver.

BUTTONS

The early pewter buttons had the design in relief of '6', the button having a roped rim (Fig. 108). The officers' silver bone-backed button of this period had a very attractive engraved design (Fig. 109).

The Dayes plates show the buttons as having '6' within what appears to be a French scroll for the other ranks and a plain '6' for officers.

Soon after the design of the antelope appeared and was shown within a crowned garter inscribed *Honi soit qui mal y pense*, the Arabic '6' below the antelope. The antelope was at first shown standing (Fig. 110) without any collar or chain. The officers' silver buttons *circa* 1810 and the later coatee and tunic buttons all showed the antelope thus. It was not until about 1840 that the collar and chain were added, although they had long been displayed on the shoulder-belt plates.

After 1881 the design on the tunic button was the antelope with collar and chain, with all four feet on the ground, within a crowned garter inscribed 'Royal Warwickshire Regiment'.

The 1900 Dress Regulations gives the design on the officers' field service cap and mess dress buttons as the badge of the antelope mounted in silver. The 1904 Regulations states that the mess dress button had the antelope in silver within a gilt garter crowned. The 1911 Regulations states the cap button die struck with same design as for mess dress button.

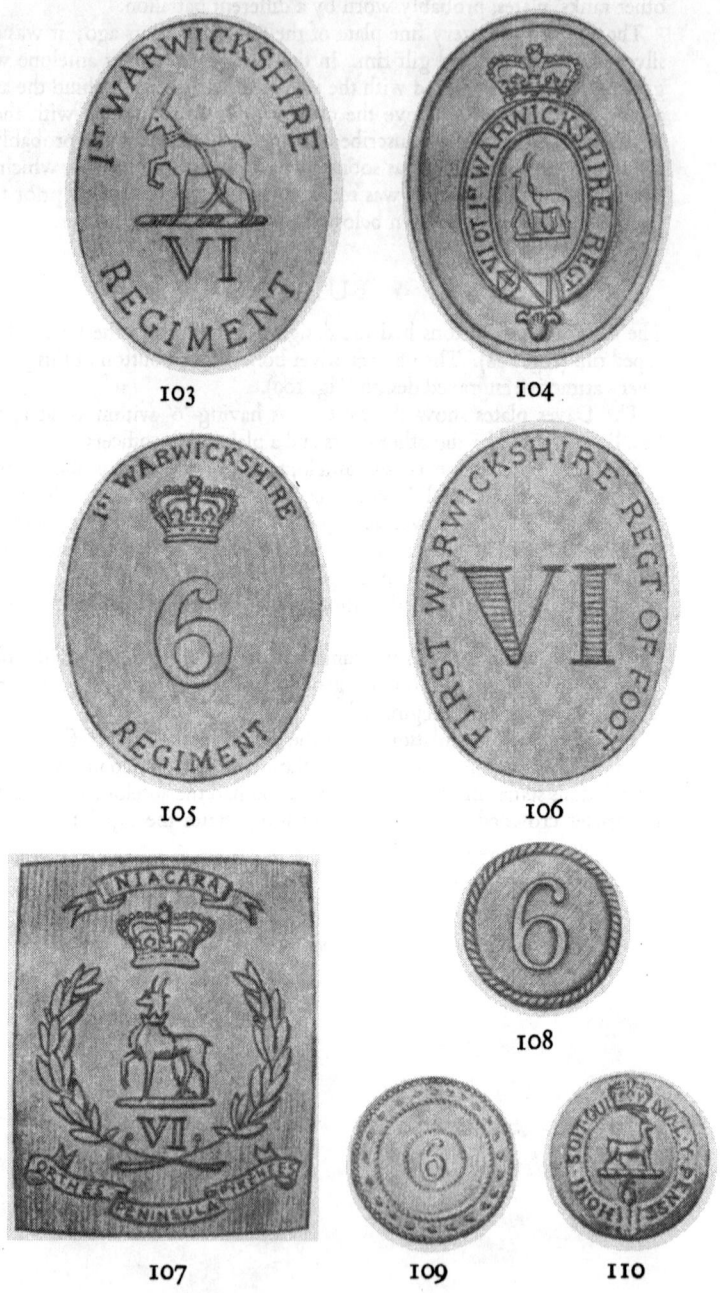

THE ROYAL FUSILIERS
(CITY OF LONDON REGIMENT)

TITLES

1685-1751   Our Royal Regiment of Fusiliers, also formerly "Our Ordnance Regiment" known by name of Colonel.

1751-1881   The 7th (or Royal Fusiliers).

1881-   The Royal Fusiliers (City of London Regiment).

BADGES

The United Red and White Rose within the Garter with Crown over it. In the Regulations for Clothing and Colours, 1747, the "Rose within the Garter and Crown over it" is directed to be displayed.

The White Horse of Hanover and the motto *Nec aspera terrent* was directed to be worn on the flap of the Grenadiers' cap in the Regulations for Clothing and Colours, 1747. After 1881 it was displayed below the Garter on the full-dress Fusiliers' cap grenade.

BATTLE HONOURS (*Dates authorized from 1815 to 1855*)

PENINSULA, 6th April, 1815.
TALAVERA, 12th November, 1819.
BADAJOZ, 12th November, 1819.
SALAMANCA, 12th November, 1819.
VITTORIA, 12th November, 1819.
PYRENEES, 12th November, 1819.
ORTHES, 12th November, 1819.
TOULOUSE, 12th November, 1819.
MARTINIQUE, 5th September, 1816.
ALBUHERA, 5th September, 1816.
ALMA, 16th October, 1855.
INKERMAN, 16th October, 1855.
SEVASTOPOL, 16th October, 1855.

SHOULDER-BELT PLATES

In Mr. Reynolds' book of notes is an officers' gilt plate as shown in Fig. 111. The star and crown were silver, the rose and garter gilt. The plate had a beaded silver edge. The other ranks' plate according to the Dayes plates was of the same design in brass.

Almack's book records a gilt oblong plate with the round corners and the design of the rose in the centre of a star of eight points, all within a crowned garter inscribed *Honi soit qui mal y pense*.

In Mr. R. W. Tilling's collection is a very attractive plate of an officer of the

Light Company of the regiment, which he dates as *circa* 1812. The plate is gilt, burnished, with a silver beaded border. In the centre of the plate a gilt rose within a crowned garter, also in gilt; the garter inscribed *Honi soit qui mal y pense*. The whole mounted on a silver cut star, below which is a Light Infantry bugle-horn. The plate has cut corners. Its size is $3\frac{1}{8} \times 2\frac{7}{8}$ inches. Mr. Reynolds also described a similar badge for the Battalion Companies of the regiment, of the same design, but without the bugle-horn or grenade.

Fig. 112 is the brass plate worn by other ranks during the Peninsular and Waterloo period. The design was engraved.

From a print on page 49 of Vol. XIX of the *Journal of the Society for Army Historical Research*, the plate worn by other ranks 1832-3 appears to have had the same design as Fig. 112, but on an oblong plate.

Fig. 113 is the officers' gilt plate *circa* 1840. Behind the garter was a blue enamel ground and behind the crown crimson cloth.

Fig. 114 is the officers' plate worn prior to 1855. The plate was dead gilt and had crimson behind the crown and blue enamel behind the pierced letters on the garter. Below the plate was a gilt bar or slide ornamented with laurel leaves. The crown was the old eight-looped crown worn by many cavalry regiments and the Rifle Brigade.

The other ranks' brass plate *circa* 1850 had the design of a large grenade, on the ball of which was the rose within a garter.

BUTTONS

The men's pewter buttons *circa* 1780 had the design shown in Fig. 115 engraved. About 1810 the design became a rose within a crowned garter, inscribed *Honi soit qui mal y pense*; in the centre of the rose, the number '7' (Fig. 116).

The officers' coatee button prior to 1855 had the design in rather low relief on a slightly convex button. This design was worn by officers until 1881 and other ranks until 1871.

After 1881 the design was the same except that the number '7' was not displayed in the centre of the rose.

In 1902 the design of the crown was changed, but otherwise there was no change.

The 1904 Dress Regulations gives the mess dress button as having the monogram 'RF' with crown above mounted in gilt.

THE KING'S REGIMENT (LIVERPOOL)

TITLES
1685-1702 The Princess Anne of Denmark's Regiment.
1702-1716 The Queen's Regiment, also by Colonel's name until 1751.
1716-1751 The King's Regiment, also by Colonel's name until 1751.
1751-1881 The 8th (The King's) Regiment.
1881   The Liverpool Regiment.
1881-1920 The King's (Liverpool Regiment).
1920-   The King's Regiment (Liverpool).

BADGES
The White Horse of Hanover and the motto *Nec aspera terrent*. The badge was directed to be worn within the Garter on the Colours of the Regiment in 1716 by King George I.
Later the badge was placed on the Colours and shown on the Grenadier caps of a number of regiments, but in 1716 it was peculiar to the 8th.
The motto was not placed on the Colours until 1846.
The representation of the horse has varied considerably. On the pre-1881 other ranks' cap badges it was even displayed "walking".
Old English lettering. This was used for a great many years.
The Sphinx superscribed 'Egypt'. Commemorates the services of the regiment in Egypt, 1801. Authorized 6th July, 1802.
The Red Rose. An old badge of the 2nd Royal Lancashire Militia and worn for a time after 1881 by all battalions of the regiment.
The Royal Cypher ensigned with the Imperial Crown. The Imperial crown was authorized in 1889. The King's cypher and crown was recorded as being on their second Colours in the Regulations for Clothing and Colours, 1747, while the Queen's Regulations of 1844 give it as the Royal cypher and the crown over it.

BATTLE HONOURS (*Dates authorized from* 1802 *to* 1855)
EGYPT AND THE SPHINX, 6th July, 1802.
NIAGARA, 19th May, 1815.
MARTINIQUE, 5th September, 1816.

SHOULDER-BELT PLATES
The officers had a gilt oval plate with a silver horse within a crowned Garter. The plate had a beaded edge. The Dayes plates showed this, and the other ranks' plate as in Fig. 117. It was almost certainly of brass and probably had the design incised.
Fig. 118 was the design on the officers' gilt plates *circa* 1800. The horse was mounted in silver. The other ranks' plate was of the same design, but of brass, die struck.

According to the Regimental History, in 1827 a scroll inscribed 'Niagara' was added to the design below the Garter. This design, if worn, was replaced by that in Fig. 119, which was on a gilt burnished plate. The crown and Garter and scroll 'King's' gilt; the horse in silver; the numerals 'VIII' in check gilt. All on a crimson background.

About 1830 the officers had a gilt oblong plate with a matted surface and burnished edge. The design was of a crowned garter inscribed *Honi soit qui mal y pense* in dead gilt. Above the garter and below the crown a label inscribed 'King's' in Old English lettering, and within the garter a scroll with motto *Nec aspera terrent*, below which was a silver horse and below the horse the Roman numerals 'VIII'. The scroll and the numerals in dead gilt; behind the centre a background of crimson velvet.

Jennen's notes state that in 1837 the plate was gilt, oblong, burnished, with a silver garter, crown and horse on a red velvet ground.

Fig. 120 is the officers' plate worn prior to 1855. The plate was burnished gilt. The design in dead gilt except for the horse, which was in solid silver, on a crimson velvet background.

In a sale at Glendining's in February, 1952, a gilt shoulder-belt plate was sold. The plate was burnished and the design mounted in bright gilt of the White Horse, below a scroll bearing in Old English lettering the motto *Nec aspera terrent*. Below the horse the Roman number 'VIII' in matted gilt. All within a crowned garter inscribed *Honi soit qui mal y pense*. A spray of laurel leaves on either side with scrolls inscribed 'Martinique' and 'Niagara'. At the foot of the plate a large gilt Sphinx on a base inscribed 'Egypt'. The approximate size was $4\frac{1}{2} \times 3\frac{1}{2}$ inches. It is not clear when this plate was worn as its size rather points to a comparatively recent date. It may even have been a colour-belt plate.

BUTTONS

The pewter buttons worn by other ranks *circa* 1780 had the design engraved as shown in Fig. 121. The button had a roped edge.

About 1810 the officers' buttons were flat gilt with the design in relief shown in Fig. 122. The coatee button prior 1855 had the same design, as did also the officers' tunic, 1855-1881, and the other ranks' tunic, 1855-1871, but with the addition of a scroll inscribed 'King's' below the Garter and superimposed on a laurel wreath. On the double-breasted tunic worn for a short time in 1855 the buttons were of two dies and displayed the horse facing inwards (Fig. 123).

After 1881 the design was of the horse below a scroll inscribed *Nec aspera terrent*, all within a crowned circle inscribed 'The Liverpool Regiment'. Below the circle superimposed on a wreath of laurel leaves was a scroll inscribed 'King's'. In one die the horse was displayed rampant, but in most it was shown galloping.

After 1920 the title on the circle was amended to read 'The King's Regiment' and the scroll below the circle replaced by the Sphinx inscribed 'Egypt'.

The 1900 Dress Regulations gives the officers' field cap and mess dress buttons as having the badge of the White Horse with a scroll above inscribed *Nec aspera terrent* mounted. In the 1911 Regulations the cap button die struck, with the design of the White Horse with a scroll below inscribed 'The King's'.

117

118

119

120

121

123

THE ROYAL NORFOLK REGIMENT

TITLES

1685-1751 Known by the names of the successive Colonels.
1751-1782 The 9th Regiment of Foot.
1782-1881 The 9th (The East Norfolk) Regiment of Foot.
1881-1935 The Norfolk Regiment.
1935- The Royal Norfolk Regiment.

BADGES

The figure of Britannia. When new Colours were presented to the regiment in 1848, the following remarks were made by General Bainbridge:
"This distinguished badge was given to you for your gallantry at the battle of Almanza (1707) during the War of Succession in Spain by Queen Anne. On the occasion of that battle it is recorded that you lost 24 officers and had 300 killed and wounded out of 467. In retiring from the field the regiment covered the retreat of General Lord Galway, a most arduous, hazardous, and difficult service. The regiment thus upheld the honour of Great Britain, and was rewarded for it by Queen Anne by allowing them to wear the figure of Britannia on their breast-plates."

The Regimental History by Mr. Loraine Petre records a letter dated 9th March, 1797, which states the design was given to the regiment after the battle of Saragossa.

The late Mr. Milne states that the first Colours of the regiment to have the badge were those of 1802.

There is also a possibility of a connection between the well-known representation of Britannia on the coinage and the regiment, as at the time of Almanza the regiment was commanded by Colonel William Steuart. The Britannia represented on the coinage was a portrait of Miss Francis Stewart, who was later Duchess of Richmond.

Which of these is the correct solution it is impossible to say.

A Horse Guards letter dated 1800 reads:

"W.O.III, No. 32.   HORSE GUARDS, 3.III.1800.

To LT.-GEN. GARTH

In reply to your letter I beg to inform you that H.M. some time ago was graciously pleased to confirm to the 9th Foot, the privilege of bearing Britannia as their badge, which I had the honour of notifying to Lt.-Gen. Bertie."

N.B.—A pencil note below stated "See No. 21, page 40", but no trace.

Britannia was at first represented armed with a spear; this was changed to a trident about 1790, while the British Lion, which for many years accompanied the figure, disappeared.

In the latest design of Britannia for the regiment the spear has been reintroduced.

On the officers' waist-belt plates, 1881-1902, the lion was shown wearing a crown.

The Castle of Norwich. Worn on the officers' waist-belt plates, 1881-1902, below the figure of Britannia. Had previously been the badge of the Norfolk Militia.

BATTLE HONOURS (*Dates authorized from 1815 to 1855*)

PENINSULA, 6th April, 1815.
BUSACO, 18th February, 1819.
SALAMANCA, 18th February, 1819.
VITTORIA, 18th February, 1819.
ST. SEBASTIAN, 18th February, 1819.
NIVE, 18th February, 1819.
ROLEIA,* 23rd September, 1820.
VIMIERA, 23rd September, 1820.
CORUNNA, 4th June, 1835.
CABOOL, 1842, 22nd June, 1844.
MOODKEE, 8th June, 1847.
FEROZESHAH, 8th June, 1847.
SOBRAON, 8th June, 1847.
SEVASTOPOL, 16th October, 1855.

SHOULDER-BELT PLATES

In the Dayes plates at Aldershot, the officer of the 9th was shown with an oval silver plate with a high beaded rim; in the centre of the plate was the figure of Britannia and below a scroll inscribed '9 Regt'. The brass plate of the other ranks had the same design, but with a crown above the figure. Mr. Hughes has in his collection a small oval silver plate of the description given in the Dayes plate; the figure of Britannia holds a halbert such as now carried by the Yeomen of the Guard.

At the sale of the Milne collection in 1913 there was an oval gilt plate with the design in silver of the number '9', surmounted by a grenade. This would appear to be the shoulder-belt plate of the Grenadier Company.

In a book entitled "The Military Costume of Europe", published 1812, the 9th are shown wearing an oblong silver plate with Britannia above a label inscribed 'IX Regt', mounted in silver.

About 1820 the officers' plates were oblong, silver, with rounded corners, and the design in relief of Britannia on a label inscribed 'IX Regt'. The other ranks' plates were of the same design, but stamped in brass (Fig. 124).

From about 1830 to 1855 the officers' plates were burnished gilt with the design mounted in silver of Britannia with the lion beside her, the whole on a label inscribed as before.

---

* An Army Order in 1911 directed the spelling to be "Rolica".

BUTTONS

The officers' bone-backed buttons of about 1780 had silver fronts with the design in low relief shown in Fig. 125.

The Dayes plates show the officers' buttons of the period as silver with the design of '9' within a half circle, possibly a French scroll. The other ranks' buttons of this time had the simple design shown in Fig. 126, which later gave place to one with the numerals 'IX' within a French scroll with a dot at the opening, the design in relief.

Fig. 127 is the officers' button worn until 1830 in silver and after that date in gilt until 1855. The number and crown are engraved on a burnished ground. The ring of points or arrow-heads are in relief on a lined ground. The button from about 1840 to 1855 had a burnished rim.

The tunic button prior to 1881 had the design of '9' below a crown within a single-line circle in relief.

After 1881 the figure of Britannia in a helmet and armed with a trident was displayed within a circle inscribed 'The Norfolk Regiment'. One die had the design within a garter and it was inscribed 'The Norfolk Regt' (Fig. 128).

In 1935 the design on the buttons became the figure of Britannia without any inscription, armed with the trident.

The 1900 Dress Regulations gives the mess waistcoat button as having the figure of Britannia mounted in silver; the button was a flat gilt one. In the 1911 Regulations the cap button is of the same design as for mess dress, but die struck.

124

125 126

127 128

THE ROYAL LINCOLNSHIRE REGIMENT

TITLES

1685-1751 Known by the names of the successive Colonels.
1751-1782 The 10th Regiment of Foot.
1782-1881 The 10th (North Lincoln) Regiment of Foot.
1881-1946 The Lincolnshire Regiment.
1946- The Royal Lincolnshire Regiment.

BADGES

The Sphinx superscribed 'Egypt'. Commemorates the services of the regiment in Egypt, 1801. Authorized 6th July, 1802.

BATTLE HONOURS (*Dates authorized from 1802 to 1855*)
EGYPT AND BADGE OF SPHINX, 6th July, 1802.
PENINSULA, 6th April, 1815.
SOBRAON, 8th June, 1847.
PUNJAUB, 14th December, 1852.
MOOLTAN, 14th December, 1852.
GOOJERAT, 14th December, 1852.

SHOULDER-BELT PLATES

According to Jennen's notes and Almack's book, the shoulder-belt plate worn 1800-1816 or before, was of a very uncommon design, having in high relief the design of a gorget ornamented with the number '10' inside a circle of dots, all in silver (Fig. 129).

The plate 1830-1836 was an oblong dead gilt matted one with the design, mounted, of a gilt crown resting on a scroll inscribed 'Peninsula'; below this a silver garter inscribed 'North Lincoln' with 'X' in gilt in its centre and a gilt wreath encircling; at the junction of the wreath a silver Sphinx inscribed 'Egypt'.

1836-1847. As above, but the plate burnished gilt with silver mounts.
1847-1855. As above with addition of scroll inscribed 'Sobraon' placed below the Sphinx (Fig. 130).

BUTTONS

The officers' buttons *circa* 1790 were flat, two piece, with the number '10' in relief. Other rank buttons were flat with the design sunk. The early buttons were of a larger size than those worn towards the end of the eighteenth century. This design was probably retained for some years.

According to the late Mr. P. W. Reynolds, the '10' on these early numbered buttons used the peculiar design of numbering 'Jo', but no actual button with this design has been discovered as far as is known.

Officers' buttons in 1786 had the number in Roman, and other ranks in Arabic figures.

1820. Officers' buttons, silver, convex, design in relief '10' within a circle of dots (Fig. 131).

1830-1855. Officers' buttons, gilt, convex, design in relief. Buttons for other ranks were of same design but in pewter (Fig. 132).

1855-1881. Officers' buttons, gilt, convex, rimmed as for coatee, Arabic numerals in place of Roman, within a crowned wreath.

1855-1871. Other ranks, design as for officers, except that there was a loop to the bow joining the sprays of leaves.

1881-1902. Officers' tunic: There were two types of this button, one showing the Sphinx with the tail up and the other with it down.

1902. Designs as above except for alteration in crown. There were different types of wreath, the number of leaves varying.

The 1904 Dress Regulations gives the mess dress button as plain gilt with the Sphinx over Egypt in silver. For the cap button the same design, but die struck.

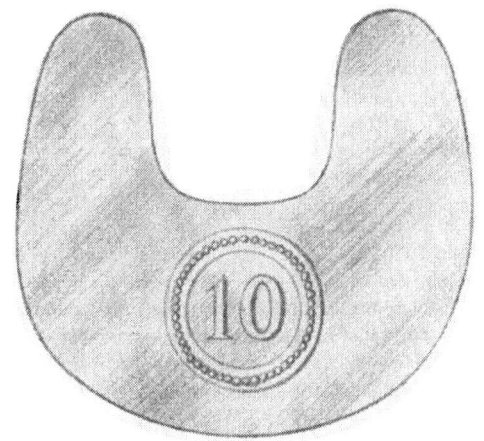

129

130

131

132

103

THE DEVONSHIRE REGIMENT

TITLES

1685-1751   Known by the name of the successive Colonels.
1751-1782   The 11th Regiment of Foot.
1782-1881   The 11th (North Devon) Regiment of Foot.
1881-   The Devonshire Regiment.

BADGES

The Castle of Exeter and the motto *Semper fidelis*, adopted as a badge by the Regular battalions in March, 1883, had been the badge of the Devon Militia for a great many years.

A United Red and White Rose. The regiment had no distinctive badge in 1881 when the Territorial system was brought in, and, in common with other regiments similarly placed, was given the badge of the Rose, changed to a united Red and White Rose in 1888, which for a short period was shown on the buttons.

BATTLE HONOURS (*Dates authorized from 1815 to 1855*)

PENINSULA, 29th March, 1815.
SALAMANCA, 9th July, 1816.
NIVELLE, 9th July, 1816.
TOULOUSE, 9th July, 1816.
PYRENEES, 3rd October, 1823.
NIVE, 3rd October, 1823.
ORTHES, 3rd October, 1823.

SHOULDER-BELT PLATES

Fig. 133 is the design worn on an early gilt plate of the regiment, probably about the 1780 period.

Fig. 134 is the plate worn about 1800. The plate was gilt with a beaded rim; the design of 'XI' within a crowned garter inscribed 'North Devon Regiment' being in gilt on a lined silver star.

After the grant of four Peninsular Honours in 1815-1816 an oblong plate with rounded corners was adopted (Fig. 135).

In Vol. XIX of the *Journal of the Society for Army Historical Research* the late Rev. P. Sumner describes a plate shown in a portrait of Captain H. K. Bloomfield. The date is put at 1832, and the description of the plate is: Gilt metal with silver star and superimposed in gilt upon it 'XI' within a crowned garter inscribed 'North Devon Regiment'.

The plate in use prior to 1855 was as shown in Fig. 136, the plate being dead gilt with gilt crown and number and a silver wreath and scroll inscribed 'Peninsula'. The other ranks' breast plate was of the same design.

BUTTONS

Very little change took place in the design shown on the buttons between the years 1800 and 1881. Both officers and other ranks had the same design. The officers' flat gilt one-piece buttons of 1800 had the design in relief of 'XI' within a crowned garter inscribed 'Regiment' and superimposed on a star (Fig. 137). Except that tunic buttons after 1855 had two differences—Roman numerals in place of Arabic and one die had 'North Devon' instead of 'Regiment'—the design did not change. For a short time after 1881 the badge of a rose was worn within a crowned circle inscribed the 'Devonshire Regt', all on a cut star. In 1883 the rose was replaced by the badge of the Castle of Exeter.

The 1904 Dress Regulations gives the design on the mess dress buttons as for the tunic button, but mounted in silver.

133

134

135

136

137

THE SUFFOLK REGIMENT

TITLES
1685-1751   Known by the successive Colonel's name.
1751-1782   The 12th Regiment of Foot.
1782-1881   The 12th (East Suffolk) Regiment of Foot.
1881-   The Suffolk Regiment.

BADGES
The Castle of Gibraltar with Key and motto *Montis Insignia Calpe*. The official date of the authorization of the castle, key and motto was 2nd May, 1836. They commemorate the part played by the regiment during the siege of 1779-1783.

In 1909 Army Order No. 180 added the dates to the Honour 'Gibraltar'.

An application for officers to be allowed to wear the castle and key on their forage caps and for the other ranks to wear brass cannons was refused, 18th June, 1866.

Oak Wreath. The Regimental History suggests that the oak wreath was connected with the arms of the Durounes. Colonel Scipio Duroune was appointed Colonel of the regiment in August, 1741, and died of wounds received at Fontenoy in 1745. It would seem a long time to elapse between 1745 and 1881, when it appeared on the regimental cap badge.

BATTLE HONOURS (*Dates authorized from 1801 to 1855*)
MINDEN, 1st January, 1801 (on Colours).
SERINGAPATAM, 28th May, 1818.
GIBRALTAR, 14th April, 1784 (the badge of castle, key and motto), 2nd Mays 1836.
INDIA, 11th June, 1836.

SHOULDER-BELT PLATES
In the Regimental History by Colonel Webb is a portrait of Colonel Charles Grey, 1797. He is shown wearing an oblong plate with cut corners and the design of the number '12' within a plain circle. According to the same book, this badge was replaced in 1799 by an oval one (Fig. 138), which in turn was succeeded in 1816 by an oblong one measuring $3\frac{1}{4} \times 2\frac{11}{16}$ inches. The plate was gilt with slightly rounded corners and had the design in dead gilt of 'XII' within a pierced garter surmounted by a crown.

The design shown in Fig. 139 was worn 1825-1842. The plate measured $3\frac{3}{4} \times 3\frac{1}{8}$ inches and was dead gilt with a silver star, and the crown, garter, wreath and number were all in gilt.

In 1843 Fig. 140 was adopted; size $4 \times 3\frac{1}{4}$ inches. The plate was burnished gilt with the design in silver except for the crown, and was worn until 1855.

The same design, all in gilt, was worn on the flap of the band pouches *circa* 1903.

BUTTONS

The design on the buttons varied very little. The men's early pewter buttons had in relief the design of the number '12' below a crown and within a spray of leaves. The officers' buttons and those for other ranks retained this design until 1881 (Fig. 141). There were various differences in the thickness of the wreath and the shape and size of the numerals owing to different dies.

After 1881 the castle, key, motto and a scroll inscribed 'Gibraltar' were displayed within a laurel wreath; across the bottom of the wreath a scroll inscribed 'The Suffolk Regt'. Above the castle was a crown. The castle was displayed until 1900 with two towers; after this, in consequence of a War Office letter, the design was regulated for all regiments entitled to the badge and was directed to be as shown in the seal of Gibraltar granted in 1502—*i.e.*, a castle with three turrets and the key suspended below the centre gateway.

The 1900 Dress Regulations states, on the mess waistcoat button the badge of the castle mounted in silver. The 1904 Regulations states, cap button same design, die struck.

Before 1900 the cap button had the design of 'SR' below a crown mounted in silver.

In the 1911 Regulations the cap button has the design of the castle, die struck.

In the 1934 Dress Regulations the design of the castle and key but without the laurel wreath.

138

139

140

141

109

THE SOMERSET LIGHT INFANTRY (PRINCE ALBERT'S)

TITLES
- 1685-1751   Known by the names of its successive Colonels.
- 1751-1782   The 13th Regiment of Foot.
- 1782-1822   The 13th (First Somersetshire) Regiment of Foot.
- 1822-1842   The 13th (First Somersetshire Light Infantry) Regiment.
- 1842-1881   The 13th (1st Somersetshire) (Prince Albert's Regiment of Light Infantry).
- 1881-1912   The Prince Albert's (Somersetshire Light Infantry).
- 1912-1920   Prince Albert's (Somerset Light Infantry).
- 1920–   The Somerset Light Infantry (Prince Albert's).

BADGES
The Sphinx superscribed 'Egypt'. Commemorates the services of the regiment in the campaign of 1801. Authorized 6th July, 1802.
A Mural Crown. Given with the Honour 'Jellalabad' in 1842 to commemorate the gallant defence of the fort by the 13th.
A Light Infantry Bugle-horn. Adopted in 1822 when the regiment became Light Infantry.
The Cypher of the late Prince Consort. Displayed between the strings of Light Infantry bugle-horn; worn since 1842.

BATTLE HONOURS (*Dates authorized from 1802 to 1855*)
EGYPT AND THE BADGE OF THE SPHINX, 6th July, 1802.
MARTINIQUE, 19th November, 1816.
AVA, 6th December, 1825.
AFFGHANISTAN, 18th July, 1840.
GHUZNEE, 18th July, 1840.
JELLALABAD AND MURAL CROWN, 20th August, 1842.
CABOOL, 1842, 22nd June, 1844.
SEVASTOPOL, 16th October, 1855.

SHOULDER-BELT PLATES

Fig. 142 is an illustration of a fine silver plate in the collection of Mr. Hughes; the plate has a sunk centre and a silver burnished rim, and would have been worn according to the Royal arms prior to 1800.

Fig. 143 is a silver plate with the design mounted in silver and had rounded corners. The Sphinx is shown on a label inscribed with Egyptian characters; according to Jennen's notes, worn 1801-1816.

About 1818 the design in Fig. 144 was adopted and displayed on a silver plate. This was probably worn until about 1825, when the design in Fig. 145 was taken into use. The plate was at first in silver and changed to gilt with the design mounted in silver. According to Jennen's notes, worn in 1831.

Fig. 146 is the plate worn prior to 1855. The plate is gilt with silver mounts.

In Messrs. Webb and Bonella's notes is a drawing of a plate similar to the above, but with a difference in the arrangement of the central ribbon, which instead of showing two ends has one which hangs down between the scrolls, inscribed 'Martinique' and 'Afghanistan'. Below these scrolls was a thin spray of leaves, in the centre of which was a scroll inscribed 'Ava'. The ends of the ribbon passing behind the scroll. Below the whole a Sphinx inscribed 'Egypt'. On the back of the drawing is a note to the effect that "General Browne gave W.B. authority to alter the form of the device and leave out the word 'Cabul'." It is dated 22nd June, 1843. This plate, if ever worn, probably lasted for a very short time; there is no trace of a General Browne in connection with the 13th at this time.

BUTTONS

The men's pewter buttons *circa* 1800 until about 1842 had the design in relief of '13' within a star of eight points (Fig. 147). The officers' silver buttons prior to 1830 had the same design; from then until 1842 the design was '13' within a circle and star, the circle inscribed 'Egypt' 'Martinique' (Fig. 148).

After the granting of the badge of the mural crown in 1842 the design became a garter, inscribed 'Prince Albert's Lt. Infantry', a wreath of laurel round and a mural crown above. Within the garter the number 'XIII'. The same design was worn on the other ranks' buttons, but with the number in Arabic figures.

On the introduction of the tunic button in 1855 the design as worn by other ranks was adopted for officers; there were several differences in dies, in the design of the numerals. After 1881 the number '13' was replaced by a bugle-horn and the garter by a circle, inscribed 'The Prince Albert's'.

The 1900 Dress Regulations give the officers' field cap button as having the bugle mounted in silver, and on the mess dress buttons the bugle surmounted by a mural crown and a scroll inscribed 'Jellalabad'. All mounted in silver on a flat button. In the 1904 Regulations the cap button has the same design, but is die struck. In the 1934 Regulations it gives "a bugle with strings in silver".

THE WEST YORKSHIRE REGIMENT (THE PRINCE OF WALES'S OWN)

TITLES

1685-1751　Known by the name of the successive Colonels.
1751-1782　The 14th Regiment of Foot.
1782-1809　The 14th (Bedfordshire) Regiment of Foot.
1809-1876　The 14th (Buckinghamshire) Regiment of Foot.
1876-1881　The 14th (Buckinghamshire or The Prince of Wales's Own) Regiment of Foot.

1881-1920　The Prince of Wales's Own (West Yorkshire Regiment).
1920-　　　The West Yorkshire Regiment (The Prince of Wales's Own).

BADGES

The White Horse and motto *Nec aspera terrent*. An old badge of the regiment, but does not appear ever to have been featured on the shoulder belt or buttons—authorized to be displayed on the Queen's Colour, 21st February, 1873.
The Royal Tiger superscribed 'India'. Authorized 1st November, 1838, to commemorate the services of the regiment in India, 1807-1831.
The Prince of Wales's Coronet, Plume and motto. Authorized at the same time as the title was given to the regiment, 26th May, 1876.

BATTLE HONOURS (*Dates authorized from 1811 to 1855*)

CORUNNA, 30th November, 1811, granted to old 2nd Battalion; (to 1st Battalion, 26th November, 1829).
WATERLOO, 2nd March, 1816, granted to old 3rd Battalion; (to 1st and 2nd Battalions, 23rd November, 1845).
JAVA, 28th May, 1818.
BHURTPORE, 6th December, 1826. Originally spelt Bhurtpoor.
TOURNAY, 24th February, 1836.
SEVASTOPOL, 16th October, 1855.

SHOULDER-BELT PLATES

The early officers' shoulder-belt plate was an oval silver polished one with the number '14' within a raised oval; the plate having a raised rim. This was replaced by another oval one, but slightly larger, with '14' within a French scroll with a dot at the opening. The Grenadier Company officers appear to have had a similar plate, but with a grenade in place of the dot. How long the oval plate was retained is not certain, but it had been replaced, according to Jennen's notes, in 1800 by an oblong silver one with rounded corners and with the design of '14' within a spray of leaves (Fig. 149).

After the granting of the Honours 'Corunna', 'Waterloo' and 'Java' a silver plate with the design mounted in gilt was worn; the other ranks' plate was of the same design, but in brass (Fig. 150).

Jennen's notes state that in 1831 the same design was worn on a gilt plate by officers. An entirely new design was adopted the following year to show the Honours, including that of 'Bhurtpore' (Fig. 151).

Fig. 152 shows the burnished gilt plate *circa* 1840-1855. The design was mounted in silver.

BUTTONS

The early pewter buttons had the simple design of '14' engraved. This button had a roped rim (Fig. 153). Another early design, either at the end of the eighteenth century or early in the next, is shown in Fig. 154. The same design was worn in relief on the officers' silver buttons for some years; the buttons were at first flat, later convex.

The officers' buttons in use when the coatee was replaced by the tunic in 1855 was as shown in Fig. 155 and was probably adopted in 1838.

The tunic 1855-1881 had the Royal Tiger above '14' with the Honours 'India' above and 'Waterloo' below.

After 1881 the button had the design of the tiger within a circle, inscribed at the top 'India' and at the bottom 'Waterloo'; outside the circle, 'Prince of Wales's Own West Yorkshire'.

In the 1900 Dress Regulations the officers' field cap button was flat gilt, with the tiger mounted in silver. The 1904 Regulations gives the same design for the mess waistcoat. In the 1911 Regulations the cap button is given as the same design.

THE EAST YORKSHIRE REGIMENT (THE DUKE OF YORK'S OWN)

TITLES

1685-1751   By the name of the successive Colonels.
1751-1782   The 15th Regiment of Foot.
1782-1881   The 15th (York East Riding) Regiment of Foot.
1881-1935   The East Yorkshire Regiment.
1935-   The East Yorkshire Regiment (The Duke of York's Own).

BADGES

The White Rose of York. An old badge of the regiment, but not displayed on the shoulder-belt plates nor the buttons until after 1881.

In 1881, in common with other infantry regiments having no distinctive badge, the badge of the Rose was given to the regiment; changed to the united Red and White Rose in 1888.

BATTLE HONOURS (*Dates authorized from* 1817 *to* 1855)

MARTINIQUE, 31st May, 1817.
GUADALOUPE, 31st May, 1817.

SHOULDER-BELT PLATES

There are on record no less than four oval shoulder-belt plates of the regiment.

The Dayes plate 1792 shows the officer wearing an oval gilt plate with a silver star of eight points. In the centre of the star a red cross within a garter (Fig. 156).

The photograph of an actual plate of this description and which is in the officers' mess of the regiment has been sent to the author by Mr. R. Jones. The plate is stated to have been worn by Colonel H. Ditmas, who served in the regiment as an Ensign, 1770. He was severely wounded in the head during the War of Independence, and it appears rather doubtful if he could have ever worn this badge.

Fig. 157 is illustrated from Almack's book. The plate was polished silver with the design engraved. This plate is stated to have been worn by officers of the 2nd Battalion, 1799-1816.

The other ranks' plate had the design of '15' surmounted by a crown, and round the top edge of the plate was inscribed 'East Riding' and round the bottom 'Yorkshire Regiment'. A specimen of this badge was found in St. Kitts, which would date it as still being worn in 1812.

The 1st Battalion officers, according to Mr. Jones, wore silver plates with the design mounted shown in Fig. 158. Jennen's notes date this plate 1801-1816. A miniature of Captain Dalrymple, who was in the 1st Battalion during this period, shows the plate with a beaded rim.

The plate in use 1833-1840 is given by Jennen's as "Gilt, oblong, with silver mounts, oval garter and crown with 'XV' in centre". With crimson velvet behind the 'XV'. (Messrs. Wilson had made this plate in 1827). The plate had rounded corners.

A similar plate was worn up to 1855, but with square-cut corners (Fig. 159).

BUTTONS

As in the case of the breast plates, there were also several designs of pewter buttons. Figs. 160, 161 and 162 are three designs in relief worn up to 1800. After that date the design for the pewter button does not appear to have changed for some time, but remained in relief 'XV' within a star of eight points. Prior to 1855 the design was '15' within a star, the whole within a French scroll without a dot.

The officers' silver buttons *circa* 1810 were flat with the design in relief of 'XV' within a star of eight points. The coatee buttons before 1855 displayed the number '15' within a continuous wreath in the centre of an eight-pointed star (Fig. 163). Between the points of the star were eight scrolls. This design was retained on the tunic button, 1855-1881, and for a time after 1881, the number being replaced by a rose. But after a short time the scrolls between the rays of the star were omitted; in some dies even the continuous wreath was changed to one of two sprays. Some of the buttons worn after 1881 had black behind the rose in memory of Wolfe.

In the 1911 Dress Regulations the cap button and the mess dress button both had the design as for the tunic button. The cap button was die struck, the mess dress button mounted with the rose in silver.

The design in the 1934 Dress Regulations is of the rose in silver on a background of black enamel, all within a star of eight points.

THE BEDFORDSHIRE AND HERTFORDSHIRE REGIMENT

TITLES

1688-1751 By the name of the successive Colonels.
1751-1782 The 16th Regiment of Foot.
1782-1809 The 16th (Buckinghamshire) Regiment of Foot.
1809-1881 The 16th (Bedfordshire) Regiment of Foot.
1881-1919 The Bedfordshire Regiment.
1919-   The Bedfordshire and Hertfordshire Regiment.

BADGES

A Hart crossing a Ford. The old badge of the Hertfordshire Militia, adopted in 1881 by the Regular battalions.
A Star and Cross. First appeared as a badge of the regiment about 1830. At first it was an exact reproduction of the star of the Order of the Bath with its wavy rays, but during the course of years the rays became straightened out. It is possible that the badge was adopted out of compliment to its new Colonel, William Carr, Viscount Beresford, G.C.B., G.C.H., who had been appointed in 1823.
The Rose. Allotted to the regiment in 1881 in common with other English infantry regiments which had no officially recognized badge; changed to the united Red and White Rose in 1888. It does not appear to have been displayed on any of the badges or buttons.
From 1874 to 1881 the Arms of Bedford were displayed as a collar badge.

SHOULDER-BELT PLATES

In the author's collection is an oval plate of beaten silver with the number '16' mounted on its centre. This plate would appear to have been worn about 1790. It has the maker's mark of John Robins, who entered the Goldsmiths' Company in 1774 (Fig. 164).

A picture by Loftie shows an officer of the regiment pre-1796 with an oval plate with the design of '16' within a star of eight points. This design is also shown in a miniature of Captain E. Stirling, who also served in the 16th from 1799 to 1802 (Fig. 165).

The late Mr. P. W. Reynolds described an oval silver plate for the regiment with the design of '16' in silver on a gilt ground within a girdle in the centre of a star of eight points. Across the top ray of the star was a corded bugle-horn. The badge was evidently that worn by the Light Company of the same period (Fig. 166). It is shown in a miniature of Captain Garrock Donald painted in 1817.

In the chapter on uniform by Mr. Carman in the forthcoming History of the Regiment by Major P. Young, it states that a tailor's book of 1824 speaks of the breast plates as being of "the old pattern," and that the late Mr. S. M. Milne took this to mean that the oval pattern was still in use.

Mr. P. W. Reynolds recorded a plate, 1822-1832, of burnished silver, but unfortunately did not state its shape.

Mr. Carman quotes Jennen's notes, 1820-1840, describing an oblong plate with the design of '16' within a circle pierced with the title 'Bedfordshire'; behind the lettering and number, a blue enamel ground, around the circle a wreath of laurel with a crown above, the whole mounted on a Maltese Cross.

In 1830 or soon after the plate would have been changed from silver to gilt.

The final shoulder-belt plate of the 16th was a very fine one with the design in gilt of a crowned Maltese Cross, in the centre of which was the regimental number within a garter inscribed 'Bedfordshire' in pierced letters on blue enamel background. The whole on a silver wavy star of the Grand Cross of the Order of the Bath, which had been assumed by the regiment in 1823 (Fig. 167).

I am indebted to Mr. L. E. Buckell for the drawings of Figs. 165, 166 and 167, and for the information concerning them.

BUTTONS

The early pewter buttons had the peculiar 'J 6' in relief (Fig. 168) within a roped border; these were replaced by one with an incised '16', the button having a lined rim (Fig. 169).

About 1800 or soon after the buttons had a design which, with various minor differences in the shape of numerals and wreath, was worn by officers and other ranks until the numbers disappeared (Fig. 170).

After 1881 the buttons displayed the hart crossing a ford within a circle inscribed 'Bedfordshire', and all in the centre of a star and cross of the Order of the Bath.

In 1919 on the change of title the present design was adopted of a hart crossing a ford within a circle inscribed 'Bedfordshire' 'Hertfordshire'.

Before 1911 the cap and mess dress button had the design as on the tunic. In the case of the cap they were die struck, in the case of the mess dress mounted in gilt.

After this both cap and mess buttons had the design as on the tunic; in the case of the cap it was die struck. The mess dress button had the design mounted in gilt with the hart in silver.

In the 1934 Dress Regulations the design for the mess buttons is of the hart crossing a ford, mounted in silver.

THE ROYAL LEICESTERSHIRE REGIMENT

TITLES
1688-1751 By the name of the successive Colonels.
1751-1782 The 17th Regiment of Foot.
1782-1881 The 17th (Leicestershire) Regiment of Foot.
1881-1946 The Leicestershire Regiment.
1946- The Royal Leicestershire Regiment.

BADGES
The Royal Tiger superscribed 'Hindoostan'. Commemorates the distinguished services of the 17th in India, 1804-1823. The badge and the Honour 'Hindoostan' were authorized 18th May, 1825, and in October, 1866, officers were allowed to wear the tiger on their forage caps.

The Badge of an Irish Harp. Was given to the Leicestershire Militia as a reward for services in Ireland. After 1881 it appeared on the officers' waist-belt plates and cap badge.

BATTLE HONOURS (*Dates authorized from 1825 to 1855*)
TIGER AND HINDOOSTAN, 18th May, 1825.
AFFGHANISTAN, 18th July, 1840.
GHUZNEE, 18th July, 1840.
KHELAT, 18th July, 1840.
SEVASTOPOL, 16th October, 1855.

SHOULDER-BELT PLATES

Fig. 171 shows the officers' silver plate worn about 1780, while Fig. 172 is from a drawing in Almack's book. The plate was burnished silver with the design mounted, and according to the Regimental History was worn by the officers of the 2nd Battalion.

Mr. P. W. Reynolds recorded an oval silver plate with ornamental rim. The design was 'XVII' below a crown within a wreath; the design was engraved. This is said to have been worn by the officers of the 1st Battalion.

Fig. 173 is a very handsome plate. The design of a tiger mounted in gilt on a cut silver star, crown and 'XVII', also in gilt, on a matted ground. The plate had a burnished edge. According to the Regimental History it was worn in 1825.

Fig. 174 is a plate worn for a short time about 1843-1845. It is the only appearance of the motto *Veni et vici*. The design was mounted on a silver gilt plate.

Fig. 175 is the plate worn prior to 1855. The tiger and '17' were in bright gilt within a gilt garter on a silver ground, the garter inscribed 'Leicestershire Regiment', all mounted on a silver cut star with silver crown and scrolls. The plate had a matted gilt surface with burnished edges.

BUTTONS

There have been a variety of early buttons of the 17th. Fig. 176 is an officers' bone-backed button with a wire-bound edge to its silver face (the peculiar shape of the numerals is noticeable); Fig. 177 an officers' bone-backed button, similar design, with wire-bound edge; Fig. 178 yet another bone-backed design. It is probable that the wire-bound buttons, although distinctive, were not very durable and were replaced by one of a slightly convex shape with the design in relief of '17' below a crown. Round the edge of the button was a continuous wreath of laurel leaves, a feature which is still shown on the buttons of today.

The early pewter buttons of the other ranks were also of three designs, probably in the case of both officers and other ranks being those of different battalions.

Fig. 179. The design in relief with a roped rim to the button.

About 1820 the officers' silver buttons were slightly convex with the design of '17' below a crown with a single-line circle. After 1830 the buttons became gilt and the design of '17' below a crown within a continuous wreath of leaves turned inwards (Fig. 180) was adopted and retained until 1881, when the Royal Tiger below a scroll inscribed 'Hindoostan' and below the tiger one inscribed 'Leicestershire', the whole within a continuous laurel wreath, was adopted.

The 1900 Dress Regulations gives the officers' field cap button as flat, gilt, with the tiger mounted in silver. The 1904 Regulations give the same design for the mess dress button.

THE ROYAL IRISH REGIMENT

TITLES

1684-1695 By the name of its successive Colonels.
1695-1751 The Royal Regiment of Ireland.
1751-1881 The 18th (The Royal Irish) Regiment of Foot.
1881-1922 The Royal Irish Regiment.
Disbanded 1922.

BADGES

The Sphinx superscribed 'Egypt'. Commemorates the services of the 18th in Egypt, 1801. Authorized 6th July, 1802.

The Arms of Nassau with the motto *Virtutis Namurcensis Præmium*. The motto and the badge were both conferred on the regiment by King William III as a reward for their gallantry in the siege and assault of Namur, 1695. The Honour 'Namur' was, however, not approved for the Colours of the regiment until February, 1910.

The Harp and Crown. Said to have been conferred on the regiment together with the arms of Nassau by King William III.

The Dragon superscribed 'China'. Commemorates the services of the 18th in China, 1840-1842. Authorized 12th January, 1843.

BATTLE HONOURS (*Dates authorized from 1802 to 1855*)

EGYPT AND THE SPHINX, 6th July, 1802.
CHINA AND THE DRAGON, 12th January, 1843.
PEGU, 20th September, 1853.
SEVASTOPOL, 16th October, 1855.

SHOULDER-BELT PLATES

Fig. 181 is the officers' oval plate worn about 1800. The plate had a matted gilt surface with a beaded rim and the harp and shamrock on a blue enamel ground within a gilt crowned garter inscribed *Virtutis Namurcensis Præmium* in pierced gilt letters on a blue ground.

Circa 1830-1840 the plate was an oblong burnished gilt one with the design of a silver star on which was mounted a gilt crowned garter with the motto of the regiment in pierced letters on a blue enamel ground. Within the garter the badge of the harp in gilt on a blue enamel ground, below the garter a gilt scroll inscribed 'XVIII' and the Sphinx inscribed 'Egypt' resting at the foot of a spray of shamrocks, all in silver. Size $3 \times 3 \frac{3}{16}$ inches.

The plate worn between 1844 and 1855 was oblong with a gilt frosted surface and polished rim, with the design mounted of a cut silver star surmounted by a crown, a wreath of shamrocks around a garter inscribed with the motto of the regiment in gilt letters on a blue enamel ground. Within the garter the badge of the harp and crown with the Roman numeral 'XVIII' below, all in gilt metal. Above the garter a gilt Sphinx inscribed 'Egypt' and below the garter a gilt dragon, above which is a scroll inscribed 'China'.

The brass shoulder-belt plate worn by other ranks before 1855 had the design of the harp surmounted by a crown and within a wreath of rose, shamrock and thistle. Above the crown was a scroll with the regimental motto, and below the wreath the badge of the Sphinx. Below this a scroll inscribed 'XVIII Royal Irish' (Fig. 183).

BUTTONS

Fig. 184 is the design in relief on the other ranks' pewter buttons *circa* 1780. About 1800 the design on the officers' flat gilt buttons and on the men's pewter buttons was of the harp and crown above the number '18'. Round the edge of the button was a continuous wreath of shamrocks (Fig. 185). This design was retained on the subsequent coatee and tunic buttons.

After 1881 the design was the harp within a crowned circle inscribed *Virtutis Namurcensis Præmium*, all within a wreath of shamrock.

The 1900 Dress Regulations gives the officers' field service cap as having mounted in silver the design of the "harp and crown and wreath" on a flat button.

The 1904 Regulations states that "on the cap and mess vest buttons the circle is omitted". The mess vest button was mounted.

181

182

183

184

185

THE GREEN HOWARDS (ALEXANDRA, PRINCESS OF WALES'S OWN YORKSHIRE REGIMENT)

TITLES

1688-1751 Known by the successive Colonel's name.
1751-1782 The 19th Regiment of Foot.
1782-1875 The 19th (1st York. North Riding) Regiment of Foot.
1875-1881 The 19th (1st York. North Riding) Princess of Wales's Own Regiment of Foot.
1881-1902 The Princess of Wales's Own (Yorkshire Regiment).
1902-1920 Alexandra, Princess of Wales's Own (Yorkshire Regiment).
1920- The Green Howards (Alexandra, Princess of Wales's Own Yorkshire Regiment).

BADGES

The White Rose of York. An old badge of the regiment.
The Princess of Wales's Cypher and Coronet. Granted when the title was conferred, 11th October, 1875.
A Dannebrog Cross. Adopted as the badge of the regiment in 1902 when Queen Alexandra became its Colonel.
The Rose. Given in 1881 to the regiment in common with other English infantry regiments having no officially recognized badge; changed to the united Red and White Rose in 1888.

BATTLE HONOURS (*Dates authorized* 1855).

ALMA, 16th October, 1855.
INKERMAN, 16th October, 1855.

SHOULDER-BELT PLATES

The early shoulder-belt plate had the design of 'XIX' below a crown; the plate was of silver. This was followed about 1790 by a gilt one with 'XIX' inside a circle within a star of eight points; the design was mounted in silver.

The star design was retained on the gilt oblong plate with rounded corners ascribed to 1816-1825. Fig. 186 shows the plate as worn by the Grenadier Company of this period.

According to an article in the Regimental Journal, the plate in use 1825-1840 was gilt, oblong, burnished, with the design of 'XIX' below a crown and within a wreath, but this may possibly be the plate of the XIX Indian Native Infantry Regiment. In 1840 the plate shown in Fig. 187 was adopted, and it seems strange for the star to have been dropped only to reappear; the 1840 plate in the Regimental Museum is gilt with a matted surface. The star cut silver and the crown and 'XIX' gilt on a green enamel ground.

About 1845 the design was practically the same. The last plate to be worn when they were abolished in 1855, it retained the star design with a slightly less pointed star and on a plate with a lined edge.

BUTTONS

The officers' flat gilt one-piece buttons *circa* 1810 had the design in relief of '19' within a French scroll and dot (Fig. 188). About 1820 the button became convex, with open back and the design in relief of '19' below a crown, all within a French scroll but with no dot at the opening (Fig. 189). This design remained in use with various minor differences in the shape and design of the numerals until 1881. The men's pewter buttons and their tunic buttons until 1871 also had this design. The jacket button worn 1860 had '19' below a crown inside a plain ring in relief.

From 1881 until 1902 the design was the cypher of H.R.H. the Princess of Wales combined with the Dannebrog Cross and surmounted by the Princess's coronet. The date '1875' which was displayed on the cross referred to the granting of the title 'Princess of Wales's Own'. On a scroll below was the title 'The Princess of Wales's Own'. In 1902, when the title was changed, the button was amended accordingly.

The 1900 Dress Regulations give the officers' field cap and mess dress buttons as having the Dannebrog Cross mounted in silver. In the 1904 Regulations it states that the scroll is omitted on the mess dress buttons and that those for the cap were die struck. In the 1911 Regulations the design for the mess dress is the Dannebrog, cypher and coronet mounted in silver; the cap button had the same design, die struck.

186

187

188

189

THE LANCASHIRE FUSILIERS

TITLES
1688-1751   Known by the name of the successive Colonels.
1751-1782   The 20th Regiment of Foot.
1782-1881   The 20th (East Devonshire) Regiment of Foot.
1881-   The Lancashire Fusiliers.

BADGES
 The Sphinx superscribed 'Egypt', within a wreath of laurel, commemorating the service of the 20th in the campaign of 1801. Authorized 6th July, 1802.
 The Red Rose of Lancaster, adopted as a badge in 1881, had been the old badge of the 7th Lancashire Militia, which became the 3rd Battalion.
 The motto *Omnia Audax* first appears in the Army List, 1901.

BATTLE HONOURS (*Dates authorized from 1802 to 1855*)
EGYPT AND SPHINX, 6th July, 1802.
MAIDA, 24th February, 1807.
PENINSULA, 6th April, 1815.
PYRENEES, 29th August, 1817.
ORTHES, 29th August, 1817.
MINDEN, 22nd December, 1820.
EGMONT-OP-ZEE, 27th March, 1820.
VITTORIA, 12th May, 1826.
TOULOUSE, 12th May, 1826.
ALMA, 16th October, 1855.
INKERMAN, 16th October, 1855.
SEVASTOPOL, 16th October, 1855.

SHOULDER-BELT PLATES

The early oval plates were of gilt with the design mounted in silver of 'XX' within a wreath, all within a raised oval (Fig. 190). This was replaced by Fig. 191, an oblong silver plate with rounded corners with the design of 'XX' below a crown within a wreath. This plate appears to have been soon replaced by another, also of silver, with the Honours awarded up to 1820 (Fig. 192).

When in 1830 the silver plate was replaced by a gilt one, the Honours awarded in 1826 were added. This plate was in turn replaced by one of a design similar to that worn about 1820; the plate was all gilt with a burnished rim.

Mr. Hughes has a photograph of a badge which was in the Lucas collection. The design was 'XX' within a garter inscribed 'Regiment', a laurel wreath round and a grenade above the garter. The plate, an oblong one, appears to have been burnished.

BUTTONS

There have been remarkably few changes in the design of the buttons worn by the 20th.

The officers' early bone-backed button had the design in relief of 'XX' within a spray of leaves; the button had a beaded rim (Fig. 193). The other ranks' button had the same design. Another design, probably later, had a plain 'XX' incised without a rim.

This design was followed for the officers and other ranks by a button, silver for officers until 1830, then gilt, with a crown at the opening of the spray (Fig. 194).

In 1855 the 'XX' was replaced by the Arabic numeral '20'. After 1881 the design on the buttons was the Sphinx below a crown and within a laurel wreath.

The cap button had the design of 'XX'. The 1934 Dress Regulations gives the mess button as having the design mounted.

190

191

192

193

194

133

THE ROYAL SCOTS FUSILIERS

TITLES

1678-1707　Colonel the Earl of Mar's Regiment of Foot, afterwards Fusiliers and popularly the Scots Fusiliers Regiment of Foot.
1707-1712　The Scots Fusiliers Regiment of Foot, also by the Colonel's name.
1712-1751　The Royal North British Fusiliers Regiment of Foot.
1751-1877　The 21st (Royal North British Fusiliers) Regiment of Foot.
1877-1881　The 21st (Royal Scots Fusiliers) Regiment of Foot.
1881-　The Royal Scots Fusiliers.

BADGES

The Thistle within the circle of St. Andrew, with the crown over it and inscribed with the motto *Nemo me impune lacessit*, was displayed on the Colours in 1747, and is recorded in the Regulations of that year.

The Royal Cypher and Crown. The Regulations for Clothing and Colours, 1747, record that the King's cypher and crown are to be displayed in the three corners of the second Colour. It is mentioned in the Army List for the first time in 1846.

The Royal Arms. Since 1881 the Royal arms have appeared on the ball of the grenades.

BATTLE HONOURS (*Dates authorized from 1854 to 1855*)

BLADENSBURG, 7th January, 1854.
ALMA, 16th October, 1855.
INKERMAN, 16th October, 1855.
SEVASTOPOL, 16th October, 1855.

SHOULDER-BELT PLATES

Circa 1786-1815 the officers' plate was oval, gilt, with the design engraved of the thistle surmounted by a crown; round the edge of the plate within a single-line oval the motto *Nemo me impune lacessit* and the number 'XXI'.

Fig. 195 is from Almack's book. The plate was gilt with the design of the crown and thistle and 'XXI' in dead gilt. The letters of the motto in raised letters on a matted ground, the centre of the plate burnished. The number 'XXI' was, it will be noticed, within the circle.

In Mr. Hughes' collection is an oblong gilt plate with the design of a grenade on the ball of which in silver was '21' within a crowned circle inscribed *Nemo me impune lacessit*.

The officers' plate *circa* 1830-1846 was a matted gilt one with a solid silver grenade (Fig. 196).

When in 1881 the Highland doublet was adopted, the sword belt was worn over the shoulder. The plate was a rectangular one of burnished gilt and had the design in silver of a thistle within a crowned circle inscribed *Nemo me impune lacessit*. In the lower curve of the circle was a small Maltese Cross and below the circle a scroll inscribed 'Royal Scots Fusiliers', and below this the date '1678'.

BUTTONS

The officers' bone-backed buttons *circa* 1777 had the design in relief on a gilt face shown in Fig. 197. The other ranks' pewter buttons of the same period had the design engraved as shown in Fig. 198.

The officers' buttons about 1800 were flat, single sheet, gilt, with the design of Fig. 199.

The convex buttons worn on the coatee by officers, 1830-1855, had the design in Fig. 200.

The tunic buttons 1855-1881 had the design of a thistle with the number '21' on the ball, with a crown above. After 1881 the design was a thistle below a crown.

The 1904 Dress Regulations give the cap and mess waistcoat as having gilt lined buttons with a burnished edge and the design of the letters 'RSF', with a crown above.

195

196

197   198   199   200

THE CHESHIRE REGIMENT

TITLES
- 1689-1751   Known by the name of the successive Colonels.
- 1751-1782   The 22nd Regiment of Foot.
- 1782-1881   The 22nd (Cheshire) Regiment of Foot.
- 1881-   The Cheshire Regiment.

BADGES

The Acorn. Tradition is that the acorn commemorates the services of the regiment at the battle of Dettingen, but no trustworthy evidence can be found to support their presence at the action, although the design has long been worn by the regiment.

A book entitled "British Battles on Land and Sea", by J. Grant, published in 1897, stated that "an aged soldier, named Robert Fergusson, who died at Paisley in 1811 in his ninety-seventh year, preserved to the last, as a precious relic, the old red coat of Handyside's Foot, the 22nd Regiment, in which he had been wounded at the battles of Dettingen and Fontenoy", which may have given rise to the tradition.

Official documents of the time of these two battles state that the regiment was employed on sea service.

The late Rev. P. Sumner, in the course of research, discovered that a sprig of acorn figured in the coat of arms of the Duke of Norfolk, the regiment's first Colonel, and also in the crest of Sir H. Bellamy, the second Colonel of the regiment, and the badge may well be derived from these. It is certainly suggestive, as four years before the Suffolk Regiment, who also have oak in their badge, had been raised by the same Duke.

Captain R. Timpson, who was a Lieutenant in the 22nd in 1761 and was one of the officers of the regiment to survive the climate of the West Indies, was in 1767 granted a coat of arms with the crest of a "sprig of oak" almost identical in design with the present collar badge of the regiment, but whether there is any connection between Timpson's crest and the regiment's badge it is impossible to say.

The Prince of Wales's Plume, Coronet and motto, worn by the Regular battalions after 1881, had been the old badge of the Royal Cheshire Militia. The Prince of Wales has the title Earl of Chester.

The Rose. In common with other regiments which had no officially recognized badge, the badge of the Rose was given in 1881 and changed to the united Red and White Rose in 1888, and for many years was shown in the Army List, but never appeared in any metal badge.

BATTLE HONOURS (*Dates authorized from 1843 to 1855*)
SCINDE, 18th August, 1843.
LOUISBURG, 2nd July, 1844.
MEEANEE, 2nd July, 1844.
HYDERABAD, 2nd July, 1844.

SHOULDER-BELT PLATES

Fig. 201 is of a plate found in St. Domingo and illustrated in the *Journal of the Society for Army Historical Research*, p. 46, Vol. XI. The plate is the one worn by other ranks and was of brass with the design incised. The regiment was stationed in the island, 1794-1796.

Almack's book illustrates (Fig. 202) a gilt matted plate with silver star, roped circle and number. The plate has a raised gilt rim. Size was $3\frac{1}{8} \times 2\frac{1}{2}$ inches. In the case of the Grenadier Company a grenade with '22' on the ball was superimposed on the top ray of the star. The Light Company would have had a bugle-horn.

In the miniature of an officer of the 22nd about 1800 he is shown wearing an oval gilt plate with the design of '22' within a crowned circle. Colonel A. Crookenden, the historian of the regiment, is doubtful if this is accurate.

Another type of oval plate had '22' within a wreath of oak in gilt, behind which was a blue enamel ground, the whole within a crowned circle, and in the centre of a silver cut star of eight points.

The plate about 1820 had the design similar to Fig. 203 on a gilt plate; the crown gilt with crimson velvet cushion; the centre design in gilt on a silver star with square ends to the rays. Below the star a gilt Roman fasces inscribed 'Cheshire'. About 1845 a similar plate was adopted with the Honours 'Scinde', 'Meeanee', 'Hyderabad' added on labels in place of the fasces (Fig. 203).

BUTTONS

The officers' bone-backed buttons *circa* 1780 had a gilt wire-bound design (Fig. 204). The other ranks' pewter buttons of the same period had the number '22' within a lined rim. They at first had the number incised, later in relief.

The officers' button *circa* 1800 were flat, single sheet, gilt, with the design in relief of '22' within a continuous wreath of laurel (Fig. 205). About 1810 this gave place to a slightly convex button with the number '22' within a spray of oak and all within a star of eight points. This button was worn until 1881, when a similar design was worn on the tunic button but with a sprig of oak in place of '22' within a circle inscribed with title. The star was retained. The other ranks' pewter buttons about 1820 were as in Fig. 206. The officers' gilt button *circa* 1840-1855 was as Fig. 207.

After 1881 the acorn with leaves was displayed within a circle inscribed 'Cheshire Regiment', and all within a star of eight points.

The officers' cap buttons were die struck; the design as on tunic buttons.

201

202

203

204

205

206

207

THE ROYAL WELCH FUSILIERS

TITLES
- 1688-1714   Colonel Lord Herbert's Regiment of Foot and by Colonel's name.
- 1714-1727   The Prince of Wales's Own Royal Regiment of Welsh Fusiliers.
- 1727-1751   The Royal Welsh Fusiliers.
- 1751-1881   The 23rd (Royal Welch Fusiliers) Regiment of Foot.
- 1881-1920   The Royal Welsh Fusiliers.
- 1920-   The Royal Welsh Fusiliers.

BADGES

The Rising Sun. The ancient badge of Edward the Black Prince. Borne on the Colours, 1747.

The Coronet, Plume and motto of the Prince of Wales. The badge of the Principality of Wales. Borne on the Colours, 1747.

The Red Dragon. An ancient badge of Edward the Black Prince. Borne on the Colours, 1747.

The Sphinx superscribed 'Egypt'. Commemorates the services of the regiment in Egypt, 1801. Authorized 6th July, 1802.

The White Horse of Hanover and the motto *Nec aspera terrent*. Described in the Clothing Regulations, 1747, as worn on the flap of the Grenadier caps and on the drums and bells of arms.

BATTLE HONOURS (*Dates authorized from 1801 to 1855*)

MINDEN, 1st January, 1801.
EGYPT AND THE SPHINX, 6th July, 1802.
PENINSULA, 6th April, 1815.
WATERLOO, 23rd November, 1815.
MARTINIQUE, 31st October, 1816.
ALBUHERA, 31st October, 1816.
BADAJOZ, 15th May, 1821.
SALAMANCA, 15th May, 1821.
VITTORIA, 15th May, 1821.
PYRENEES, 15th May, 1821.
NIVELLE, 15th May, 1821.
ORTHES, 15th May, 1821.
TOULOUSE, 15th May, 1821.
CORUNNA, February, 1835.
ALMA, 16th October, 1855.
INKERMAN, 16th October, 1855.
SEVASTOPOL, 16th October, 1855.

SHOULDER-BELT PLATES

An Inspection Report of the 23rd Regiment dated 1788 records: "Breast-plates uniform with 3 Feathers engraved. The 3 Feathers of Wales worn in the Hats of the Battalions appear showy and give height to Battalion men in their undress."

Fig. 208 is an officers' plate *circa* 1800. The plate was gilt, with the plume and motto in silver and a burnished rim.

In Vol. XXX of the *Journal of the Society for Army Historical Research* is an illustration of the other ranks' plate in the collection of Mr. A. R. Cattley. The plate, which is brass, is described as die struck, with the design deeply incised, the design being the number '23' below the Prince of Wales's plume, coronet and motto.

Fig. 209 is a gilt plate with rounded corners and the design in gilt except for the feathers, which are silver.

Fig. 210 probably came into use about 1835 and was worn until about 1840, when a gilt matted plate with a burnished rim was in use until 1855. The design on the plate was a grenade with a crowned circle on the ball, inscribed 'Royal Welch Fusiliers' within the circle, the number 'XXIII' surmounted by the Prince of Wales's plume, coronet and mttoo. The design mounted in dead gilt on a burnished grenade.

BUTTONS

The officers' bone-backed buttons *circa* 1788 had gilt faces with the design of the Prince of Wales's plumes above the number '23', round the edge of the button a circle of leaves turned inwards (Fig. 211). This design was, in relief, also worn on the other ranks' pewter buttons.

Later the design worn on the other ranks' buttons was '23' engraved (Fig. 212) the button having a roped rim. About 1800 the other ranks' buttons had the design in relief of the Prince of Wales's crown plume and motto above the number 'XXIII' (Fig. 213). The button had a beaded border. The officers' buttons about 1810 were gilt, slightly convex, open backed, with the design of the crown plume and motto within a crowned circle inscribed 'Royal Welch Fusiliers'; below the circle, the number 'XXIII'. This design was retained on the coatee button up to 1855 (Fig. 214).

For a short time after the introduction of the tunic in 1855 the design worn was as on the coatee, but with the number in Arabic characters. This design was replaced by a button with the design of the crown plume and motto above '23', within a beaded circle; worn by other ranks until 1871.

In 1881 the design had little change except that the number disappeared and was replaced by the title. The buttons retained the beaded circle so long associated with the regiment. Some dies had the word 'Welch' spelt with a 'c' others with a 's'.

The 1900 Dress Regulations give the cap and mess waistcoat buttons as having gilt lined buttons with burnished edge. Below the plume the letters 'RWF'.

208

209

210

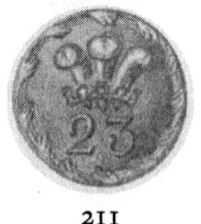
211

212

213

214

THE SOUTH WALES BORDERERS

TITLES
1689-1751   Known by the Colonel's name.
1751-1782   The 24th Regiment of Foot.
1782-1881   The 24th (2nd Warwickshire) Regiment of Foot.
1881-   The South Wales Borderers.

BADGES

The Sphinx superscribed 'Egypt'. Commemorates the services of the regiment in Egypt, 1801. Authorized 6th July, 1802.

A Wreath of Immortelles. Queen Victoria directed that a silver wreath should be borne on the staff of the Queen's Colour of battalions to commemorate the devoted gallantry of Lieutenants Melville and Coghill in saving that Colour after the battle of Isandlwana, and in memory of the defence of Rorke's Drift. Authorized 15th December, 1880.

The Dragon of Wales. Adopted in 1881. Had previously been the badge of the Royal South Wales Borderers Militia, who became the 3rd Battalion in 1881.

BATTLE HONOURS (*Dates authorized from 1802 to 1855*)

EGYPT AND THE SPHINX, 6th July, 1802.
PENINSULA, 29th March, 1815. To old 2nd Battalion (conferred on regiment 15th February, 1825.)
TALAVERA, 29th July, 1817.
FUENTES D'ONOR, 29th July, 1817.
PYRENEES, 29th July, 1817.
ORTHES, 29th July, 1817.
CAPE OF GOOD HOPE, 21st June, 1824.
NIVELLE, 24th July, 1824.
SALAMANCA, 20th September, 1824.
VITTORIA, 20th September, 1824.
PUNJAUB, 14th December, 1852.
CHILLIANWALLAH, 14th December, 1852.
GOOJERAT, 14th December, 1852.

SHOULDER-BELT PLATES

Almack's book shows a silver oval plate (Fig. 215). The plate had a silver cast matted surface with a beaded border; the design was of the star engraved, a garter and number 'XXIV' mounted in gilt.

The oval silver shoulder-belt plate (Fig. 216) *circa* 1802 was adopted after the granting of the Sphinx as a Battle Honour.

About 1815 the plate was oblong, silver, with the design of a crown over the Sphinx and '24' surrounded by a wreath of laurel. This plate is shown on page 199, Vol. XXIV, of the *Journal of the Society for Army Historical Research*. The officers' plates in 1850 were burnished gilt with the design mounted in silver (Fig. 217).

In the Royal United Service Institution collection is a brass other ranks' plate with the design of '24' within a crowned garter inscribed 'Warwickshire'. Below the garter are the Sphinx on straight label inscribed 'Egypt' and below this one inscribed 'Peninsula'.

BUTTONS

The officers' buttons in 1800 were flat, silver, with '24' engraved. This design was retained on the later convex ones until 1830. The men's early pewter buttons were of several varieties, '24' in relief on a plain button, and '24' with a roped rim to the button (Fig. 218). This gave way to one with '24' in relief with a continuous circle of leaves round the edge. Soon after 1810 the men's button had the design of '24' within a wreath, but the button had scalloped edges. This design, which was worn by both officers and other ranks, was retained by officers until 1881 and by other ranks until 1871. After 1881 the officers' button displayed the Welsh Dragon within a wreath, the scalloped rim being retained. There are several dies of these buttons as well as of the 1855-1881 period, with minor differences in shape of numbers and thickness of the wreath.

The tunic button after 1881 had the design of the Welsh Dragon within a wreath of laurel.

The 1900 Dress Regulations gives the mess dress button as having the "Dragon mounted in silver" on a plain gilt button. Later this was changed to one with the design mounted in silver of 'XXIV' within a wreath of Immortelles.

215

216

217

218

145

THE KING'S OWN SCOTTISH BORDERERS

TITLES
- 1689-1751 Known by the Colonel's name; also as The Edinburgh Regiment of Foot.
- 1751-1782 The 25th (Edinburgh) Regiment of Foot.
- 1782-1805 The 25th (Sussex) Regiment of Foot.
- 1805-1881 The 25th (The King's Own Borderers) Regiment of Foot.
- 1881-1887 The King's Own Borderers.
- 1887- The King's Own Scottish Borderers.

BADGES

The Royal Crest. Conferred on the regiment by King George III with the title in 1805.

The motto *In Veritate Religionis confido* given to the regiment in 1805 by King George III on the change of title. Authority to retain the motto was dated 26th May, 1828.

The Castle of Edinburgh and motto *Nisi Dominus frustra*, authorized 8th March, 1832. The motto is that of the city of Edinburgh.

The White Horse of Hanover and motto *Nec aspera terrent* was displayed on the Colours previous to 1805.

The Sphinx superscribed 'Egypt'. Commemorates the services of the regiment in Egypt, 1801. Authorized 6th July, 1802.

BATTLE HONOURS (*Dates authorized from 1801 to 1855*)

MINDEN, 1st January, 1801.
EGYPT AND THE SPHINX, 6th July, 1802.
MARTINIQUE, TO FLANK COMPANIES, 9th December, 1819.
EGMONT-OP-ZEE, 10th February, 1820.

SHOULDER-BELT PLATES

Fig. 219 is the officers' shoulder-belt plate worn about 1782-1805. The plate was gilt with the design engraved.

Prior to 1855 the plate with slide in Fig. 220 was worn. The plate was matted gilt with the design of the White Horse and Sphinx in silver. The scroll inscribed with the motto *In Veritate Religionis confido* had pierced letters with a blue enamel ground. There were two dies of the plate, in one of which the horse was shown prancing.

The brass plate worn by other ranks *circa* 1850 had the design stamped on the shields, one with the White Horse inside an oval inscribed with the motto *Nec aspera terrent* and the other Edinburgh Castle inside an oval inscribed with the motto *Nisi Dominus frustra*. Above the shields a scroll inscribed with the motto *In Veritate Religionis confido* and surmounted by the Royal crest.

Below the shields the number 'XXV' and a scroll inscribed 'The King's Own Borderers'. Below the scroll a Sphinx. The whole on a cut star and the cross of St. Andrew, on which were inscribed 'Egmont-Op-Zee', 'Martinique', 'Egypt' and 'Minden'.

The late Captain Campbell's notes contain a photograph of an oblong plate with a design similar to that worn by other ranks, but with the following differences. The Sphinx was displayed above the number 'XXV', and the scroll with presumably the title was placed lower in the ovals. Unfortunately no description of the plate is with the photograph. The date of the plate is probably about 1840.

BUTTONS

The pewter buttons of the other ranks *circa* 1790 to 1805 had the design in relief of '25' within a single-line circle with the word 'Sussex' above (Fig. 221).

Circa 1820 the officers' buttons had the design of '25' below a crown with the title 'King's Own Borderers' round the top edge. The buttons were gilt, convex, with open backs. The same design but in higher relief was displayed on the coatee button, 1840-1855 period, with the addition of the word 'The' before the title.

This design was worn until 1881, after which date the crown was changed to the Royal crest. When in 1887 the title was changed, the necessary alteration was made on the button.

The pipers' silver diamond-shaped doublet button *circa* 1870 (Fig. 222) had the design of '25' below a crown, and the title around the button had a lined surface.

The 1900 Dress Regulations gives for the mess dress button a plain gilt button with the Royal crest above the letters 'KOSB' mounted in silver.

The 1911 Regulations gives the cap button as die struck with the same design as for the mess dress.

219

221

222

220

THE CAMERONIANS (SCOTTISH RIFLES)

TITLES

1ST BATTALION

1689-1751 Known by the names of successive Colonels, Regiment of Foot. Also for some time as 'The Cameronians'.
1751-1786 The 26th Regiment of Foot.
1786-1881 The 26th (Cameronians) Regiment of Foot.

2ND BATTALION

1759-1783 The number '90' was also that of two regiments, both disbanded:
(a) 1759-1763: The 90th (Irish Light Infantry) Regiment.
(b) 1775-1783: The 90th Regiment of Foot.
1794-1815 The 90th (Perthshire Volunteers) Regiment.
1815-1881 The 90th (Perthshire Volunteers) (Light Infantry).
1881- July-November: The Cameronians Regiment (Scotch Rifles).
1881- November: The Cameronians (Scottish Rifles).

BADGES

A Light Infantry Bugle-horn. The old badge of the 90th (Perthshire Volunteers) Light Infantry, adopted when the title Light Infantry was given in 1815. On certain of the shako plates the bugle-horn was of the French horn pattern. The Sphinx superscribed 'Egypt', which was at first displayed on the Colours between two laurel branches, commemorates the services of both battalions in Egypt, 1801. Authorized 6th July, 1802.
The Dragon superscribed 'China'. Commemorates the services of the 26th Regiment in China.
A Mullet or Spur Rowel. The crest of the Grahams. The 26th Regiment was raised by Mr. Thomas Graham, Laird of Balgowan, who later became Lord Lynedoch.
The Arms of Perth. Authorized to be worn on the glengarry of the 90th in 1873.

BATTLE HONOURS (*Dates authorized from 1802 to 1855*)

26TH
EGYPT AND THE SPHINX, 6th July, 1802.
CORUNNA, 17th April, 1823.
CHINA WITH THE DRAGON, 12th January, 1843.

90TH
EGYPT AND THE SPHINX, 6th July, 1802.
MANDORA, 7th March, 1817.
MARTINIQUE, 7th March, 1817.
GUADALOUPE, 7th March, 1817.
SEVASTOPOL, 16th October, 1855.

SHOULDER-BELT PLATES

26TH

About 1790-1800 the officers' oval silver shoulder-belt plate was of small size with the design mounted of '26' above a thistle.

Fig. 223 is the plate in use *circa* 1802-1830; the plate was still of silver but with the design mounted in gilt, and had rounded corners. This plate may have retained its design but with the metals reversed until 1843, when the Chinese Dragon and the word 'China' were added to the plate.

Fig. 224 is the plate worn until 1855. The plate was burnished gilt with a gilt crown, circle, number '26', Sphinx and wreath. The scrolls, Sphinx, star and back to the number were silver.

90TH

Almack's book illustrates an oval gilt plate of the 90th with the design of '90' below 'GR' engraved on a lined ground, all within a crowned garter inscribed 'Perthshire Regiment'.

Fig. 225 is of brass and probably worn by other ranks; the design was incised.

Fig. 226. This plate is of brass and the design incised. Probably worn by other ranks, date 1796-1805.

Fig. 227. The plate was gilt with the design mounted in silver, date about 1815-1830.

Fig. 228. Probable date 1830-1845.

The other ranks' brass oblong plate of this period had the design of 'XC' below a Light Infantry bugle-horn inside a crowned garter inscribed 'Perthshire Light Infantry'. On either side of the garter a spray of laurel, across the bottom of which were scrolls inscribed 'Martinique' and 'Guadaloupe'. Below the garter a Sphinx on a label inscribed 'Egypt', and below this a scroll inscribed 'Mandora'.

After Fig. 228 the plate was an oblong gilt one with a silver bugle-horn below a crown and the number '90' between the strings; the cords were tied in a bow.

BUTTONS

26TH

The officers' bone-backed buttons *circa* 1780 had the design in relief shown in Fig. 229 on a silver face. The other ranks' pewter buttons of the period 1767-1800 had the design shown in Fig. 230. The button had a roped rim and the design in relief. Another other ranks' design was '26' within a continuous wreath of leaves, introduced soon after 1800. This design was retained on the pewter buttons for a number of years, and was also worn by the officers on their flat single-piece buttons from 1800 to 1820.

The officers' buttons of the period 1830-1855 were gilt with the design shown in Fig. 231.

When in 1855 the tunic was introduced, the older design of '26' within a continuous wreath was adopted and worn by officers and other ranks (Fig. 232).

90TH

The officers' buttons *circa* 1800 were gilt, flat, with the design in relief of '90' within a single-line circle. Other ranks had the same design on their pewter buttons.

This design was retained on the subsequent coatee button—which, although with a closed back, was almost flat—and also on the tunic buttons.

For a short time a button with the design of '90' between the strings of a bugle-horn, the strings running straight into a crown and showing no bow to the cord, was used.

After becoming Rifles in 1881, the button became black and had the design of a bugle-horn with bow below a crown, within a spray of thistles. The pipers' diamond-shaped buttons were of white metal with the design of a bugle-horn interwoven with three thistles.

THE ROYAL INNISKILLING FUSILIERS

TITLES

1ST BATTALION

1689-1751   Colonel Zachariah Tiffin's (or by name of the successive Colonels) Regiment of Foot.
1751-1840   The 27th (Enniskillen) Regiment of Foot.
1840-1881   The 27th (Inniskilling) Regiment of Foot.

2ND BATTALION

1760-1796   Two regiments had the number 108th during this period, both being disbanded.
           (a) 1761-1763   The 108th Regiment of Foot.
           (b) 1794-1795   The 108th Regiment of Foot.
1854-1858   The Hon. East India Company 3rd (Madras European Infantry).
1858-1862   The 3rd (Madras) European Infantry Regiment.
1862-1881   The 108th (Madras Infantry) Regiment.
1881-   The Royal Inniskilling Fusiliers.

The 2nd Battalion was disbanded on reduction of the Army in 1922, re-formed in 1924 as part of the corps of the Royal Irish Fusiliers, and in 1938 once more became 2nd Battalion Royal Inniskilling Fusiliers, to be disbanded as such in 1948 on the Army being again reduced, and was again re-formed in 1951.

BADGES

The Castle of Inniskilling with St. George's colours flying in a blue field and the name 'Inniskilling' over it. Mentioned in the Royal Warrant of 1751 as a castle with three turrets.

The White Horse of Hanover and motto. Received authority to bear the badge and motto on its Colours for service during the Rebellion of 1715.

The Sphinx superscribed 'Egypt'. Commemorates the services of the 27th in Egypt, 1801. Authorized 6th July, 1802.

BATTLE HONOURS (Dates authorized from 1802 to 1855)

EGYPT AND THE SPHINX, 6th July, 1802.
MAIDA, 24th February, 1807.
PENINSULA, 6th April, 1815.
WATERLOO, 8th December, 1815.
BADAJOZ, 22nd October, 1821.
SALAMANCA, 22nd October, 1821.
VITTORIA, 22nd October, 1821.
PYRENEES, 22nd October, 1821.
NIVELLE, 22nd October, 1821.
ORTHES, 22nd October, 1821.
TOULOUSE, 22nd October, 1821.
ST. LUCIA, 28th March, 1836.

SHOULDER-BELT PLATES

Two oval gilt plates are recorded as having been worn, both displaying the ancient badge of the regiment. They were of gilt metal. Fig. 233 had the design mounted in silver, and the plate was of dead gilt with a beaded border. In Fig. 234 the castle and star rays at the back of the castle are silver. Size $3\frac{1}{4} \times 2\frac{5}{8}$ inches.

Fig. 235. The plate gilt with silver castle and number; the scroll with the title was gilt. The *Journal of the Society for Army Historical Research* records this plate in Vol. XXII, page 156, but with the addition of a bugle in silver for the light company, and does not mention the regimental number. The size of the plate is given as $3\frac{1}{4} \times 2\frac{5}{8}$ inches.

Fig. 236. A gilt matted plate with burnished edges and the design mounted in silver.

Fig. 237. A matted gilt plate, diamond cut star, the crown and Sphinx dead gilt. Castle and letters silver, gilt matted '27'.

The plate worn by other ranks *circa* 1800 had the design of the castle with the flag flying to the right. Above the castle a scroll inscribed 'Enniskillen', and below the castle the number '27'. The plate was brass. Size $2\frac{11}{16} \times 2\frac{1}{16}$ inches.

This design with a change in the showing of the numerals, which previously had been enclosed in a sunk octagonal square, was still worn in 1815.

A photograph of apparently an other ranks' plate appeared in the Regimental Journal, but unfortunately without any description except a note that the badge might have been struck. The castle is shown without a flag, resting on a scroll inscribed 'Enniskillen' and with '27' below. Above the castle, a crown. This plate may have followed the one mentioned above.

The other ranks' plate in 1850 was of the same design as for officers', but stamped in brass.

BUTTONS

27TH

The Inspection Report of 1768 records buttons not numbered; that of 1775, "Buttons with badge and number of Regiment". The design remained the same with little change until 1881, the chief difference being the spelling of Inniskilling; at first this was Enniskillen, later Inniskilling was adopted.

On page 156, Vol. XXII, of the *Journal of the Society for Army Historical Research*, the buttons on the jackets of the 27th Foot in the Regimental Museum at Omagh are described by the late Rev. P. Sumner: On the earlier jacket, 1813, as single piece, quite flat, with the design of the castle, with '27' below and 'Enniskillen' in a half-circle above (Fig. 238). The second jacket's date is given as 1816, and the buttons by then had become convex but had the same design.

The Regimental Journal illustrated a small size button with the design of a single tower, below which was the number '27', and above the tower the title 'Inniskilling Foot'. It is dated in the plate as the end of the eighteenth century.

Another button, probably worn about 1855 for a short time, had the design of the Sphinx below the castle; round the top edge of the button were ornamental scrolls, and below the Sphinx one inscribed 'Inniskilling'.

108TH

The other ranks' pewter buttons of the 108th Regiment of 1794-5 had the design of '108' within a French scroll, with a dot at the opening.

Prior to 1881 the design on the tunic buttons was the regimental number within a crowned garter inscribed 'Madras Infantry'.

After 1881 the buttons displayed the Castle of Inniskilling with the word 'Inniskilling' superscribed. In some dies the flag flew towards the right and in others to the left. One die displayed it as a Union Jack instead of St. George's Cross.

The 1900 Dress Regulations gives for the cap and mess dress buttons a plain gilt button with the castle mounted in silver. The 1904 Regulations states that the same design was worn on the cap button, but was die struck.

THE GLOUCESTERSHIRE REGIMENT

TITLES

1ST BATTALION

1694-1751   Known by the name of the Colonel.
1751-1782   The 28th Regiment of Foot.
1782-1881   The 28th (North Gloucestershire) Regiment of Foot.

2ND BATTALION

1756-1768   The 61st Regiment of Foot. Raised as the 2nd Battalion 3rd Regiment of Foot. Renumbered 61st in 1758.
1758-1782   The 61st Regiment of Foot.
1782-1881   The 61st (South Gloucestershire) Regiment of Foot.
1881-   The Gloucestershire Regiment.

BADGES

The Royal Crest. An old badge of the 28th. It appears on the old bone-backed officers' buttons of the 1780 period.

The Sphinx superscribed 'Egypt'. Awarded to the 28th and the 61st to commemorate their services in Egypt, 1801. Authorized 6th July, 1802.

The Back Badge. To commemorate the gallantry of the 28th at the Battle of Alexandria, when they were attacked by the French from both front and rear, the 28th were authorized to wear a special badge at the back of their head-dress. According to an excellent article on the badge by Lieutenant-Colonel R. M. Grazebrook which appeared in the *Journal of the Society for Army Historical Research*, Vol. XXIV, it was not officially authorized until 1830, but had been worn for many years before.

The Arms of the City of Gloucester. Had been the old badge of the Gloucester Militia. After 1881 it was worn on the officers' round-peaked forage cap in gilt metal and red enamel surmounted by a gilt Sphinx.

BATTLE HONOURS (*Dates authorized from 1802 to 1855*)

28TH

EGYPT AND THE SPHINX, 6th July, 1802.
BARROSA, 30th November, 1814.
PENINSULA, 6th April, 1815.
WATERLOO, 8th December, 1815.
ALBUHERA, 28th May, 1816.
VITTORIA, 30th November, 1816.
PYRENEES, 28th May, 1820.
NIVELLE, 28th May, 1820.
NIVE, 28th May, 1820.
ORTHES, 28th May, 1820.

CORUNNA, 11th June, 1832.
ALMA, 16th October, 1855.
INKERMAN, 16th October, 1855.
SEVASTOPOL, 16th October, 1855.

61ST
EGYPT AND THE SPHINX, 6th July, 1802.
MAIDA, 10th February, 1808.
PENINSULA, 6th April, 1815.
SALAMANCA, 9th July, 1816.
TOULOUSE, 9th July, 1816.
NIVELLE, 9th July, 1816.
TALAVERA, 8th October, 1821.
PYRENEES, 7th June, 1823.
NIVE, 7th June, 1823.
ORTHES, 7th June, 1823.
PUNJAUB, 14th December, 1852.
CHILLIANWALLAH, 14th December, 1852.
GOOJERAT, 14th December, 1852.

SHOULDER-BELT PLATES

28TH

Fig. 239 illustrates a solid silver engraved plate dug up in New York; from the fastenings at the back it is obvious the plate was worn on a shoulder belt. At its back was engraved 'Lieut. James Edwards, 28th Regt'.

I am indebted to Colonel R. M. Grazebrook, the Hon. Curator of the Gloucestershire Regiment Museum, for the following information concerning plates in their collection:

(1) Silver oval plate with the design of the Royal crest above the number '28', worn about 1790.

(2) A small silver oblong plate with rounded corners, size $3\frac{1}{2} \times 2\frac{5}{8}$ inches, the design as above. The plate is hall-marked '1820'.

Colonel Grazebrook agrees that later there may have been another plate of the 1820 design, but larger.

The officers' plate prior to 1855 was a gilt burnished plate with the design mounted in silver (Fig. 240).

On page 48 of Vol. XX, *Journal of the Society for Army Historical Research*, the other ranks' plate of 1852-1854 is described: "Was a brass rectangular plate with the number all cast in one; the sergeants had the same pattern, only in better metal, *e.g.*, a copper gilt metal".

61ST

The shoulder-belt plate worn by the 61st from 1802 to 1855 was unique in its simplicity, being a silver buckle slide and tip as shown in Fig. 241.

Of the 61st Colonel Grazebrook writes: "We have the special buckle-tip and slide plate in both silver and gilt. There are one or two slight differences in these. The 'LXI' and wreath on the tip is of various designs. The slide sometimes has 'Egypt' on one side and 'South Gloucestershire' on the reverse. I have seen no other LXI plates, but Herbert's No. 1 book gives 61st shoulder belt 3-inch with silver square buckle, solid tip and silver engraved. C. Smith's book, *circa* 1825: Belt buckle, tip and slide Jennen's (Herbert's) No. 2 book, *circa* 1842: Buff shoulder belt with gilt buckle tip and slide."

Page 78, Vol. XXIII, of the *Journal of the Society for Army Historical Research* states: "It was the only regiment which retained the old buckle, tip and slide sword belt for officers up to the introduction of the waist-belt plate in 1854. A Horse Guards letter, 31st October, 1843, gave permission for the 61st to continue to wear buckles and slides on their buff belts. The tip of the belt usually bore the figures 'LXI' between sprays of laurel, and the slide the distinction 'Egypt'."

Officers of the Light Company also bore on the belt a scroll inscribed 'Maida', which had been authorized for the flank companies of the 61st in 1808.

BUTTONS

28TH

The design on the face of the officers' buttons of the 28th had hardly any change between 1767 and 1881. Fig. 242 shows the officers' bone-backed button *circa* 1780; the face was silver and the design in relief.

Prior to 1830 the officers' buttons were silver, convex in shape, with open backs, and the design as before in low relief. After 1830 the buttons became gilt, still with the same design but in much stronger relief, which was worn until 1881.

The other ranks' early pewter buttons had a plain '28' (Fig. 243) in relief, but from about 1800 they had the same design as for officers.

61st

The 61st, like the 28th, had little if any change in the design of their buttons, having the design of '61' below a crown inside a single-line circle until 1881.

After 1881 the King's crest above the cypher 'GR' inside a border of leaves turned inwards, an old feature of the buttons of the 28th, was adopted and is still worn (Fig. 244). In some dies the old representation of the lion above the crown is used—*i.e.*, without a crown.

The 1900 Dress Regulations states the mess dress button as having the same design as on the tunic, but with the wreath and the design engraved. The 1911 Regulations give the cap button as having the Royal crest on a plain gilt button, die struck.

239

240

241

242  243  244

THE WORCESTERSHIRE REGIMENT

TITLES
1ST BATTALION
1694-1751   Known by the name of the successive Colonels.
1751-1782   The 29th Regiment of Foot.
1782-1881   The 29th (Worcestershire) Regiment of Foot.

2ND BATTALION
1702-1751   Known by the name of the successive Colonels.
1751-1782   The 36th Regiment of Foot.
1782-1881   The 36th (Herefordshire) Regiment of Foot.

1881-   The Worcestershire Regiment.

BADGES
 The Lion and the Royal Crest. An old badge of the 29th.
 An Eight-pointed Star. An old badge of the 29th. When in 1784 the pouch badges were discontinued, the 29th were allowed to continue to wear their star, according to tradition, through the influence of Queen Charlotte.
 The Motto 'Firm'. The origin is not known, but it had been the motto of the 36th from 1773, if not before.
 The Royal Crest. An old badge of the 36th.
 A Round Tower of Worcester Castle. An old badge of the Worcestershire Militia, worn after 1881 for a time in the centre of the officers' waist-belt plates.
 The United Red and White Rose. The badge of the Rose was given to the regiment in 1881 in common with other regiments which had no particular design. It does not appear to have ever been displayed by the regiment in its metal badges. It was changed to the United Red and White Rose in 1888.
 A Naval Crown superscribed '1st June, 1794'. Commemorates the services of the 29th at Lord Howe's victory on that date. Authorized 1909.

BATTLE HONOURS *(Dates authorized from 1812 to 1855)*
29TH
 ROLEIA,* 2nd March, 1812.
 PENINSULA, 6th April, 1815.
 VIMIERA, 8th August, 1818.
 TALAVERA, 8th August, 1818.
 ALBUHERA, 8th August, 1818.
 FEROZESHAH, 8th June, 1847.
 SOBRAON, 8th June, 1847.

* An Army Order in 1911 directed the spelling to be "Rolica".

36TH
    PENINSULA, 6th April, 1815.
    SALAMANCA, 9th July, 1816.
    NIVELLE, 9th July, 1816.
    TOULOUSE, 9th July, 1816.
    VIMIERA, 26th July, 1816.
    PYRENEES, 12th November, 1825.
    NIVE, 12th November, 1825.
    CORUNNA, 26th May, 1833.
    ROLEIA,* 26th May, 1833.
    HINDOOSTAN, 16th October, 1835.
    ORTHES, 5th February, 1836.

SHOULDER-BELT PLATES

29TH

The Regimental History records that in 1797 the officers had a silver plate 3 inches long and $2\frac{1}{4}$ inches wide. It was engraved round the edge with a wreath of laurels; in the centre in relief was mounted the device of a lion crowned statant gardant within a crowned garter, the garter inscribed *Honi soit qui mal y pense*. This is stated to be the earliest display of the lion. The same design was worn in 1812, but with a scroll inscribed 'Roleia' added below the wreath.

The late Mr. Reynolds stated that a miniature of an officer of the 29th had been seen in Ireland wearing an oval plate with the design of '29' within two wreaths.

Colonel H. E. Everard also records an oval plate with the design of '29' within a laurel wreath worn by an officer who joined the 29th in 1810 or 1811; and Colonel Everard says the plate was probably an old one worn previous to 1792.

The hall-mark on a silver plate with the design shown in Fig. 245 is '1818'.

In 1825 the plate, still silver, had the device in gilt of '29' within a crowned garter. Below the garter a scroll inscribed 'Peninsula', and on either side two scrolls, those on the left inscribed 'Roleia' and 'Vimiera', those on the right 'Talavera' and 'Albuhera'.

Prior to 1830 the 29th officers wore a silver octagonal engraved plate with a gilt lion cast within a crowned garter.

Fig. 246 is the officers' plate, 1832-1855; the plate was burnished gilt with gilt mounts. Within the crowned garter a crowned lion in dead gilt on a crimson velvet background The garter had pierced letters with the motto on blue enamel. The other ranks' plate *circa* 1830-1850 was a plain brass one with the number '29'.

36TH

Almack's book illustrates the 36th's badge *circa* 1800 as shown in Fig. 247. The plate was gilt with a silver beaded border and had the design mounted.

---

* An Army Order in 1911 directed the spelling to be "Rolica".

Fig. 248 is the silver plate probably worn about 1812 or a little later. The plate was an oblong gilt one with rounded corners with the design mounted in silver of '36', surmounted by a crown, and a scroll below inscribed 'Firm'. Mr. Reynolds states that a plate of this design but all gilt is given in the Morphen's pattern book. Another plate of this design was in the Ferle collection which was sold at Messrs. Sotheby's in 1921, but in the catalogue the plate was described as "gilt".

In a photograph of the Lucas collection lent by Mr. Hughes is an oblong plate with the design of '36' below a lion and crown and within a circle, all in the centre of an eight-pointed star. Above the star a scroll inscribed 'Peninsula' and below the star one with the motto 'Firm'. Below this a wreath of what appears to be laurel with four scrolls interwoven, according to Mr. Reynolds inscribed 'Vimiera', 'Nivelle', 'Salamanca', 'Toulouse', and worn about 1830.

The plate probably worn 1840-1855 had the design of '36' and the motto 'Firm' within a crowned garter inscribed 'Herefordshire Regiment'. The garter within a laurel wreath interwoven with scrolls inscribed 'Nive', 'Roleia', 'Pyrenees', 'Peninsula,' 'Corunna', 'Nivelle', 'Salamanca', 'Toulouse', 'Vimiera'; below the wreath a scroll inscribed 'Hindoostan' and 'Orthes'. All in gilt on a silver star.

The other ranks' plate of the period 1849-1850 was as shown in Fig. 249.

BUTTONS

29TH

The officers' bone-backed silver-faced buttons *circa* 1780 and the other ranks' pewter buttons of the period were of the same design. Whether Fig. 250 or Fig. 251 is the earlier is uncertain; probably Fig. 250, which was engraved, while Fig. 251 is in relief.

The late Mr. Milne recorded an other ranks' pewter button with the design of '29' in the centre of a star of eight points.

About 1800 the pewter buttons had the design in relief of '29' within a raised circle. This design was retained on all subsequent buttons for other ranks of the 29th until 1871.

Fig. 252 is the officers' silver button worn soon after 1813. It was very slightly convex with open back.

After 1825 the buttons became gilt and had in relief the design of '29' within a wreath of laurel leaves, and were worn on the coatee until 1855, when the newly introduced tunic had a button with '29' within a raised circle, which remained in use until 1881.

36TH

The officers' buttons of the 36th were always gilt.

According to Mr. P. W. Reynolds, in 1776 the buttons had the design of '36' within a thick circle. His information is from a portrait of Captain A. Napier.

The early pewter buttons worn by other ranks' had the design of '36' incised. The button had a roped rim.

In those worn about 1800, the design was almost flat, single sheet, with the design in relief, as shown in Fig. 253. There was no dot at the opening of the French scroll. The other ranks' pewter buttons were of the same design.

About 1830 a dot was placed at the opening of the scroll, and this design was continued on the tunic buttons.

After 1881 the design on the buttons became the lion within a crowned circle inscribed 'The Worcestershire Regiment'; below the circle a label with the motto 'Firm'. All this on a star. In some dies the lion was shown crowned, in others not.

After 1909 the design was an elongated star of eight points with the lion crowned on a label inscribed 'Firm', displayed within a garter inscribed with the motto of the Order of the Garter.

The Dress Regulations, 1900, gives the mess dress button as having the design as for the tunic, but engraved. In the 1904 Regulations the mess dress button is still engraved, but the crown is omitted and a garter is substituted for the circle.

THE EAST LANCASHIRE REGIMENT

TITLES
1st Battalion
1714-1751 Known by the name of the successive Colonels.
1751-1782 The 30th Regiment of Foot.
1782-1881 The 30th (Cambridgeshire) Regiment of Foot.

2nd Battalion
1755-1757 The 61st Regiment of Foot, renumbered as 59.
1757-1782 The 59th Regiment of Foot.
1782-1881 The 59th (2nd Nottinghamshire) Regiment of Foot.
1881-   The East Lancashire Regiment.

BADGES
The Sphinx superscribed 'Egypt', awarded to the 30th Regiment for services in Egypt, 1801. Authorized 6th July, 1802.
The Red Rose of Lancaster. Adopted in 1881 with the change of title. Had been the old badge of the 5th Royal Lancashire Militia, which in 1881 became the 3rd (Militia) Battalion of the regiment.
Motto: *Spectamur Agendo*. Authorized by Army Order No. 150, June, 1911. It had been used for some years previously.

BATTLE HONOURS (*Dates authorized from 1802 to 1855*)
30TH
EGYPT AND THE SPHINX, 6th July, 1802.
PENINSULA, 6th April, 1815 ⎫ To old 2nd Battalion. To the regiment
WATERLOO, 8th December, 1815 ⎭ as a whole, 10th April, 1827
BADAJOZ, 26th March, 1825.
SALAMANCA, 26th March, 1825.
ALMA, 16th October, 1855.
INKERMAN, 16th October, 1855.
SEVASTOPOL, 16th October, 1855.

59TH
CORUNNA, 29th April, 1812, to the old 2nd Battalion.
PENINSULA, 29th March, 1815, to the old 2nd Battalion, and to the regiment as a whole, 5th June, 1816.
VITTORIA, 16th April, 1818.
ST. SEBASTIAN, 16th April, 1818.
NIVE, 16th April, 1818.
JAVA, 28th May, 1818.
BHURTPORE, 6th December, 1826.
CAPE OF GOOD HOPE, 3rd March, 1836.

SHOULDER-BELT PLATES

30TH

Almack's book shows an oval plate for the 30th Regiment, '30' within a raised oval, the plate having a deep rim; the whole being of burnished silver, polished.

In a miniature of Captain A. Macnab, who was killed at Waterloo, he is shown wearing an oval silver breast plate with the design of '30' below a crown within a laurel wreath.

A portrait of Major T. Tongue, who served in the regiment during the Peninsular War, shows him wearing an oblong silver plate with the design of '30' surmounted by a crown in gilt metal.

Mr. P. W. Reynolds' notes record that about 1816 was worn an oval silver plate engraved with the design of 'XXX' with a roped circle, below this the Royal arms, and below them three scrolls inscribed 'Peninsula', 'Egypt', 'Waterloo'. The plate had an ornamental design round the rim. This plate appears to have been the last of the oval badges worn by the regiment.

Mr. P. W. Reynolds also writes that the shoulder-belt plate, 1830-1840, had the design of 'XXX' within a gilt garter inscribed with the motto *Spectamur Agendo*. Above this a scroll inscribed 'Peninsula', and below the garter one inscribed 'Waterloo'. On the left of the garter a scroll inscribed 'Salamanca' and on the right one inscribed 'Badajoz'. All within a wreath of laurel in gilt and on a diamond cut star of eight points. Above the garter a crown, and at the bottom of the wreath a gilt Sphinx inscribed 'Egypt'.

Prior to 1855 the plate was gilt burnished with the design mounted in dead gilt on a silver cut star of eight points. The design was 'XXX' within a garter inscribed with the motto *Spectamur Agendo*; above the garter a scroll inscribed 'Peninsula', and round the bottom part of the garter three scrolls inscribed 'Salamanca', 'Waterloo', 'Badajoz'. The scroll superimposed on a wreath of leaves, above which is a crown, and below the wreath a Sphinx. Size 3 ⅛ × 3 ⅞ inches (Fig. 254).

59TH

Mr. H. Y. Usher has in his collection an oval gilt plate with the design in silver of '59' below a crown and within a wreath, while Mr. A. R. Cattley has one of the same design, silver, hall-marked '1808-09', probably worn by a different battalion of the 59th.

In the books of uniforms compiled by the late Mr. P. W. Reynolds is a plate copied from an engraving showing the uniform of the 1769-1800 period. In this the plate is an oval one, with a plain '59'. Later in the same book is an illustration of a portrait of Lieutenant John Cowper, who served in the regiment from 1799 to 1810. The plate he wears is an oblong gilt one with the design of '59' within a spray of leaves.

Another plate illustrated by Mr. Reynolds was a gilt burnished oval one with a bright silver star, the rays of which are described as on red enamel.

Fig. 255 shows the silver plate with rounded corners worn prior to the change from silver to gold lace in 1830.

Fig. 256 was probably adopted soon after 1820; the plate was gilt with the design mounted in silver. This was replaced by the design in Fig. 257, a gilt plate with the design mounted in silver, which in turn gave way to that shown in Fig. 258, the plate worn 1846-1855; it is drawn from one in the collection of Mr. H. Y. Usher. The plate, a very handsome one, is of dead gilt with a frosted ground. The wreath and garter are in enamel with a red enamel back to the centre. The star is cut silver.

Since the above was written, Mr. H. Y. Usher has drawn the author's attention to the following shoulder-belt plates of the 59th.

(a) The Montray Sale included an oblong gilt plate of similar design to 257, but with the honour 'Bhurtpoor' added below the number 'LIX'.

(b) At the Cattley Sale, 1955, was a large gilt burnished plate with a similar design to 258, but with the star rays all straight.

Mr. Usher is of opinion that this was the last design worn.

BUTTONS

30TH

The officers' bone-backed button had the design in relief of '30' within a deep ornamental design of leaves turned inwards round the rim to the button (Fig. 259).

The officers' silver buttons of 1800 period were flat with the design of '30' in relief within a single circle (Fig. 260).

The other ranks' pewter button *circa* 1800 had the design in relief of '30' within a circle of continuous leaves. The button had a roped rim.

The gilt convex coatee button 1840-1855 had the design in relief of 'XXX' within a crowned garter inscribed 'Cambridge', a wreath of laurel round the garter with a spray of rose, thistle and shamrock at the bottom. The other ranks' pewter buttons had the same design (Fig. 261).

When in 1855 the tunic buttons came in, this design of spray was retained on the button until 1881, but the Roman numerals were replaced by Arabic.

59TH

The early pewter buttons worn by the other ranks of the 59th had the design in relief of '59'. The button had a roped rim (Fig. 262).

The men's pewter buttons 1840-1855 had the design of '59' below a crown within a plain single circle. The officers' buttons about 1825 were convex, of silver, and with the design of '59' on a lined ground within a crowned garter, the garter inscribed '2nd Nottingham'. This design was retained on the gilt buttons which came into use after 1830. The early designs have the title on the garter incised, the later in relief (Fig. 263).

The tunic button of 1855 had in relief the number '59' below a crown within a plain single circle. There were several varieties in the size and shape of the numerals.

After 1881 the design on the buttons was the Sphinx on a label inscribed 'Egypt'. Below this a rose, the whole within a circle inscribed 'The East Lancashire Regiment'.

The 1904 Dress Regulations gives for the mess dress button the Sphinx and rose in silver, mounted. The cap button was die struck.

THE EAST SURREY REGIMENT

TITLES

1ST BATTALION
- 1713-1751   Known by the name of the successive Colonels.
- 1751-1782   The 31st Regiment of Foot.
- 1782-1881   The 31st (Huntingdonshire) Regiment of Foot.

2ND BATTALION
- 1756-1758   The 31st Regiment of Foot, 2nd Battalion.
- 1758-1782   The 70th Regiment of Foot.
- 1782-1812   The 70th (Surrey) Regiment of Foot.
- 1812-1825   The 70th (or Glasgow Lowland) Regiment of Foot.
- 1825-1881   The 70th (The Surrey) Regiment of Foot.
- 1881-   The East Surrey Regiment.

BADGES

The Arms of Guildford. Adopted as a badge by the regiment in 1881.

A Star. Adopted in 1881 by the Regular battalions; had been the old badge of the 3rd Royal Surrey Militia.

In 1881 the regiment was issued, with other regiments having no distinctive badge, with the badge of the Rose, changed to the United Red and White Rose in 1888. It does not appear to have ever figured in any of the metal badges worn by the regiment.

BATTLE HONOURS (*Dates authorized from 1815 to 1855*)

31ST

PENINSULA, 29th March, 1815, to the old 2nd Battalion. To the regiment as a whole, 29th January, 1825.

ALBUHERA, 5th June, 1816.

TALAVERA, 4th January, 1823.

VITTORIA, 4th January, 1823.

NIVELLE, 4th January, 1823.

NIVE, 4th January, 1823.

PYRENEES, 4th January, 1823.

CABOOL, 1842, 22nd June, 1844.

MOODKEE, 3rd June, 1847.

FEROZESHAH, 3rd June, 1847.

ALIWAL, 3rd June, 1847.

ORTHES, 7th June, 1847.

SOBRAON, 8th June, 1847.

SEVASTOPOL, 16th October, 1855.

SHOULDER-BELT PLATES

31ST

Mr. Reynolds records a plate shown in the miniature of an officer in the uniform of the period 1769-1800. The plate is oval, silver, with the number '31', and has what appears to be a matted surface. Almack's book illustrated an oval polished silver plate with the design in relief of '31' within a double circle; the plate was burnished.

Mr. Reynolds records later in his book another plate of the 31st shown in a miniature of an officer about 1795. This plate is oval with the design of '31' within a crowned garter; the plate has a beaded rim. The plate in Almack's book may have been worn by the officers of the 2nd Battalion, which was raised on the renewal of the French War and disbanded in 1814.

About 1824 the plate was silver with the design shown in Fig. 264. After 1830 the plate remained of the same design, but the metal was gilt with the design in silver. An oblong gilt plate with the design of 'XXXI' within a crowned garter inscribed 'Huntingdonshire', with a laurel wreath, around which was interwoven a riband bearing the Peninsula, Afghan, 1842, and the Sikh Honours, was worn 1847-1855.

70TH

The 70th plate illustrated in Almack's book had the design of '70' within a wreath, with a crown at the opening. The plate was oval, gilt, with the design mounted in silver.

About 1820 a gilt plate (Fig. 265) with rounded corners was worn. The design of '70' within a crowned garter inscribed 'Surry Regiment' was incised.

The Grenadier Company plate *circa* 1820 was oblong, gilt, with the design of '70' below a grenade, all within a wreath of laurel.

Fig. 266 shows the plate worn *circa* 1840-1855. The plate had a gilt matted surface with a bevelled rim. The star was silver, the crown, garter and scrolls in dead gilt.

BUTTONS

31ST

The early officers' buttons of the 31st had the design of '31' engraved. The button had a roped rim (Fig. 267).

About 1800 the design for both officers and other ranks was the number in relief within a single-line circle.

The coatee buttons 1840-1855 had the design of 'XXXI' within a crowned garter inscribed 'Huntingdonshire', and with a wreath of rose, shamrock and thistle. The design was worn by both officers and other ranks.

After 1855 the button remained of the same design except that the 'XXXI' was replaced by '31', and in some dies the design of the crown was distinctive. The spray of rose, thistle and shamrock, which had been displayed for many years superimposed on the wreath at the bottom of the garter, disappeared in 1881.

70TH

The 70th early pewter button had the number engraved on a button with a roped rim (Fig. 268). This gave way to one (Fig. 269) with '70' below 'Surry', and below the number a spray of leaves. This design was worn by other ranks for a considerable time.

The officers' coatee button of 1848 had the number 'LXX' within a crowned garter inscribed 'Surry' and having a scalloped rim.

It was followed by a very plain button with '70' in relief within a single plain ring (Fig. 270). This design was used until 1881.

After 1881 the design on the tunic button was of the arms of Guildford within a crowned circle inscribed 'East Surrey'. On the bottom of the circle a spray of laurel leaves, the whole on a star of eight points.

The 1904 Dress Regulations give the mess dress button design as for the tunic button, but mounted in silver. The cap button had the same design, die struck.

264

265

266

267

268

269

270

THE DUKE OF CORNWALL'S LIGHT INFANTRY

TITLES

1st Battalion

1702-1714 Colonel Edward Fox's or Jacob Borr's (Regiment of Marines).
1714-1751 Colonel Jacob Borr's Regiment of Foot, or by the name of the successive Colonels.
1751-1782 The 32nd Regiment of Foot.
1782-1858 The 32nd (Cornwall) Regiment of Foot.
1858-1881 The 32nd (Cornwall) Light Infantry.

2nd Battalion

1741-1751 Colonel James Price's Regiment of Foot, or by names of the successive Colonels.
1751-1782 The 46th Regiment of Foot.
1782-1881 The 46th (South Devonshire) Regiment of Foot.
1881- The Duke of Cornwall's Light Infantry.

BADGES

Bugle-horn. Adopted by the 32nd in 1858 when the regiment was given the title Light Infantry as a distinction for their gallantry in the defence of the Residency at Lucknow during the Indian Mutiny.

The Coronet of the Duke of Cornwall and the arms of the Duchy, with the motto "One and All". Adopted as a collar badge by the Regular battalions in 1876. Had been the badge of the Royal Cornwall Rangers Militia, who in 1881 became the 3rd Battalion of the regiment. The Coronet was later displayed on the buttons in conjunction with the bugle-horn.

Two Red Feathers. A distinction of the 46th, whose Light Company, when forming part of a light Battalion during the American War of 1777, so harassed the enemy that the Americans said they would give "no quarter" to the "Light Bobs". To prevent mistakes the Light Battalion dyed their feathers red.

A Turreted Archway. After the introduction of the Territorial system in 1881, the helmet plate centre displayed a turreted archway in conjunction with the bugle-horn and the badge of the two red feathers.

The archway was more accurately shown on the buttons which came into use after 1929, and was described as the "Gateway as shown on His Royal Highness' Great Seal as Duke of Cornwall". The design is of the ancient gateway of Launceston Castle.

The United Red and White Rose. Was given as a badge to the regiment in 1881 in common with other English infantry regiments without officially distinctive badges, but was never included in the metal badges of the regiment. At first shown as the Rose; changed to the United Red and White Rose in 1888.

BATTLE HONOURS (*Dates authorized from 1815 to 1855*)

32ND

PENINSULA, 6th April, 1815.
WATERLOO, 8th December, 1815.
SALAMANCA, 9th July, 1816.
NIVELLE, 9th July, 1816.
ROLEIA,* 9th July, 1816.
VIMIERA, 23rd January, 1826.
PYRENEES, 23rd January, 1826.
ORTHES, 23rd January, 1826.
NIVE, 14th November, 1831.
CORUNNA, 8th April, 1842.
PUNJAUB, 14th December, 1852.
MOOLTAN, 14th December, 1852.
GOOJERAT, 14th December, 1852.

46TH

DOMINICA, 9th February, 1808.
SEVASTOPOL, 16th October, 1855.

SHOULDER-BELT PLATES

32ND

Fig. 271 is of an early officers' plate given in the late Mr. Reynolds' notes.

The same notes illustrate two oval brass plates, now in the Dublin Museum. One plate had the design of '32' within a crowned garter inscribed 'Cornwall Regt', all on a star of eight points. The regiment was in Ireland in 1782, in which year they received the title "Cornwall". They proceeded to Gibraltar in 1783.

This plate was either followed by another design, or possibly worn by a different battalion. The plate was oval, brass, with the design engraved of '32' surmounted by a crown.

The Regimental History illustrates a small gilt oblong plate with rounded corners and the design in silver of '32' within a crowned garter inscribed 'Cornwall'.

Mr. Reynolds records a gilt oblong plate with rounded corners with the design in silver of '32' within a spray of leaves; above at the opening a scroll inscribed 'Peninsula', surmounted by a crown. Below the wreath a scroll inscribed 'Waterloo'.

About 1830 the plate was oblong, gilt, with the design mounted in silver of '32' within a crowned circle inscribed 'Cornwall Regt', all within a spray of laurel leaves and mounted on a star of eight points; the ends of the points not

---

* An Army Order in 1911 directed this honour to be spelt "Rolica".

being pointed, and the eight main rays inscribed 'Nive', 'Salamanca', 'Orthes', 'Pyrenees', 'Peninsula', 'Nivelle', 'Roleia' and 'Vimiera'. Below the wreath a scroll inscribed 'Waterloo'. The other ranks' brass plate had the same design.

46TH

In the catalogue of the sale of the Moutray Collection, May, 1954, is given an oval silver engraved plate of the regiment with the design of '46' below a crown within a circle and star.

The officers' plate worn prior to 1855 was of burnished gilt with a silver beaded star of eight points on which was mounted the design of '46' within a crowned garter; the garter inscribed 'South Devon'. The garter within a wreath of half laurel and half palm; below the garter and superimposed on the join of the wreath, a scroll inscribed 'Dominica'. All in gilt. The garter having a matted ground. (Fig. 272).

The brass plate worn by other ranks had the design of '46' below a crown and within a wreath of half laurel and half palm, on the bottom of the wreath a scroll inscribed 'Dominica'. The design was stamped.

BUTTONS

32ND

The early gilt bone-backed button worn by the officers of the 32nd was as shown in Fig. 273.

This was followed by a flat two-piece button with a gilt face and the design in relief (Fig. 274). This button apparently had a short existence and was replaced by a single-piece flat button with the design in relief shown in Fig. 275. This design was also worn on the other ranks' pewter buttons and was retained on the tunic buttons by both officers and other ranks; in the case of officers until 1881, and by other ranks until 1871.

46TH

The early 46th pewter button had the design in relief of '46'. The button had a roped border (Fig. 276). About 1800 the men's button displayed '46' within a French scroll with a dot at the opening. The officers' silver buttons about 1820 were convex with the simple design of '46' incised.

Circa 1840 the officers' coatee button had the design of '46' within a crowned garter and a wreath, half of laurel and half of palm. The garter was inscribed 'South Devon'.

After the introduction of the tunic the old design of '46' within a French scroll with a dot at the opening was resumed.

After 1881 the design on the buttons was a bugle with strings surmounted by a crown. Round the edge of the button the title of the regiment.

Later the crown was changed to the coronet of the Prince of Wales, as shown on the great seal of His Royal Highness as Duke of Cornwall.

After 1929 the design was changed to a bugle with strings surmounted by the coronet, and the gateway of Launceston as shown on His Royal Highness's Great Seal as Duke of Cornwall, and with the title round.

The 1904 Dress Regulations gives the design on the mess dress button as for the tunic button, but mounted in silver. Before this the design was of a bugle-horn, surmounted by a coronet mounted in gilt. The 1911 Regulations gives the cap button as the same design, die struck.

271

272

273

274

275

276

THE DUKE OF WELLINGTON'S REGIMENT (WEST RIDING)

TITLES
1ST BATTALION
1702-1751 Colonel the Earl of Huntingdon's Regiment of Foot, or by the names of the successive Colonels.
1751-1782 The 33rd Regiment of Foot.
1782-1853 The 33rd (1st Yorkshire West Riding) Regiment of Foot.
1853-1881 The 33rd (The Duke of Wellington's) Regiment.

2ND BATTALION
1756-1768 The 61st Regiment of Foot.
1758-1763 The 76th Regiment of Foot. Disbanded.
1787-1807 The 76th Regiment of Foot.
1807-1812 The 76th (Hindoostan) Regiment of Foot.
1812-1881 The 76th Regiment of Foot.
1881-1920 The Duke of Wellington's (West Riding Regiment).
1920- The Duke of Wellington's Regiment (West Riding).

BADGES
The Crest and Motto of the Duke of Wellington. The 33rd was the first regiment to be commanded by the Duke and is now the only one to be named after a subject. The Crest and Motto authorized as badge for the 33rd, 18th June, 1853.

The Elephant with Howdah. Conferred on the 76th Regiment, 17th January, 1807, to commemorate their long and distinguished service in India, 1788-1806.

BATTLE HONOURS (*Dates authorized from 1806 to 1855*)
33RD
WATERLOO, 8th December, 1815.
SERINGAPATAM, 28th May, 1818.
ALMA, 16th October, 1855.
INKERMAN, 16th October, 1855.
SEVASTOPOL, 16th October, 1855.

76TH
HINDOOSTAN, 20th October, 1806; to this Honour was added the badge of an Elephant with Howdah on 17th January, 1807.
PENINSULA, 6th April, 1815.
NIVE, 1st January, 1845.

SHOULDER-BELT PLATES

33RD

The officers' oval silver shoulder-belt plate *circa* 1800 had the design engraved of '33' with a lined background within a crowned garter inscribed 'First Yorkshire West Riding'.

The late Mr. P. W. Reynolds records a silver plate of similar design, but with 'Waterloo' added below the garter.

In Mr. Tilling's collection of photographs of plates is one of similar design to the 1800 one, but the garter is more oblong and there is only one scroll below, which is inscribed 'Waterloo'. The plate was burnished. This is probably identical with the one mentioned by Mr. Reynolds.

Fig. 277 is the oblong all-silver plate worn until after 1830, when the plate became burnished gilt with the design mounted in silver. The scroll below the garter was prolonged and inscribed 'Seringapatam', 'Waterloo'. The plate was worn up to 1855.

76TH

Almack's book shows the oval plate of the 76th (Fig. 278). It is described as "silver polished plate with bright engraved border and metal chased crown and Palm. Gilt dead colour and number '76' (within a spray of laurel and with a crown above) engraved on the plate in the centre and blacked with wax."

Mr. Reynolds states that after the grant of the Hindoostan honours in 1807 a new plate, oblong with the corners slightly rounded, was adopted. This plate was silver with gilt mounts; the elephant without howdah cloth in centre surmounted by a crown, and the regimental number in Roman numerals below it. The whole surmounted by two laurel branches. Below these and just above the lower edge of the plate a scroll inscribed 'Hindoostan'.

Fig. 279 is a polished gilt plate with the scrolls, crown and numerals in silver.

Fig. 280 is from a plate in Mr. Young's collection. The plate is entirely silver, in spite of the Battle Honour, 'Nive', which was not granted to the 76th in 1845.

Prior to 1855 the plate had a matted gilt surface with burnished rim. The design (as in Fig. 280) was mounted on a silver cut star and cross and had the elephant in burnished silver and the number 'LXXVI' in silver with a matted surface. The crown, wreath and scrolls were in bright gilt. Size $3\frac{3}{8} \times 2\frac{13}{16}$ inches. The scroll inscribed 'Peninsula' in some dies was shorter, and the elephant was without a howdah cloth.

BUTTONS

33RD

The early officers' buttons of the 33rd were flat, silver, with the design of '33' engraved.

The other ranks' pewter buttons (Fig. 281) of the same period had the number '33' engraved on a button with a roped rim. Later this was replaced by one with '33' within a continuous wreath. This design was worn on the coatee by officers and men until about 1840. The coatee and tunic buttons 1848-1881 had '33' below a crown within a garter inscribed the 'Duke of Wellington's

Regt'. In the case of the coatee the button was flat. The men's pewter buttons at first had '33' incised, the button having a roped rim; later, one with the design in relief (Fig. 282) was adopted.

76TH

The early officers' buttons were of a very handsome design (Fig. 283); the men's pewter buttons having the same design. The officers' silver buttons *circa* 1800-1810 had the design of '76' below a crown, at first incised on a flat single-piece button; later, in low relief on a slightly convex button. Soon after 1807 the design for officers was as shown in Fig. 285, the same design being used by other ranks but with the omission of the crown and wreath, and the elephant had a howdah (Fig. 284).

The howdah does not appear to have been shown on the officers' buttons until after 1855.

The gilt coatee button for officers, 1830-1855, had the same design as on the former silver one with the addition of the Honour 'Peninsula' to the top rim of the button. The men's buttons also had the addition of 'Peninsula'.

After 1881 the elephant, fully equipped and with howdah, was shown with the title 'Duke of Wellington's' round top edge of the button and 'West Riding Regt' at the bottom.

The design of the howdah has varied considerably.

The 1900 Dress Regulations describe the cap and mess dress as having the elephant and howdah mounted in silver on a plain button. An earlier mess button had the crest of the Duke of Wellington mounted in silver on a flat gilt button. In the 1911 Regulations the cap button has the title omitted.

181

THE BORDER REGIMENT

TITLES

1st Battalion

1702-1751 Colonel Lord Lucas's Regiment of Foot, or by the names of the successive Colonels.

1751-1782 The 34th Regiment of Foot.

1782-1881 The 34th (Cumberland) Regiment of Foot.

2nd Battalion

1755-1757 The 57th Regiment of Foot, renumbered 55th.

1757-1782 The 55th Regiment of Foot.

1782-1881 The 55th (Westmoreland) Regiment of Foot.

1881-   The Border Regiment.

BADGES

A Laurel Wreath. An old badge of the 34th, and which tradition says is in memory of the battle of Fontenoy.

The Dragon superscribed 'China'. Given to the 55th Regiment, 12th January, 1843, to commemorate their services in the China War. Colonel M. Smyth, the Hon. Curator of the Border Regiment's Regimental Museum, who also has done an immense amount of research into the design of the regiment's badges and buttons, stated that the officer's shako plate 1869-1878 displayed the dragon as one of "Imperial design"—*i.e.*, five claws and wearing a crown. The 55th appear to have been the only British regiment to display it thus, but after 1878 to have adopted one of the universal design.

A Maltese Cross. Although not officially authorized until 22nd July, 1881, had figured on the shoulder-belt plates and shako badges of the 34th for some years previously.

The Star of the Garter. Displayed on the officers' waist-belt plates, 1881-1902; was originally the badge of the Royal Westmoreland Militia.

The Red and White Tuft. For many years the 34th Regiment had the distinction of wearing red and white feathers, later tufts, in their head-dress in memory of their gallantry at the action of Arroyo dos Molinos. When red and white tufts became general for regiments of Foot other than Light Infantry and Rifles, the distinction was lost, but the name of the action was placed on the Colours. Previously only general actions had been awarded this honour. Later the wearing of a red and white tuft with red at the top instead of as usual at the bottom was sanctioned.

On the introduction of the helmet the distinction was commemorated by a red and white background to the plate and to the cap and collar badges.

BATTLE HONOURS (*Dates authorized from 1815 to 1855*)

34TH
PENINSULA, 29th March, 1815, to old 2nd Battalion; to 34th, 18th September, 1817.
ALBUHERA, 13th June, 1817, to old 2nd Battalion; to 34th, 18th September, 1817.
VITTORIA, 3rd July, 1817.
PYRENEES, 16th August, 1823.
NIVELLE, 16th August, 1823.
NIVE, 16th August, 1823.
ORTHES, 16th August, 1823.
ARROYO DOS MOLINOS, 30th May, 1845.
SEVASTOPOL, 16th October, 1855.

55TH
CHINA, with the badge of the Imperial Dragon of China, 12th January, 1843.
ALMA, 16th October, 1855.
INKERMAN, 16th October, 1855.
SEVASTOPOL, 16th October, 1855.

SHOULDER-BELT PLATES

34TH

Before 1800 the officers' oval silver shoulder-belt plate had the design engraved of '34' within a laurel wreath. This was replaced about 1806 by an oblong silver one with rounded corners with the same design. The design was mounted. The other ranks' plate of about this period had the design in Fig. 286 on a brass plate.

Mr. Reynolds in his book on uniforms records the officers' plate of 1826 as silver, oblong, square corners, with the design of '34' within a laurel wreath and a scroll below inscribed 'Vittoria', 'Peninsula', 'Albuhera'.

This plate does not appear to have been worn for long and was replaced by one with the design of a Maltese Cross surmounted by a crown. Within the circle in the centre of the cross the number '34' on a silver background; the circle inscribed 'Cumberland'. Lions between the limbs of the cross and a wreath of laurel behind showing between the limbs. The limbs inscribed with the Honours 'Peninsula', 'Pyrenees', 'Nive', 'Vittoria', 'Orthes', 'Nivelle' and 'Albuhera'. This design, all in gilt, was mounted on a silver cut star of eight points, probably—according to Mr. Reynolds—about 1832.

After the change of the colour of the lace from silver to gold, which took place in 1830, the plate was of the same design as the previous one, but the plate was gilt burnished.

In 1845 the Honour 'Arroyo dos Molinos' was added on a scroll below the cross. This was the plate in use up to 1855. The brass plate worn by other ranks in the 1840-1850 period had the design of '34' within a wreath with crown above.

55TH

The 55th were a gold-laced regiment from its early days. The early officers' plate was gilt with the design (Fig. 287) engraved. Fig. 288 is an early brass plate worn by other ranks and is from the collection of Mr. Usher. The design was engraved.

The officers' gilt oblong plate worn up to 1843 was gilt burnished plate with the silver design of '55' within a crowned wreath. When in 1843 the Honour 'China' with the dragon was awarded, the plate became as in Fig. 289. The plate was gilt matted with burnished edge; the design mounted in gilt and a burnished background to the centre.

BUTTONS

34TH

The officers' bone-backed buttons *circa* 1780 had silver faces with the design in relief of '34', round the edge of the button a border of leaves turned inwards (Fig. 290).

The other ranks' pewter buttons of the same period had the same design, later changed to '34' in relief, the button having a roped rim; while for a short time they had the design of '34' within a continuous wreath.

The officers' buttons about 1800 were silver, slightly convex, with a plain '34' incised. About 1826 the officers' silver buttons had the design incised of '34' within a wreath. This design was retained on the gilt coatee button worn until 1855, and was retained in relief on the tunic buttons. The other ranks' pewter buttons prior to 1855 had the same design also in relief.

55TH

The early pewter buttons had the design in relief shown in Fig. 291. The officers' gilt buttons *circa* 1800 were flat, one piece, the design being evidently copied from the old wire-bound buttons worn by several regiments about 1780 (Fig. 292).

Prior to 1855 the design was the Chinese dragon above the number '55' within a crowned wreath. This design was also worn on the first tunic buttons.

After 1881 the buttons had the design of the Chinese dragon with the word 'China' above. There was also another type worn with the dragon below a scroll inscribed 'China' and within a laurel wreath. Above and around the top half of the wreath was inscribed 'The Border Regiment'.

The 1904 Dress Regulations gives the mess dress button as flat, design as for the collar badge, but with the lions and scroll omitted. On the cap button the dragon.

THE ROYAL SUSSEX REGIMENT

TITLES
1ST BATTALION
- 1701-1751   Colonel the Earl of Donegal's Regiment of Foot and by the names of its successive Colonels.
- 1751-1782   The 35th Regiment of Foot.
- 1782-1805   The 35th (Dorsetshire) Regiment of Foot.
- 1805-1832   The 35th (Sussex) Regiment of Foot.
- 1832-1881   The 35th (Royal Sussex) Regiment of Foot.

2ND BATTALION
- 1760-1763   The 107th (Queen's Own Royal British Volunteers) Regiment of Foot.
- 1794-1795   107th Regiment of Foot.
- 1854-1858   The H.E.I.C.'s 3rd Bengal European Light Infantry Regiment.
- 1858-1862   The 3rd (Bengal European Light Infantry) Regiment.
- 1862-1881   The 107th (Bengal Infantry) Regiment.
- 1881-   The Royal Sussex Regiment.

BADGES
The badge of a Plume was originally adopted in 1759, but was not officially authorized until 30th June, 1880. Commemorates the service of the 35th at the battle of Quebec, when they are said to have taken the white plumes from the caps of the defeated members of the Royal Roussillon Grenadiers.

The Maltese Cross. Said to commemorate the capture of Malta, 1800.

The Star of the Order of the Garter, worn since 1881, was the old badge of the Royal Sussex Light Infantry Militia.

The Rose. Given to the regiment in 1881 and changed to the United Red and White Rose in 1888. Does not appear to have ever figured in any of the metal badges of the regiment.

BATTLE HONOURS (*Dates authorized from* 1808 *to* 1855)
MAIDA. To flank companies, 10th February, 1808; to regiment, 27th June, 1818.

SHOULDER-BELT PLATES
In the Reynolds' MSS. books is recorded an oval silver plate with the design in gilt of the numeral '2' within the cords of a bugle-horn and the number '35' above, all within a crowned garter. The information is from a portrait in a sale in 1917.

Almack's book illustrates a silver gilt oval plate with circle, crown and '35' mounted in silver. Worn early in the nineteenth century and probably before.

The circle was inscribed 'Dorsetshire Regiment'. The same design was apparently worn in 1805 when the title was changed to that of Sussex.

Prior to 1830 the officers' plate was silver (Fig. 293). It had rounded corners and the design was mounted. On the plate being changed to gilt after 1830 the same design mounted in silver was worn, the size of the plate being slightly larger.

The plate in 1832 was gilt, oblong, with a silver frosted Maltese Cross, '35' within a crowned garter inscribed 'Royal Sussex Regt', with wreath round. The number, garter, crown and wreath all gilt (Fig. 294).

Another plate of the same design but with Roman numerals instead of Arabic was worn before 1855.

The other ranks' plate *circa* 1840 was brass, die struck, and had the design of 'XXXV' within a wreath of leaves, with a crown at the opening. At the junction of the two sprays of the wreath was a scroll inscribed 'Maida'.

BUTTONS

35TH

The officers' early bone-backed buttons were silver with the design of '35' within a deep scalloped edge. The early pewter buttons, 1780 period, had the design engraved of '35'. The button had a roped border (Fig. 295).This design was replaced by one which had '35' inside a star of eight points in relief (Fig. 296).

The officers' silver buttons were of the same design.

The coatee button, 1832-1855, and the tunic button had the design of '35' within a crowned garter inscribed 'Royal Sussex Regt'.

107TH

The design on the tunic buttons, 1862-1881, was the number '107' inside a plain garter and wreath, in the centre of a Maltese Cross, the top limb of which was inscribed 'Bengal' and the bottom limb 'Infantry'.

For a short time after 1881 the design on the tunic buttons was a crowned garter inscribed 'Royal Sussex Regt', in the centre of the garter a lined cross, the whole superimposed on a star. The button had a scalloped edge.

This was replaced by the design still worn of a Maltese Cross within a circle inscribed 'Royal Sussex Regt'. Behind the Maltese Cross a feather and in the centre of the cross a wreath enclosing the cross of St. George.

The 1900 Dress Regulations gives for the cap and mess dress buttons the design as shown in the centre of the tunic button, the design mounted in gilt. In the 1911 Regulations the design on the cap button is the same, but die struck.

293

294

295

296

THE ROYAL HAMPSHIRE REGIMENT

TITLES

1ST BATTALION

1702-1751 Known by the name of its successive Colonels.
1751-1782 The 37th Regiment of Foot.
1782-1881 The 37th (North Hampshire) Regiment.

2ND BATTALION

1758-1782 The 67th Regiment of Foot, raised as 2nd Battalion 20th Regiment in 1756.
1782-1881 The 67th (South Hampshire) Regiment of Foot.
1881-1946 The Hampshire Regiment.
1946-   The Royal Hampshire Regiment.

BADGES

The Royal Tiger. The badge and 'India' were given to the 67th to commemorate their service in that country, 1805-1826. Authorized 20th December, 1826.

The Hampshire Rose. Adopted as a badge by the Regular Battalions in 1881. Had been the old badge of the Hampshire Militia.

BATTLE HONOURS (*Dates authorized from* 1801 *to* 1855)

37TH

MINDEN, 1st January, 1801.
PENINSULA, 6th April, 1815.
TOURNAY, 13th June, 1826.

67TH

PENINSULA, 6th April, 1815.
BARROSA, 26th May, 1817.

SHOULDER-BELT PLATES

37TH

An oblong plate of the 37th Regiment was found in the remains of the British Fort at Richmond, Staten Island, New York City. The design was a plain '37' incised, as shown in Fig. 297. From the fact that the plate is engraved lengthways it may be a converted waist-belt plate. About 1800 the other ranks' belt plate had the design of '37' within a two-lined oval and a wreath of laurel leaves, the design being incised.

Mr. Hughes has an oval silver burnished plate with '37' below a crown within a wreath; the plate has a beaded rim. There was also another oval silver plate with the design, also in silver, of '37' within a laurel wreath. The plate had a raised rim. This may have been worn by another battalion of the 37th.

Soon after 1826 a gilt oblong plate with rounded corners had the design mounted in silver of '37' below a crown and within a laurel wreath, 'Minden' on a scroll above and 'Peninsula' below. A plate of this description with the Birmingham hall-mark 1827 is in the collection of Mr. Tilling. Its measurements are 3¾ × 2 15/16 inches.

Fig. 298 shows the plate worn up to 1855. The plate was gilt and had the design mounted in gilt except for the number 'XXXVII', which was in silver. Its measurements were 4⅛ × 3¼ inches.

67TH

Two oval silver plates are recorded for the 67th.
  (a) A plain burnished plate with the number '67' engraved.
  (b) One described by Mr. G. O. Rickwood in the *Journal of the Society for Army Historical Research* (Vol. XXVIII, page 141), from the miniature of an officer of the 67th, as oval with the design of '67' surmounted by a crown (Fig. 299). The date of the miniature showing the badge is about 1795.

Fig. 300 is the plate worn by officers from about 1826 until 1855. Before 1845 the plate was of silver, after that date gilt.

Page 185 of Volume XXI, *Journal of the Society for Army Historical Research*, records a letter dated 1st January, 1845:

"With regard to the silver breastplates worn by the officers of the 67th Regiment, however much disposed the Commander-in-Chief may be to be indulgent towards officers in allowing articles of dress actually in wear to be worn out, on any general change of uniform, yet inasmuch as the case now brought under observation is a palpable deviation from Her Majesty's Regulations for the Dress of the Army, the officers of the 67th Regiment must be ordered to change, or gild, their breastplates by the period of the next inspection, as no Regiment can, under the existing orders, be suffered to wear silver breastplates, except as a temporary expedient, for the accommodation of the officers."

The other ranks' plate was brass with the design of '67' with a wreath below a crown, above the crown a scroll inscribed 'Barrosa', below the wreath a scroll inscribed 'Peninsula'.

BUTTONS

37TH

The early type of officers' bone-backed button was '37' engraved on a flat silver face, the button having an ornamental rim (Fig. 301). The other ranks' pewter button had the design in relief of '37' within a laurel wreath (Fig. 302).

The design shown in Fig. 303 was retained until 1830, being worn by the officers on their almost flat single-piece buttons, and also on the other ranks' pewter buttons.

After the introduction of gold lace in 1830 the design for both officers and other ranks was '37' within a lined, crowned garter on a flat button, and was retained until 1855, when one with '37' below a crown and within the laurel wreath was adopted.

67TH

The pewter buttons of the 67th prior to 1800 had the design of '67' within a French scroll with a dot at the opening, and round the rim of the button a beaded rim of dots (Fig. 304). This design was also worn on the early buttons by officers. The men's design was replaced by one of similar design, but with a plain rim, which remained the design for other ranks until 1871.

The officers' buttons *circa* 1810 were flat, single piece, with the design in relief of '67' within a garter inscribed *Honi soit qui mal y pense*. It is quite possible that these buttons were retained in use, like the silver shoulder-belt plate, until 1845, but there is no evidence either way. When gilt buttons were adopted they were convex with the design in relief of '67' below a crown within a French scroll, but with no dot at the opening; at the top of the button was the Honour 'Barrosa' and at the bottom 'Peninsula' (Fig. 305).

The officers' tunic button adopted in 1855 had the design of '67' within a French scroll with a dot at the opening. The other ranks' was of the same design.

The early tunic buttons made by Messrs. William Jervis, however, had an outer circle of dots to the French scroll, very like the early pewter buttons.

After 1881 the buttons displayed the tiger above a rose within a wreath of laurel. In some dies the tail of the tiger was curled over its back, in others it was down.

The 1900 Dress Regulations gives for the cap and mess dress the design of the Royal tiger mounted in silver. There was also a die-struck button.

297
298
299
300
301   302
303   304   305

192

THE SOUTH STAFFORDSHIRE REGIMENT

TITLES

1ST BATTALION

1705-1751   Known by the names of the successive Colonels.
1751-1782   The 38th Regiment of Foot.
1782-1881   The 38th (1st Staffordshire) Regiment of Foot.

2ND BATTALION

1758-1763   The 80th (Light-armed) Regiment of Foot. Disbanded.
1778-1784   The 80th (Royal Edinburgh Volunteers) Regiment of Foot. Disbanded.
1793-1881   The 80th (Staffordshire Volunteers) Regiment of Foot.
1881-   The South Staffordshire Regiment.

BADGES

The Sphinx superscribed 'Egypt'. The badge and Battle Honour commemorates the services of the 80th in Egypt, 1800. Authorized 6th July, 1802.
The Royal Cypher and Crown. Appears in Queen's Regulations of 1844.
The Stafford Knot. An old badge of both battalions.
An Oak Wreath. For a short time the pre-1881 cap badge of the 38th had a wreath of half oak and half laurel in place of the usual one of laurel.
The Round Tower of Windsor Castle, an old badge of the King's Own Staffordshire Militia, adopted by regular battalions in 1881 and worn on the officers' waist-belt plate.

BATTLE HONOURS *(Dates authorized from 1802 to 1855)*

38TH

PENINSULA, 6th April, 1815.
MONTE VIDEO, 19th March, 1817.
SALAMANCA, 19th March, 1817.
ST. SEBASTIAN, 19th March, 1817.
AVA, 6th December, 1826.
BUSACO, 29th August, 1831.
BADAJOZ, 29th August, 1831.
VITTORIA, 29th August, 1831.
NIVE, 29th August, 1831.
ROLEIA*, 14th November, 1831.
VIMIERA, 14th November, 1831.
CORUNNA, 14th November, 1831.
ALMA, 18th October, 1855.
INKERMAN, 18th October, 1855.
SEVASTOPOL, 18th October, 1855.

---

* The spelling was changed to "Rolica" in an Army Order, 1911.

80TH

EGYPT WITH THE BADGE OF THE SPHINX, 6th July, 1802.
FEROZESHAH, 8th June, 1847.
SOBRAON, 8th June, 1847.
PEGU, 20th September, 1853.

SHOULDER-BELT PLATES

38TH

The late Mr. Calver, of New York, sent the author a photograph of the plate shown in Fig. 306. The plate was silver with the design in relief. Its fastenings were two studs and a hook. The date would be about 1780.

Two oval silver plates are recorded as having been worn. One in Almack's book with the design of '38' below a crown and above the knot. The plate was described as of polished silver, with a metal crown, number, and Stafford Knot in dead gilt.

In Mr. P. W. Reynolds' book is a copy of a miniature of Captain Robert Barclay, who, according to the History of the Regiment, left the 38th in 1804. The shoulder-belt plate is of the same design except that in place of a crown is a bugle-horn; the plate was evidently that worn by the officers of the Light Company.

Thanks to careful research by Mr. L. E. Buckell, it is now definitely proved that the design mentioned in Almack's book was worn in 1802 or earlier, while that shown in Fig. 307 replaced it and was worn by both battalions of the regiment about 1805 or a little later. The later plate was silver with the design mounted in silver. The plate had a raised rim.

Fig. 308 was the design worn from before 1830 until 1855. Prior to 1830 the plate was silver with the design in gilt.

80TH

Information as to plates worn by the 80th is scarce. The oval gilt plate of 1800 was probably worn until 1815 or even later. It had the design of '80' below a Stafford Knot within a crowned oval inscribed 'Staffordshire : G.R.: Volunteers'. The plate had a raised rim.

In the *Journal of the Society for Army Historical Research*, Vol. XXI, the late Rev. P. Sumner records the following information concerning breast plates worn by the 80th: "1816-17. Rectangular gilt plate with silver mountings, laurel wreath, crown at top, with Sphinx, Stafford Knot and '80' underneath."

In Herbert's book is a drawing of a belt plate, dated August, 1817, marked "Pattern for 80 not fixed on", "Showing a crown over garter inscribed 'Staffordshire Volunteers' and enclosing a Stafford Knot over '80' with the Sphinx at the base of the plate"; also another drawing similarly dated and marked "Not fixed on", the design being a crown over a scroll inscribed 'Egypt', '80' in centre of plate, with Stafford Knot below, with sprays of laurel at each side of the knot and a label with 'Staffordshire Volunteers'.

This plate was followed by one of similar design but with an extra spray of laurel at the bottom of the wreath. The plate was burnished gilt with the design in silver, and was worn until 1855.

A shoulder-belt plate with the design of '80' surmounted by a Sphinx and with the knot shown upside down, all within a wreath of laurel mounted in silver on a gilt plate, is supposed to have been worn; but Colonel R. Savage, the late Honorary Curator of the Regimental Museum and an authority on the badges and buttons of the Regiment, states he has never seen this plate, but has a drawing of an officers' shako plate, 80th Foot, 1830-1844, with the knot shown upside down.

In the author's collection is a plate of the design in Fig. 309 which shows distinct marks of the knot having been at one time upside down. Colonel Savage writes: "I think that this mistake must have crept in between 1830 and 1844; probably some tailor was to blame."

BUTTONS

38TH

The early officers' bone-backed buttons *circa* 1780 had silver faces with the design in relief of '38' within a continuous wreath of leaves. The button had a raised rim. Another button of this period, probably worn by a different battalion, was bone-backed and had the design in relief of '38' surmounted by a lion and crown; round the rim of the buttons was a border of leaves turned inwards (Fig. 310).

The pewter buttons of the other ranks had two designs, the earlier one having '38' within a continuous wreath (Fig. 311) and '38' below a crown; both designs were in relief.

About 1800 the design for both officers and other ranks was '38' surmounted by the knot and crown. The officers' buttons remained of silver until 1830, after which they became gilt with the same design, which was continued on the later coatee and tunic buttons.

80TH

Figs. 312 and 313 are designs worn on the bone-backed buttons of the 80th Royal Edinburgh Volunteers Regiment, disbanded 1784.

The buttons had the design in relief on a silver face. Other ranks had the same design on their pewter buttons. Later one with '80' incised was worn. This button had a lined rim (Fig. 314). About 1820 the design for both officers and other ranks was '80' below a knot and crown within a laurel wreath. This design was retained on the tunic button which was introduced in 1855, with various minor differences in the size and shape of the numerals and wreath.

After 1881 the design on the tunic buttons was the Staffordshire knot surmounted by a crown.

The 1904 Dress Regulations gives the mess waistcoat buttons as flat, gilt, with the design of the Crown and Stafford knot mounted in silver. The 1911 Regulations gives the cap button as having the same design, but die struck.

THE DORSET REGIMENT

TITLES

1ST BATTALION
- 1702-1751 Known by the name of the successive Colonels.
- 1751-1782 The 39th Regiment of Foot.
- 1782-1807 The 39th (East Middlesex) Regiment of Foot.
- 1807-1881 The 39th (Dorsetshire) Regiment of Foot.

2ND BATTALION
- 1755-1757 The 56th Regiment of Foot, renumbered.
- 1757-1782 The 54th Regiment of Foot.
- 1782-1881 The 54th (West Norfolk) Regiment of Foot.
- 1881-1951 The Dorsetshire Regiment.
- 1951- The Dorset Regiment.

BADGES

The Castle, Key and Motto *Montis insignia Calpe*. Commemorates the services of the 39th Regiment during the great siege of Gibraltar, 1779-1783.

The Sphinx superscribed 'Marabout'. Commemorates the services of the 54th in Egypt, 1801. Authorized 6th July, 1802.

Motto: *Primus in Indis*. Commemorates the fact that the 39th were the first Regiment of the Line to serve in India.

Permission to resume the motto *Primus in Indis* and the Honour 'Plassey', also to have the Castle and Key in addition to the Honour 'Gibraltar', were authorized 17th November, 1835. These distinctions had been removed by the Inspector of Colours in 1807.

The green ground to the badge is in memory of the old green facings of the 39th.

BATTLE HONOURS (*Dates authorized from 1784 to 1855*)

39TH
- GIBRALTAR, 14th April, 1784.
- PENINSULA, 6th April, 1815.
- ALBUHERA, 22nd October, 1816.
- VITTORIA, 29th May, 1824.
- PYRENEES, 29th May, 1824.
- NIVELLE, 29th May, 1824.
- NIVE, 29th May, 1824.
- ORTHES, 29th May, 1824.
- PLASSEY, 17th November, 1835.
- MAHARAJPORE, 22nd June, 1844.
- SEVASTOPOL, 16th October, 1855.

54TH
- EGYPT AND SPHINX, 6th July, 1802.
- AVA, 6th December, 1826.
- MARABOUT, 18th December, 1841.

SHOULDER-BELT PLATES

39TH

The earliest known plate of the 39th was an oval one found in the River Lagan at Ballynahinch, Co. Down. The regiment was at Belfast until 1789. The design on the plate was '39' surmounted by a crown and with the word 'Gibraltar' below the number. On either side of the crown the letters 'G.R.'. The plate had a roped rim.

Almack's book illustrates an oval gilt plate with silver mounted design of '39' within a double French scroll with a dot at the opening. This, according to the book, was worn 1800-1815 on a scroll; below the scroll is a label inscribed 'Gibraltar' in raised gilt letters on a matted ground. About 1820 the plate was oblong with rounded corners. Fig. 315 is from the drawing of one in Mr. Reynolds' book. It is evidently that worn by the Light Company.

Fig. 316 is the plate worn after the resumption of the motto *Primus in Indis* in 1835; the plate was retained until 1855. The plate was matted gilt with a burnished rim, the badge of the castle with two towers, the key and scroll in gilt within a gilt pierced garter with a green enamel ground, the garter inscribed '39th or Dorsetshire', behind the letters a dark blue enamel ground, a gilt crown, all on a polished silver star. The scrolls above and below dead gilt.

Another plate of similar design but with the following differences is in the collection of Mr. Tilling. Size 3¼ × 3¼ inches. The number '39' below the castle, the key above, all in silver. The garter inscribed 'Gibraltar'. The motto *Montis insignia Calpe* is omitted, the Battle Honour scrolls are closer to the star and the one 'Plassey' is omitted, as is also the scroll inscribed *Primus in Indis*. It would appear as if this plate was in use prior to the one shown in Fig. 316. The plate does not have a burnished rim.

54TH

The oval silver plate Fig. 317 is from an illustration in Almack's book.

Fig. 318 is from a drawing in Mr. Reynolds' book and is taken from a portrait of Colonel Daniel in 1821; the plate would have been all silver.

Fig. 319 was worn about 1826 when the Honour 'Ava' was added on a scroll below that inscribed 'Egypt'. The plates were silver with the design in gilt, the scrolls being pierced.

Fig. 320 is the plate in use prior to 1855. It was gilt with the design in silver.

BUTTONS

39TH

According to the drawing of a pewter button found in Canada, the design in 1814 was a very uncommon one, being '39' within a French scroll with the opening and dot below the number. The design may have been due to a mistake in the die, but at any rate was not worn for long, and the usual representation of the design with the opening and dot above the number was adopted and used from about 1800 until 1855.

The design of officers' buttons showed practically no change, having in relief the number '39' below a crown within a French scroll without a dot at the opening. With the introduction of the tunic several different dies were used which differed in the size and design of the numerals, and in one case a small scroll appeared at the opening of the French scroll.

54TH

The officers' early bone-backed buttons had silver faces with the design in Fig. 321.

There are three designs of the 1800 period pewter buttons on record: A plain '54' (Fig. 322); design engraved; as shown in Fig. 323 in relief. This design (Fig. 323) was also worn by the officers on their flat silver buttons. In the case of the other ranks' buttons it was replaced by one with the design of '54' within a French scroll with a dot at the opening; the button had a lined rim. Soon after 1800 the design for both officers and other ranks was '54' below a crown and within a laurel wreath; this design was retained on the coatee and tunic buttons. As usual, different makers made variations in the size of the numerals and shape of the wreath.

After 1881 the badge of the castle, key and motto with the Sphinx below and a scroll 'Gibraltar' above the key and castle, and title 'the Dorsetshire Regt' round the top edge of the button, was adopted. In 1900 the castle was changed to one with three towers with the key below (Fig. 324).

The 1904 Dress Regulations stated the cap button, which was die struck, had the design as for the cap badge, but with the title and motto *Primus in Indis* omitted. On the mess waistcoat the castle and key mounted in silver. In 1934 the mess dress button had the castle and key in silver on a flat button.

THE SOUTH LANCASHIRE REGIMENT (THE PRINCE OF WALES'S VOLUNTEERS)

TITLES

1ST BATTALION

1717-1751   By the name of the successive Colonels.
1751-1782   The 40th Regiment of Foot.
1782-1881   The 40th (2nd Somersetshire) Regiment of Foot.

2ND BATTALION

1758-1763   The 82nd Regiment of Foot. Disbanded.
1778-1784   The 82nd Regiment of Foot. Disbanded.
1793-1881   The 82nd (Prince of Wales's Volunteers) Regiment of Foot.
1881-1920   The Prince of Wales's Volunteers (South Lancashire Regiment).
1920-1938   The Prince of Wales's Volunteers (South Lancashire).
1938-   The South Lancashire Regiment (The Prince of Wales's Volunteers).

BADGES

The Prince of Wales's Coronet, Plume and motto. This design was worn on the badges and buttons from the formation of the 82nd in 1793. The Colonel of the 82nd at the time was attached to the household of the Prince of Wales. The badge was authorized 20th December, 1831, and permission given to wear the design on the officers' forage cap 29th September, 1868.
The Sphinx. The badge of the Sphinx superscribed 'Egypt' commemorates the services of the 40th in Egypt, 1801; was given to the flank companies of the 40th, 6th July, 1802.

BATTLE HONOURS (*Dates authorized from 1802 to 1855*)

40TH

EGYPT AND SPHINX, 6th July, 1802.
PENINSULA, 6th April, 1815.
WATERLOO, 8th December, 1815.
ROLEIA,* 6th April, 1824.
VIMIERA, 6th April, 1824.
TALAVERA, 6th April, 1824.
BADAJOZ, 6th April, 1824.
SALAMANCA, 6th April, 1824.
VITTORIA, 6th April, 1824.
PYRENEES, 6th April, 1824.
NIVELLE, 6th April, 1824.
ORTHES, 6th April, 1824.

---
* The spelling was changed to "Rolica" in an Army Order, 1911.

TOULOUSE, 6th April, 1824.
MONTE VIDEO, 27th April, 1824.
MAHARAJPORE, 22nd June, 1844.
CANDAHAR, 2nd March, 1844.
GHUZNEE,* 20th March, 1844.
CABOOL, 1842, 20th March, 1844.

82ND
PENINSULA, 6th April, 1815.
NIAGARA, 27th June, 1816.
ROLEIA,† 7th September, 1824.
VIMIERA, 20th September, 1824.
VITTORIA, 20th September, 1824.
PYRENEES, 20th September, 1824.
NIVELLE, 20th September, 1824.
ORTHES, 20TH September, 1824.
SEVASTOPOL, 16th October, 1855.

SHOULDER-BELT PLATES

40TH

In Mr. Hughes' collection is an oval gilt plate with the design incised of '40' within a wreath and the title 'Somerset' above.

The officers' plate *circa* 1789-1818 was oval, of gilt metal, with the design mounted in silver of '40' within a wreath of laurel. The plate had a raised silver rim.

About 1818 the plate became an oblong gilt one of the design shown in Fig. 325, the design being mounted in silver and the plate having a burnished edge. From 1824 to 1844 (Fig. 326) the plate was a gilt burnished one with a cut silver star; the crown, number, wreath and honours being in gilt; the back to the number '40' being burnished.

Fig. 327 is the plate in use from 1844 to 1855.

The Flank Companies displayed a Sphinx at the foot of the garter.

82ND

The oval silver plate illustrated in Almack's book had the design of '82' below the Prince of Wales's plume within a French scroll with a dot at the opening. The oval was a much broader one than usual and had a lined centre with burnished edges. The design was mounted in silver.

About 1817 the plate became oblong, was of silver, with the design shown in Fig. 328 mounted; it had rounded corners. In the case of the Light Company a bugle-horn was displayed pendent from the scroll.

Fig. 329 shows the design worn 1824-1832; the plate was silver with silver mounts and with a blue enamel background to the Prince of Wales's plume. In 1832 the plate was changed to a gilt one with the same design mounted in silver.

---

* Army Order 208, 1907, changed this to read Ghuznee and Candahar, 1842.

† The spelling was changed to "Rolica" in an Army Order, 1911.

BUTTONS

40TH

It was not until 1769 that Inspection Report records the button as numbered. The previous year's report states "no number on them". The early pewter buttons *circa* 1782 had the design in relief of '40' within a wreath, with 'Somerset' at the opening of the wreath (Fig. 331).

This button appears to have soon been replaced by one with the number '40' within a wreath and an ornamental circle with dots, which in turn was replaced by a design which, with slight differences in the thickness of the wreath and shape of the numerals, lasted until 1881. The design of '40' within a spray of leaves was worn by other ranks as well as officers.

82ND

Prior to 1830 the officers' buttons of the 82nd were silver, slightly convex, with the design in relief of '82' below the Prince of Wales's coronet, plume and motto. The earlier buttons had the number and rim sunk, but soon after all was in relief. This was retained with various minor alterations in the numerals and scroll with the motto until 1881 (Fig. 333).

The coatee 1830-1855 for officers was a gilt frosted button, slightly convex, with the design in high relief and with a narrow burnished rim.

The tunic buttons had the design of the Sphinx inscribed 'Egypt' below the Prince of Wales's coronet, plume and motto, within a crowned circle above the scroll inscribed 'The South Lancashire Regiment'; below the circle a scroll with spray of leaves, the scroll inscribed 'Prince of Wales's Vol'.

The 1900 Dress Regulations states that the cap and mess dress buttons had the design mounted of the Prince of Wales's plume in silver, the monogram P.W.V. below in gilt. Later the plume and motto were shown mounted in silver. In the 1911 Regulations the design on the cap button is die struck.

325 326

327 328

329 330 331

332 333

THE WELCH REGIMENT

TITLES

1ST BATTALION

1719-1751	Independent Companies of Invalids, known by the Commanding Officer's name.
1751-1787	41st Regiment of Invalids.
1787-1831	The 41st Regiment of Foot.
1831-1838	The 41st or the Welch Regiment of Infantry.
1838-1852	41st (Welch) Regiment.
1852-1862	41st (the Welch).
1862-1881	The 41st the Welsh Regiment of Foot.

2ND BATTALION

1756-1758	2nd Battalion. 24th Regiment of Foot renumbered.
1758-1782	The 69th Regiment of Foot.
1782-1881	The 69th (South Lincolnshire) Regiment of Foot.
1881-1920	The Welsh Regiment.
1920-	The Welch Regiment.

BADGES

The Rose and Thistle within the Garter and with a crown over it. Was displayed on the Colours in 1747.

The Prince of Wales's Coronet, Plumes and motto. Authorized for the 41st Regiment, 16th December, 1831.

The Red Dragon of Wales. Was adopted as a collar badge by the 1st and 2nd Battalions in 1881. It had previously been the badge of the Royal Glamorgan Militia, which in 1881 became the 3rd Battalion of the Regiment.

A Naval Crown superscribed with the date of Admiral Sir George Rodney's victory, 12th April, 1782, in which the 41st Regiment took part. Authorized 1909.

Motto: *Gwell Angau na Chywilydd*. The motto was authorized 16th December, 1831. The origin is not clear. The Regimental History states that the following reason may or may not be the correct one. Lieutenant-Colonel Sir Edmund Williams applying for it on the ground that the motto was that of the Mackworths of Glen Usk, Monmouthshire. Sir Edmund was a native of Monmouthshire, and it is quite within the bounds of possibility that when he chose the Welsh designation for the regiment, he asked the head of the Mackworth family for the 41st to be allowed to use the motto. The spelling of the motto has varied considerably. Original spelling in 1831, Gwell Angau Neughwilydd; on the buttons, 1834-1855, Gwell Augau Neuchwilydd; on the shako plate, 1845-1847, Gwell Augau Neu Chwilydd; and in several instances Gwell Augau na chwilydd and Gwell Augau Newchwilydd.

BATTLE HONOURS (*Dates authorized from 1816 to 1855*)

41ST

> DETROIT, 2nd April, 1816.
> QUEENSTOWN, 2nd April, 1816.
> MIAMI, 2nd April, 1816.
> NIAGARA, 20th September, 1824. The Flank Companies had been granted the Honour, 19th May, 1815.
> AVA, 6th December, 1826.
> *CANDAHAR, 28th July, 1843.
> *GHUZNEE, 22nd June, 1844.
> CABOOL, 22nd June, 1844.
> ALMA, 16th October, 1855.
> INKERMAN, 16th October, 1855.
> SEVASTOPOL, 16th October, 1855.

69TH

> WATERLOO, 8th December, 1815, to old 2nd Battalion. To the regiment as a whole, 22nd January, 1818.
> JAVA, 28th May, 1818.
> INDIA, 13th April, 1826.
> BOURBON, 13th June, 1826.

SHOULDER-BELT PLATES

41ST

There are on record no less than three oval silver plates as having been worn by the officers of the 41st. There were two battalions of the 41st for a short time during the early part of the nineteenth century. Fig. 334 is the plate worn in 1799 and is from an illustration of Captain Fuller in the Regimental History.

Almack's book illustrates an officers' plate with the design of '41' within an ornamental oval and star of eight points. The plate had a rim described as "a large hollow between a very small cut". The other ranks' brass oblong plate *circa* 1790 had the design incised of '41' below a crown; the design was retained for many years on the subsequent oval brass plate.

Fig. 335 is from a portrait of Lieutenant-Colonel R. Place, reproduced in the Regimental History. Colonel Place served in the regiment, according to the Regimental History, in 1827.

The design as shown in Fig. 336 is reproduced from the Regimental History, and is dated as being worn 1826-1829.

This plate does not appear to have been retained for very long and was replaced by a burnished gilt one, in the centre of which was a cut silver star of eight points on which was mounted in gilt the design of a rose and thistle, the old badge of the "Invalids", within a crowned garter inscribed *Honi soit qui mal y pense*; below the garter a scroll inscribed 'Queenstown', and between this and the scrolls inscribed 'Niagara' and 'Ava' was the number 'XLI'. A wreath of laurel on either side of the garter with scrolls inscribed 'Detroit' and 'Miami'.

---

* Army Orders 208, 1907, added the date to both honours.

Soon after 1831 the design in the centre of the garter was changed to that of the Prince of Wales's plume, etc., in silver on a blue enamel ground. Apart from this and that the plate now had a gilt frosted surface there was no further change (Fig. 337).

69TH

Fig. 338 is of the officers' gilt oval plate *circa* 1800. The number and star were in silver, the garter and ground gilt.

Fig. 339 is the officers' plate, 1826-1855. It is recorded that the plates were changed in 1826 before the regiment returned from India, just at a time when two new Honours, 'India' and 'Bourbon', had been given. The plate was gilt with silver star and gilt crown, number, garter, wreath and scrolls.

BUTTONS

41ST

The early officers' silver buttons of the 41st had the design in relief of an eight-pointed star, in the centre of which was the number '41' (Fig. 340).

In 1813 this was discarded for a gilt button; the star was retained, but the number replaced by a cross inside a plain circle. Above the star was a crown and below the star '41'; on either side of the design from the rim was a design of leaves turned inwards (Fig. 341).

At about this period the men's small gaiter buttons had the number '41' in relief. Their coatee buttons had the design as for the early buttons, which was retained until 1831, in which year the badge of the Prince of Wales's plume, coronet and motto was given to the regiment. The officers' coatee buttons displayed the design in high relief with '41' below inside a circle, with the motto *Gwell Augau Neu Chivillydd*. The men's buttons had the same design without the motto and circle.

Officers' tunic buttons 1855-1881 had the design of '41' surmounted by the Prince of Wales's coronet, plume and motto, all within a raised circle. The other ranks' buttons 1855-1871 had a similar design.

69TH

The early other ranks' pewter buttons of the 69th had the design of '69' in relief. The button had a sunk rim ornamented with a series of small leaves.

The officers' buttons *circa* 1800 were flat gilt with the design of '69' in relief on the sunk centre of a circle inside a star of eight points; the star sunk. This design was worn for some thirty or more years until about 1830, when the design of '69' below a crown and within a wreath was adopted, and was retained on the tunic until 1881.

After 1881 the design was the Prince of Wales's coronet, plume and motto within a crowned circle inscribed 'The Welsh Regiment', with a wreath of laurel below.

This design is still worn with a difference of crown and the spelling of 'Welsh' with a 'c'.

On the field cap and mess dress the dragon is mounted in silver. In the 1904 Dress Regulations the design is changed to the Prince of Wales's plume. The 1911 Regulations states the mess dress button (mounted). The cap button was presumably die struck.

334 335

336 337

338 339

340 341

THE BLACK WATCH
(ROYAL HIGHLAND REGIMENT)

TITLES
1ST BATTALION
1739-1751   The Highland Regiment. Also by Colonel's name.
1751-1758   The 42nd Highland Regiment.
1758-1861   The 42nd Royal Highland Regiment of Foot.
1861-1881   The 42nd Royal Highland (The Black Watch) Regiment of Foot.

2ND BATTALION
1758-1786   The 2nd Battalion 42nd Royal Highland Regiment, regimented.
1786-1809   The 73rd Highland Regiment of Foot.
1809-1862   The 73rd Regiment of Foot.
1862-1881   The 73rd (Perthshire) Regiment.

1881-1934   The Black Watch (Royal Highlanders).
1934-   The Black Watch (Royal Highland Regiment).

BADGES
The Royal Cypher within the Garter. First appears in the Monthly Army List in 1868.
The Sphinx superscribed 'Egypt'. Commemorates the services of the 42nd Royal Highlanders in Egypt, 1801. Authorized 6th July, 1802.
The Thistle and Crown. An old badge of the Regiment. Was displayed on the Colours in 1747.
The Badge and Motto of the Order of the Thistle (St. Andrew).
The Royal Cypher within the collar of St. Andrew and the crown over it.
Motto: *Nemo me impune lacessit.* Was borne on the Colours of the 42nd in 1751 and had been displayed before.
The Arms of Perth. Worn as a collar badge by the 73rd, 1874-1881.

BATTLE HONOURS (*Dates authorized from 1800 to 1855*)
42ND
EGYPT AND THE SPHINX, 6th July, 1802.
CORUNNA, 20th February, 1812.
PENINSULA, 29th March, 1815.
WATERLOO, 8th December, 1815.
TOULOUSE, 26th July, 1816.
FUENTES D'ONOR, 4th December, 1817.
PYRENEES, 4th December, 1817.
NIVELLE, 4th December, 1817.
NIVE, 4th December, 1817.
ORTHES, 4th December, 1817.
ALMA, 16th October, 1855.
INKERMAN, 16th October, 1855.
SEVASTOPOL, 16th October, 1855.

73RD

MANGALORE. The Honour was awarded during Lord Lake's colonelcy of the Regiment between November, 1796, and February, 1800. It appears in the Yearly Army List first in 1814: 1813 was the first year in which Honours were shown, and it was not until 1818 that Battle Honours appeared in the Monthly Army List.

WATERLOO, 23rd November, 1815. To the old 2nd Battalion, 8th December, 1815.

SERINGAPATAM, 28th May, 1818.

SHOULDER-BELT PLATES

42ND

An excellent article on the regimental shoulder-belt plates appeared in the *Red Hackle*, dated October, 1932, and January, 1933, from which the following details have been taken:

The officers' plate, 1786-1790, was a small engraved one, oval in shape, and having the design of '42' within a ring surmounted by St. Andrew and his cross. Behind the head of the saint the rays of a halo; above the figure a scroll inscribed *Nemo me impune lacessit*; below the number a spray of thistle and rose. The plate had an ornamental rim.

The other ranks' brass plate *circa* 1818-1830 had the design engraved of '42' within an oval, in the centre of a star of the Order of the Thistle. The size of the plate was $3\frac{1}{8} \times 2\frac{5}{8}$ inches, and the corners were very slightly rounded (Fig. 342). The late Captain G. Campbell considered the plate to have been worn earlier than 1818.

The officers' plate of 1790-1805 was almost of the same design as before, but the plate was slightly larger, more oval in shape, and the figure of St. Andrew considerably larger, and the head of the saint had no halo behind it. The thistle had two leaves and the rose seven; the spray was lower on the plate, which had a lined rim.

From 1805 to 1812 the plate was gilt, oval, with the design engraved very similar to the one before, but '42' larger and not enclosed in a ring. The figure of St. Andrew considerably smaller and the title 'Royal Highlanders' above, in place of the scroll with motto. The plate had no design round the rim.

In the Scottish United Services Museum is a brass oval plate engraved with the design of the letters 'N D', below which is the number '42', the whole in a plain oval within a star of the Order of the Thistle. It is dated 1800-1818.

According to the late Captain E. A. Campbell's notes, the officers' plate 1812-1820 was gilt, burnished, with rounded corners, and the design of St. Andrew and the cross in silver within a crowned garter, the garter gilt with the title 'The Royal Highlanders' in silver. Below the garter a Sphinx inscribed 'Egypt'.

Fig. 343 is assigned as being worn 1820-1845. The plate was gilt with the design in silver except for the circle and motto, which were in gilt. The size was $2\frac{3}{4} \times 3\frac{3}{8}$ inches.

The officers' plate, 1845-1850 (Fig. 344), was gilt, oblong, burnished, with the design in silver of '42' within a wreath of thistle, rose and shamrock; above the number was a crown. In 1850 this was changed to a gilt matted plate with a burnished rim. In the centre of the plate was a cut silver star of the Order of the Thistle, with '42' within a gilt circle inscribed with the motto of the order, a wreath of thistle round and a crown above; below the wreath a Sphinx. These were all in gilt except for the silver star.

Since 1881 the design on the shoulder-belt plate has been the same as for the officers' glengarry badge, but unofficially many 1st Battalion officers wore the number '42' instead of St. Andrew in the centre.

Fig. 345 is the brass plate worn by other ranks, 1845-1852. The design was stamped.

73RD

Figs. 346 and 347 are silver plates of the regiment in the R.U.S.I. Museum. Both are of the 1780 period. Which is the earlier it is hard to say; from its size and shape one would expect Fig. 346 to be.

Almack's book illustrates an oval plate, gilt with a roped border. The design is described as the "King's Arms" in the centre and '73' within an oval below. Above the arms a scroll inscribed 'Mangalore'. This Honour was given in 1814, so the plate would be after that date. In the Waterloo Museum there was an oblong plate of the 73rd which had the corners cut and the number within a spray of thistle; at the bottom of the plate a scroll inscribed 'Mangalore'.

The other ranks' brass plate *circa* 1815 had the design of '73' within a spray of two thistles. Above the number a crown and below the spray a scroll inscribed 'Mangalore'. The plate had rounded corners.

In a book entitled "Armies of Europe, 1800-1812", the plate is oblong, gilt, with the design in silver, as above, but the Honour 'Mangalore' is on a separate bar to the plate and was evidently in the form of a slide. Fig. 348 is a gilt burnished plate with the design mounted in silver; the scrolls had roped edges. Below the plate was a slide, but by 1850 this had been discarded.

The plate in use prior to 1855 had the design of '73' between two scrolls inscribed 'Mangalore' and 'Seringapatam'; above the upper scroll a crown; a wreath of half thistle and half laurel around. Below the wreath a scroll inscribed 'Waterloo'. The plate was gilt, with a gilt crown wreath and scrolls; with silver letters the number was in silver.

BUTTONS

42ND

A portrait of Lieutenant Valentine Chisholm, who was in the 42nd in 1770, shows him with buttons bearing a plain '42' like that worn by the other ranks.

The late Mr. Calver, of New York, described a button of the 42nd which he discovered as having the number inside a French scroll and dot.

The design for the early buttons of both officers and other ranks was the number '42' below a crown and with a spray at top and bottom of a thistle and rose (Fig. 349). This was replaced soon after in the case of the other ranks by a button with a plain '42', a design which was worn by them until 1871.

About 1810 the officers' buttons had a star of the Order of the Thistle with '42' in its centre. In the case of the coatee buttons the design of the star was sharper in both coatee and tunic; the design was displayed incised (Fig. 350).

For a short time the design on the officers' coatee was as above with the title 'Royal Highlanders' above the star and a spray of thistle below, all in relief.

73RD

The officers' buttons of the 73rd *circa* 1800 were flat, with the design in relief of '73', with sprays at top and bottom of thistle and rose.

This was replaced by a flat button with '73' below a crown, and a thistle and rose spray below (Fig. 351), which was also the design on the other ranks' buttons.

The same design was retained on the coatee buttons of 1820.

The coatee button, 1840-1855, had '73' within a crowned circle inscribed 'Seringapatam, Mangalore', while below the circle, superimposed on a wreath of thistle and rose, was a scroll inscribed 'Waterloo'.

The tunic buttons, 1855-1881, reverted to the earlier design of '73' below a crown and with a thistle and rose spray. There were different dies of this button, one in very high relief having different shaped numerals to the other.

After 1881 the star of St. Andrew in an incised design was used, the title of the regiment round the edge.

The present design of the button is of the star without any title but without a rim.

342

343

344

345

346

347

348

349

350

351

THE OXFORDSHIRE AND BUCKINGHAMSHIRE LIGHT INFANTRY

TITLES

1ST BATTALION

1741-1751 Colonel Thomas Fowkes' Regiment of Foot, or by the name of the successive Colonels.
1751-1782 The 43rd Regiment of Foot.
1782-1803 The 43rd (Monmouthshire) Regiment of Foot.
1803-1881 The 43rd (Monmouthshire Light Infantry) Regiment.

2ND BATTALION

1755-1757 The 54th Regiment of Foot, renumbered 52nd Regiment of Foot.
1757-1782 The 52nd Regiment of Foot.
1782-1803 The 52nd (Oxfordshire) Regiment of Foot.
1803-1881 The 52nd (Oxfordshire Light Infantry) Regiment.

1881-1908 The Oxfordshire Light Infantry.
1908- The Oxfordshire and Buckinghamshire Light Infantry.

BADGES

43RD

The Bugle-horn. The distinguishing badge of both the 43rd and 52nd has been the Light Infantry bugle-horn since 1803. The arrangement of the cords has varied considerably. The 52nd do not appear to have displayed the bugle-horn except for a short time on their shoulder-belt plates, although it was worn as a hat and later shako badge by both regiments.
In 1881 they were one of the regiments given the badge of the Rose; it was changed in 1888 to the United Red and White one, but it does not appear to have ever been worn on badges or buttons.

BATTLE HONOURS (*Dates authorized from 1815 to 1855*)

43RD

PENINSULA, to 1st Battalion, 6th April, 1815; to old 2nd Battalion, 1st March, 1816.
VIMIERA, 13th February, 1821.
BUSACO, 13th February, 1821.
FUENTES D'ONOR, 13th February, 1821.
CIUDAD RODRIGO, 13th February, 1821.
BADAJOZ, 13th February, 1821.
SALAMANCA, 13th February, 1821.
VITTORIA, 13th February, 1821.
NIVELLE, 13th February, 1821.
NIVE, 13th February, 1821.
CORUNNA, 8th March, 1821.

52ND

PENINSULA, 6th April, 1815.
WATERLOO, 8th December, 1815.
VIMIERA, 13th February, 1821.
BUSACO, 13th February, 1821.
FUENTES D'ONOR, 13th February, 1821.
CIUDAD RODRIGO, 13th February, 1821.
BADAJOZ, 13th February, 1821.
SALAMANCA, 13th February, 1821.
VITTORIA, 13th February, 1821.
NIVELLE, 13th February, 1821.
NIVE, 13th February, 1821.
ORTHES, 13th February, 1821.
TOULOUSE, 13th February, 1821.
CORUNNA, 20th February, 1821.
HINDOOSTAN, 20th February, 1821.

SHOULDER-BELT PLATES

43RD

Almack's book and a portrait of Major R. Elers which was reproduced in the *Regimental Chronicle* of 1908 show the design of the oval plate worn by the Light Company officer *circa* 1800, with the design of '43' below a stringed bugle-horn within a raised oval. In Almack's book it states that the plate was gilt with a flat silver rim, and that the Battalion Companies of the regiment did not have the bugle-horn.

The late Colonel Mockler-Ferryman, in a letter to the author dated 1912, wrote that, after becoming a Light Infantry regiment in 1803, the officers' shoulder-belt plate had "a bugle (good shape, deep curve) with strings and tassels, and '43' under, but there was no crown." Shortly afterwards (date unknown) the crown was added.

In the 1894 *Regimental Chronicle* is a portrait of Lieutenant-Colonel H. Booth, who had joined the regiment in 1807 and was Lieutenant-Colonel in 1830. The plate he is wearing has the tassels of the bugle cords hanging down between the cords. The other ranks' plate *circa* 1815 had a plain '43' stamped on it.

Another design of the oval plate is given in Fig. 352. The plate was gilt with the design mounted in silver. The wearing of gilt plates is curious, as the 43rd were a silver-laced regiment and had silver buttons until 1830.

Fig. 353 is of a silver plate with rounded corners worn *circa* 1820-1830. In the 1895 *Regimental Chronicle* is reproduced a portrait of General Sir James Fergusson; he wears a plate of similar design, but without a crown. The other ranks' brass stamped plate was of similar design, but with the ends of the cords hanging between the strings of the bugle-horn.

Fig. 354 is the officers' plate, 1831-1855. The design was in silver on a gilt burnished plate.

52ND

Almack's book illustrates a small oblong officers plate of 1798-1812, silver, with rounded corners, and the design engraved of '52' within a crowned garter inscribed 'Oxford Regiment'.

In the 1907 *Regimental Chronicle* is a miniature of Ensign Robert Burnett wearing an oblong plate with the design an oval below which was the number '52'. This officer was gazetted to the 52nd in 1805, and was promoted two years later into the 15th Foot.

It is hard to say which was the earlier plate, but one is inclined to favour Almack.

In a print by Hamilton Smith, the officers' plate is shown as oblong, silver, with a large '52'; the other ranks' having the same design, only in brass.

A portrait of W. Crawley Yonge *circa* 1810-1823 shows an oblong plate with 'LII' within a crowned garter surrounded by a wreath.

A portrait of Colonel Considene about 1828 shows him wearing an oblong silver plate, in the centre a bugle-horn, below which was the number 'LII', all within a crowned garter inscribed 'Oxfordshire Regiment'. Outside the garter a laurel wreath.

There are also recorded two other plates of this period, the same design as before, but the plate burnished gilt with the design mounted in silver, probably adopted with the change of lace from silver to gold in 1830. This plate was inscribed 'Oxfordshire' only, the word Regiment being omitted.

Another plate, which probably either took the place of the above or was made by a different firm of badge makers, or worn by a different battalion, had the same design but with '52' in place of 'LII'.

The *Regimental Chronicle* states that in 1830 the officers' plate had the design of a silver star with the Battle Honours on the rays, but this would appear to have come into use at a later date and been retained until 1855 (Fig. 355). Other ranks had a similar design but all brass.

According to notes written in 1901 by Bugler Johnson of the 52nd, published in the *Journal of the Society for Army Historical Research*, 1941 the shoulder belts were worn until the end of the Indian Mutiny.

43RD
BUTTONS

The early pewter buttons of the 43rd had the design of '43' engraved; the button had a roped rim. This was replaced by one with '43' within a laurel wreath, which design was retained on the other ranks' buttons until 1871.

The officers' silver buttons of about 1810 were flat, one piece, with the design in relief of '43' within a crowned garter lined (Fig. 356). About 1820 they became convex and had the design of '43' within the strings of a crowned bugle-horn. The strings went into the crown and showed no bow (Fig. 357).

About 1830 the gilt buttons of the officers had the same design. This design was also worn on the tunic button after 1855, but the official design was of the same design as the men's—*i.e.*, '43' within a laurel wreath—but it is very doubtful if this was ever worn. The late Colonel Mockler-Ferryman, in a letter to the author, stated: "The bugle-horn buttons were always worn except at inspections, when the official one mysteriously appeared."

52ND

The other ranks' pewter buttons *circa* 1780 had the design of '52' in low relief. The button had a roped rim; this was replaced by the design of '52' within a laurel wreath, the button having a cut rim. This design was also worn on the tunic buttons, 1855-1871.

The officers' silver buttons *circa* 1810 were slightly convex, with the design in relief shown in Fig. 358. This design was retained on the gilt coatee button up to 1855. On the tunic button, 1855-1881, the officers wore '52' within a laurel wreath, the button having cut rims (Fig. 359).

Bugler Johnson, in his notes of the Indian Mutiny, states that he thinks the number of buttons down the front of the khaki dyed jacket was nine. He calls the buttons lead, but must mean pewter. He goes on: "Officers had no distinction whatever in their dress, only their small gilt buttons".

After 1881 the design was a bugle-horn above the word 'Oxfordshire' and within a laurel wreath; the button retained its cut rim in one die; the ends of the bugle-horn cords as a rule being down between the cords, but in some dies the design was shown going into the crown.

After the change of title in 1908 the design remained as before with the new title round the bugle-horn.

The 1900 Dress Regulations gives the mess dress button as having the bugle-horn, crown and wreath, with the title below; the cap button had the same design.

352   353

354   355

356   357   358   359

THE ESSEX REGIMENT

TITLES

1st Battalion

- 1741-1751   By the name of the successive Colonels.
- 1751-1782   The 44th Regiment of Foot.
- 1782-1881   The 44th (East Essex) Regiment of Foot.

2nd Battalion

- 1755-1757   The 58th Regiment of Foot, renumbered 56th.
- 1757-1782   The 56th Regiment of Foot.
- 1782-1881   The 56th (West Essex) Regiment of Foot.
- 1881-   The Essex Regiment.

BADGES

The Castle Key and Motto *Montis insignia Calpe*. Conferred on the 56th for services during the defence of Gibraltar, 1779-1783. By Army Order 180, July, 1909, the dates 1779-1783 were added to the badge.

The Sphinx superscribed 'Egypt'. Conferred on the 44th for service in Egypt, 1801. Authorized 6th July, 1802.

The Arms of the County of Essex. The badge was displayed as part of the pre-1881 cap badge of the 56th.

An Oak Wreath. In 1881 an oak wreath was adopted and displayed on the officers' helmet plate instead of the usual one of laurel.

An Eagle. Conferred on the 44th Regiment in 1922 to commemorate the capture of a French eagle at the battle of Salamanca. It was worn as a collar badge in mess dress and on the buttons of the Regiment.

BATTLE HONOURS (*Dates authorized from 1784 to 1855*)

44TH

EGYPT AND THE SPHINX, 6th July, 1802.
PENINSULA, 6th April, 1815.
WATERLOO, 26th July, 1816.
BADAJOZ, 4th January, 1820.
SALAMANCA, 4th January, 1820.
AVA, 6th December, 1826.
BLADENSBURG, 31st May, 1827.
ALMA, 16th October, 1855.
INKERMAN, 16th October, 1855.
SEVASTOPOL, 16th October, 1855.

56TH

GIBRALTAR, 14th April, 1784.
PENINSULA, 29th March, 1815.
MORO, permission to retain, 27th December, 1827.
SEVASTOPOL, 16th October, 1855.

SHOULDER-BELT PLATES

44TH

Fig. 360 was probably worn *circa* 1802. The plate was all silver with a raised rim. The angle of showing the Sphinx is peculiar.

About 1812 the plate, still silver, had become a small oblong one with rounded corners and with the design in silver of the Sphinx on a label inscribed with Egyptian characters, all within a crowned garter inscribed 'Forty Four'.

Fig. 361, according to Mr. P. W. Reynolds, is of the silver plate prior to 1830. The crown, Sphinx and wreath in gilt, the number '44' in silver.

Fig. 362 was a gilt polished plate with the design mounted in dead gilt and with bright matted letters. The circle and scrolls all had corded edges. The size of the plate was $3\frac{3}{4} \times 3$ inches. It was worn approximately 1830-1855.

56TH

Fig. 363, silver, design engraved, probable date about 1790, drawn from one in Mr. Tilling's collection. The plate has a lined rim.

In Almack's book is illustrated an oval silver polished plate of the 56th with the design of '56' within a laurel wreath, with crown above and the Honour 'Gibraltar' engraved below.

Mr. P. W. Reynolds records a similar plate but without 'Gibraltar'. This would almost certainly have been of an earlier date and very probably worn by the 2nd Battalion, who were not in the siege.

In Mr. Tilling's collection is a gilt burnished oblong plate with the design mounted in silver of a castle with three towers and the key displayed perpendicularly; a scroll inscribed 'Gibraltar' is superimposed on the bottom of a wreath, and the number of the regiment in Roman numerals has a matted surface. It was probably worn about 1830.

BUTTONS

44TH

1760-1800. The Inspection Report of May, 1768, records that the officers' buttons were numbered. The bone-backed ones had the design in relief as in Fig. 364. The same design was worn on the men's early pewter buttons.

The design was replaced by one for both officers and men which had the design of '44' below a crown. This design was retained until 1881 on the officers' buttons, and on those of the other ranks until 1871.

56TH

The early pewter buttons of the 56th had the design in relief of the number within a spray of leaves with a crown at the opening (Fig. 365). This design remained in use with various minor differences in the wreath and shape of the numerals until 1881 by officers and until 1871 by other ranks.

In 1881 the tunic button displayed the arms of Essex surmounted by a Sphinx inscribed 'Egypt'; below the shield the castle and key of Gibraltar, on either side a spray of oak leaves.

In 1902 the eagle replaced the Sphinx and shield with the arms of Essex, and in 1900 the castle was shown with three towers.

The 1900 Dress Regulations gives the mess jacket button as having the

Sphinx over 'Egypt' and the castle and key engraved. On the mess waistcoat the castle was mounted in silver. The 1904 Regulations state that the design on the mess dress button was the eagle mounted in silver while the cap button had the county arms.

In the 1911 Regulations the cap button had the Sphinx above the county arms.

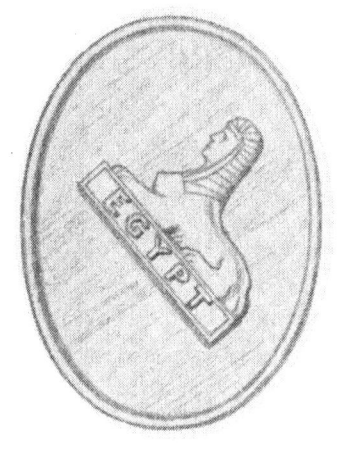

360

361

362

363

364

365

THE SHERWOOD FORESTERS (NOTTINGHAMSHIRE AND DERBYSHIRE) REGIMENT

TITLES

1ST BATTALION

1741-1751   Colonel D. Houghton's Regiment of Foot, or by the names of the successive Colonels.

1751-1782   The 45th Regiment of Foot.

1782-1866   The 45th (Nottinghamshire) Regiment of Foot.

1866-1881   The 45th (Nottinghamshire Sherwood Foresters) Regiment.

2ND BATTALION

1760-1763   The 95th Regiment of Foot. Disbanded.

1780-1783   The 95th Regiment of Foot. Disbanded.

1794-1796   The 95th Regiment of Foot. Disbanded.

1803-1816   The 95th now The Rifle Brigade.

1816-1818   The 95th Regiment of Foot raised as a 2nd Battalion of the 52nd and formed into a separate regiment as 96th in 1803. Disbanded as 95th in 1818.

1823-1825   The 95th Regiment of Foot.

1825-1881   The 95th (The Derbyshire) Regiment of Foot.

1881-1902   The Sherwood Foresters (Derbyshire) Regiment.

1902-   The Sherwood Foresters (Nottinghamshire and Derbyshire) Regiment.

BADGES

A Maltese Cross. "Records and Badges of the British Army" states that when raised in 1823 there were in the regiment a good many officers and men of the old 95th Rifles and that the Maltese Cross was adopted as its badge, but there is no evidence to support the statement.

A White Hart lodged within Park Gates on an azure field. The old badge of the Derby Militia, adopted by the Regular battalions of the regiment in 1881.

The Rose. The badge was given to the regiment in 1881 in common with other regiments which had no particular regimental design. It does not appear to have ever been displayed by the regiment in any of its metal badges. It was changed to that of the United Red and White Rose in 1888.

BATTLE HONOURS (*Dates authorized from 1815 to 1855*)

45TH

  PENINSULA, 6th April, 1815.
  ROLEIA,* 4th December, 1817.
  VIMIERA, 4th December, 1817.
  CIUDAD RODRIGO, 4th December, 1817.
  BADAJOZ, 4th December, 1817.
  SALAMANCA. 4th December, 1817.
  VITTORIA, 4th December, 1817.
  PYRENEES, 4th December, 1817.
  NIVELLE, 4th December, 1817.
  ORTHES, 4th December, 1817.
  TOULOUSE, 4th December, 1817.
  TALAVERA, 30th January, 1817.
  BUSACO, 30th January, 1817.
  FUENTES D'ONOR, 22nd December, 1820.
  AVA, 6th December, 1826.

95TH

  ALMA, 16th October, 1855.
  INKERMAN, 16th October, 1855.
  SEVASTOPOL, 16th October, 1855.

SHOULDER-BELT PLATES

45TH

Almack's book illustrates an officers' silver plate *circa* 1809-1813. The plate was polished silver with the design shown in Fig. 366 mounted in silver.

About 1817 a silver oblong plate with rounded corners was worn. The design was '45' within a crowned circle inscribed 'Nottingham Regiment', all on the centre of a star; below the star a scroll inscribed 'Peninsula'; on either side of the crown, scrolls inscribed 'Busaco' and 'Talavera'.

This was worn until about 1832, when a gilt plate of the design in Fig. 367 was adopted. The plate had a silver star; the fourteen major rays were in gilt and inscribed with Peninsular Honours. A similar design was worn on the brass plate of other ranks. These plates were probably worn until the 1850 period. Another shoulder-belt plate of the 45th worn by other ranks had the design of 'XLV' within a crowned garter inscribed 'Nottinghamshire'; round the garter a wreath of laurel. The plate was brass, stamped, and had square-cut corners.

---

* An Army Order in 1911 directed this honour to be spelt "Rolica".

95TH

Mr. P. W. Reynolds records the officers' plate, 1823-1840, as being oblong, silver, with a gilt crowned garter and the number '95' within. The figures had a matted surface. The garter, which had roped edges, was inscribed *Honi soit qui mal y pense*. The Light Company plate was of similar design, but the number '95' was between the cords of a Light Infantry bugle-horn.

Fig. 368. The officers' plate of the 95th, 1840-1855, was an oblong gilt burnished plate with an exact replica of the Star of the Grand Cross of the Order of the Bath. Below a lower limb of the cross was a silver lined label bearing the number '95' in relief in silver.

BUTTONS

45TH

The early officers' buttons of the 45th are said to have had the design of '45' within a French scroll with a dot at the opening. It appears to be uncertain if they were gold or silver. The Inspection Report of July, 1768, states "Buttons silver numbered", but the late Mr. W. Calver, of the U.S.A., was not sure whether those found were of silver or gilt. Those of 1780 had the design in relief of '45' on a gilt button with a roped border (Fig. 369). The whole on a bone back.

The men's pewter buttons of this period had a plain '45' (Fig. 370). Later this gave place to one with '45' inside a French scroll with a dot at the opening (Fig. 371). Whether the officers' buttons had this design with a dot is not known. There appears to have been little change in the design of their buttons between 1820 and 1881. The design for officers was of the number below a crown inside a French scroll, being used on both silver and gilt coatee buttons and on the tunic. There was no dot at the opening.

95TH

The other ranks' pewter buttons, 1828-1855, had the design in relief of '95' below a crown within a single-line circle. The officers' coatee button had '95' within a crowned wreath at first and later '95' inside a crowned garter inscribed *Honi soit qui mal y pense*. The tunic buttons in 1855 had the number and crown design as a rule inside a single-line circle. There were different dies, some with large numerals, others small, while one die omitted the circle.

After 1881 the design was a crowned Maltese Cross on which, within an oak wreath on the cross, was a hart lodged. A half scroll on the left limb of the cross inscribed 'Sherwood' and another on the right inscribed 'Foresters', on the lower limb of the cross one inscribed 'Derbyshire'. On the change of title in 1902 the lower scroll was amended to read 'Notts and Derby'.

The 1904 Dress Regulations gives the mess dress button as having the same design as the tunic, but mounted.

366

367

368

369

370 371

THE LOYAL REGIMENT (NORTH LANCASHIRE)

TITLES

1st Battalion
1741-1751 By the name of its successive Colonels.
1751-1782 The 47th Regiment of Foot.
1782-1881 The 47th (The Lancashire) Regiment of Foot.

2nd Battalion
1758-1769 The 81st Invalid Regiment of Foot renumbered 71st.
1778-1794 The 81st (Aberdeen Highlanders) Regiment of Foot. Disbanded.
1793-1794 The 81st (Loyal Lincoln Volunteers) Regiment of Foot.
1794-1832 The 81st Regiment of Foot.
1832-1881 The 81st (Loyal Lincoln Volunteers) Regiment of Foot.
1881-1920 The Loyal North Lancashire Regiment.

1920- The Loyal Regiment (North Lancashire).

BADGES

The Royal Crest, which was also the crest of the Duchy of Lancaster, was displayed on the buttons of the 47th found at Ticonderoga, so it was evidently worn prior to 1781, in which year they returned to England.

The Red Rose of Lancaster. An old badge of the 47th appears to have been first displayed on the shoulder-belt plates about 1818.

The Arms of the City of Lincoln. The 81st were raised in the city of Lincoln and were given the title Loyal Lincoln Volunteers and the badge to commemorate the fact that they were raised almost entirely from the Lincoln Militia, whose badge was the arms of the city at whose expense the regiment was formed.

Motto: *Loyauté m'oblige.* Authorized 1934.

BATTLE HONOURS (*Dates authorized from 1807 to 1855*)

47th
PENINSULA, 13th June, 1816.
TARIFA, 13th June, 1816.
VITTORIA, 28th May, 1818.
ST. SEBASTIAN, 28th May, 1818.
AVA, 6th December, 1826.
ALMA, 16th October, 1855.
INKERMAN, 16th October, 1855.
SEVASTOPOL, 16th October, 1855.

81st
MAIDA, 2nd February, 1807.
PENINSULA, 6th April, 1815.
CORUNNA, to the old 2nd Battalion, 20th February, 1812; to the regiment as a whole, 18th July, 1816.

SHOULDER-BELT PLATES

47TH

Fig. 372 is of an officers' silver plate, design engraved. The date would be about 1782. The officers' silver plate, design in relief, worn *circa* 1820 is shown in Fig. 373. This was followed by the design shown in Fig. 374 and was worn up to 1830 in silver, and after that the same design was worn but on a gilt plate with the design mounted in silver. The plate worn before 1830 was without the Honours 'Ava' and 'Tarifa'.

Fig. 375 is the plate worn prior to 1855. The plate was gilt with the design mounted in silver.

81ST

A portrait of G. H. Reade, of the 81st Aberdeen Highlanders, reproduced in the *Journal of the Society for Army Historical Research*, Vol. XV, page 180, shows him wearing an oblong plate with what appears to be the design of '81' below a crown.

Almack's book records an oval silver polished plate with the design in relief of '81' inside a double circle.

During the period of about 1807-1818 two oval silver plates appear to have been worn, possibly by different battalions of the regiment:

(a) The design of '81' inside a circle with a scroll above inscribed in pierced letters 'Maida'. The Honour had been awarded in 1807.

(b) The design shown in Fig. 376. The plate was still silver, with garter and centre gilt. The numerals were of silver. The Honour 'Corunna' was given in 1812 to the 2nd Battalion which then existed of the regiment but was not given to the regiment as a whole until 1816.

The oval plate was succeeded by a silver oblong one bearing the simple design of 'LXXXI'. After 1830 the same design was retained, but the plate became gilt.

BUTTONS

47TH

There were two designs of officers' bone-backed buttons. Fig. 377 had the design in relief on a silver face. The other ranks' pewter buttons had the designs shown in Figs. 378 and 379. The design on Fig. 379 was also worn on the officers' flat single-piece buttons *circa* 1800-1818, about 1817 when the design in Fig. 380 was adopted.

This design was also worn on the men's pewter buttons and on the officers' gilt coatee buttons and the tunic buttons until 1881 and 1871 in the case of other ranks.

It was not until after 1881 that the lion was displayed crowned.

81ST

The 81st, like the 47th, were a silver-laced regiment and had silver buttons until 1830.

The 1800 button had the number '81' in relief within a raised circle. In 1807 the Honour 'Maida' was added above the circle, and in 1812 the Honour

'Corunna' was given to the regiment; this was placed below the circle. With small roses between the two Honours, the design was retained until 1881 by the officers and 1871 by other ranks.

The officers' tunic buttons, 1881-1902, had the design of a shield with the arms of Lincoln, the old badge of the 81st, surmounted by the Royal crest, the badge of the 47th. This design in relief was superimposed on a circle inscribed 'Loyal North Lancashire Regiment'.

The present design is of the shield and Royal crest within a wreath of laurel leaves and with the Honour 'Tarifa' above the lion and the title 'Loyal North Lancashire' round the bottom half of the button.

After 1902 the cap button was die struck, the design as for the tunic.

THE NORTHAMPTONSHIRE REGIMENT

TITLES
1st Battalion
1741-1751   Known by the name of the successive Colonels.
1751-1782   The 48th Regiment of Foot.
1782-1881   The 48th (Northamptonshire) Regiment of Foot.

2nd Battalion
1755-1757   The 58th Regiment of Foot renumbered 56.
1755-1757   The 60th Regiment of Foot renumbered 58.
1757-1782   The 58th Regiment of Foot.
1782-1881   The 58th (Rutlandshire) Regiment of Foot.
1881-   The Northamptonshire Regiment.

BADGES
The Castle, Key and Motto *Montis insignia Calpe*, awarded to the 58th for having served in the defence of the Rock, 1779-1783. Officially authorized 2nd May, 1836, but had been worn before. Army Order 180, July, 1909, added the date '1779-83' to the Honour.

The Sphinx superscribed 'Egypt'. Awarded to the 58th, 6th July, 1802.

A Golden Horseshoe. The old badge of the Rutland Militia, and was added to the Regular battalions' badges in 1881. The horseshoe was derived from the arms of Oakham, which has as arms a black horseshoe with silver nails on a gold ground; the origin of this being that when Queen Elizabeth was riding through the town her horse cast a shoe. From this the town acquired the right of claiming a horseshoe from any Royal or noble personage who entered it.

BATTLE HONOURS (*Dates authorized from 1784 to 1855*)
48th
PENINSULA, 6th April, 1815.
TALAVERA, 6th November, 1816.
ALBUHERA, 22nd January, 1818.
BADAJOZ, 22nd January, 1818.
SALAMANCA, 22nd January, 1818.
VITTORIA, 22nd January, 1818.
PYRENEES, 22nd January, 1818.
NIVELLE, 22nd January, 1818.
ORTHES, 22nd January, 1818.
TOULOUSE, 22nd January, 1818.
DOURO, 22nd January, 1818.
SEVASTOPOL, 16th October, 1855.

58TH

GIBRALTAR, 22nd April, 1784.
EGYPT AND SPHINX, 6th July, 1802.
MAIDA, 12th February, 1807.
PENINSULA, 6th April, 1815.
SALAMANCA, 14th February, 1821.
VITTORIA, 14th February, 1821.
PYRENEES, 14th February, 1821.
NIVELLE, 14th February, 1821.
ORTHES, 14th February, 1821.

Badge of the Castle, Key and Motto to be displayed in addition to 'Gibraltar', 2nd May, 1836.

SHOULDER-BELT PLATES

48TH

In the Regimental Museum is an early oval brass plate with the design of '48' surmounted by a crown. Round the top edge of the plate the title 'Northamptonshire', and at the bottom 'Regiment'. A plate found in America had the design of the Royal cypher and '48'.

About 1792 the officers' gilt plate had the design in relief as shown in Fig. 381. Another oval plate was worn towards the close of the eighteenth century; the plate was gilt with a silver half-bound corner and silver '48' on a matted ground inside a crowned oval.

From 1820 to 1855 the plate which was oblong was gilt, with the design mounted in silver (Fig. 382).

58TH

An early oval plate of the 58th had the design engraved of the Royal cypher in script characters; above this was a crown, on either side of which were the numbers '5' and '8'.

About 1800 the officers' plates were gilt, oval, with the number surmounted by a crown; this design probably remained in use until about 1816.

Fig. 383 shows the plate worn prior to 1855. A similar plate to this was sold at Messrs. Glendinings in 1924, but it had no Sphinx and had a narrower rim to the plate.

Figs. 384 and 385 are of other ranks' plates, both of brass. From the number of Honours displayed, Fig. 385 would appear to be the earlier, but the Honours are too indistinct to be made out.

BUTTONS

48TH

The officers' early bone-backed button of the 48th was of a handsome design; the face of the button was of gilt metal with the design in relief (Fig. 386). No record exists of the men's buttons of this period, but the design of a crown, number and twisted bar was adopted early in the nineteenth century, if not before. An officers' silver button with the design was found in America and said to be of the 1776-1783 period.

The design of '48' on a twisted bar with a crown above was used by the regiment for a considerable time. About 1810 the design was shown incised on a convex button with open back.

The officers' coatee buttons, 1830-1855 period, had the design of '48' below a crown and within a wreath. Above the crown was the Honour 'Peninsula' and below the wreath 'Talavera'. On the introduction of the tunic button in 1855, the earlier design of a crown, number and twisted bar was reverted to and worn until 1881.

There were two or more designs of this button, one with a large '48' and one with a small, also one without the twisted bar.

58TH

An Inspection Report dated 30th May, 1768, reports buttons as "yellow and unnumbered". The early pewter button had the design of '58' inside a scroll with a dot at the opening. The button had a roped rim. This was followed by a design of the number '58' inside a circle with a border of dots; the circle inscribed 'Gibraltar', 'Egypt', 'Maida'.

The tunic buttons, 1855-1881, had two types of numeral, one large and the other small.

After 1881 the design on the tunic buttons was the castle with key below and with a crown above, around the bottom half of the button a scroll inscribed 'The Northamptonshire Regiment'.

Before 1900 the castle was shown with two towers; after that date it had three.

The 1904 Dress Regulations gives the cap button as having the same design as for the tunic but without the title. The mess dress button had the same design mounted. Another type of cap and mess dress button had the design of a scroll inscribed 'Talavera' with a crown above. The button was mounted. In the 1911 Regulations the cap button is as for the tunic, but with scroll omitted. The mess dress button had the castle and key in silver.

THE ROYAL BERKSHIRE REGIMENT (PRINCESS CHARLOTTE OF WALES'S)

TITLES
1ST BATTALION
1743-1751   Colonel Edward Trelawney's (or Colonel's name) Regiment of Foot.
1751-1782   The 49th Regiment of Foot.
1782-1816   The 49th (Hertfordshire) Regiment of Foot.
1816-1881   The 49th (or the Princess Charlotte of Wales's or Hertfordshire).

2ND BATTALION
1756-1758   The 19th (2nd Battalion) Regiment of Foot renumbered.
1758-1782   The 66th Regiment of Foot.
1782-1881   The 66th (Berkshire) Regiment of Foot.
1881-1885   Princess Charlotte of Wales's (Berkshire Regiment).
1885-1920   Princess Charlotte of Wales's (Royal Berkshire Regiment).
1920-   The Royal Berkshire Regiment (Princess Charlotte of Wales's).

BADGES
The Dragon of China awarded to the 49th for service during the China War of 1840-1842. Date of award, 12th January, 1843.

From 1881 until the helmet was abolished the regiment displayed, in the centre of the plate, the badge of the old Royal Berkshire Militia, a Stag under an oak tree.

Application for permission to wear a badge in memory of Lord Rodney's victory on 12th April, 1782, and the word 'St. Vincent' on its Colours, was made but refused in September, 1854; while in November, 1880, an application for officers to wear a laurel wreath on their forage caps and for the word 'St. Vincent' to be placed on the Colours was also refused. But in October, 1951, it was authorized for a Naval Crown, to be associated with the Honour 'Copenhagen', awarded the 49th in 1820.

On the front of the officers' blue peaked cap is the badge of a coiled rope in gilt metal to commemorate the sea service of the '49'.

BATTLE HONOURS (*Dates authorized from 1815 to 1855*)
49TH
QUEENSTOWN, 27th January, 1816.
EGMONT OP ZEE, 19th February, 1820.
COPENHAGEN, 19th February, 1820.
CHINA WITH BADGE OF DRAGON, 12th January, 1843.
ALMA, 16th October, 1855.
INKERMAN, 16th October, 1855.
SEVASTOPOL, 16th October, 1855.

66TH

PENINSULA, 6th April, 1815. Regranted 30th July, 1823.
DOURO, 14th August, 1815.
TALAVERA, 11th January, 1823.
ALBUHERA, 11th January, 1823.
VITTORIA, 11th January, 1823.
PYRENEES, 11th January, 1823.
NIVELLE, 11th January, 1823.
NIVE, 11th January, 1823.
ORTHES, 11th January, 1823.

SHOULDER-BELT PLATES

49TH

The officers' oval shoulder-belt plate, 1790–1812 or later, had the design of '49' below a crown. The plate for other ranks was a brass one with a plain '49' incised.

In a portrait of Lieutenant John Day, of the Grenadier Company, 49th Foot, reproduced in the Day Papers by S. H. Day (privately printed in 1911), the portrait was evidently painted before 1813 as the oval shoulder-belt plate (with crown at the top, '49' in centre and grenade at bottom) is depicted. Another portrait of a Grenadier Company officer of the regiment painted later shows a rectangular breast plate with Battle Honours.

The *Journal of the Society for Army Historical Research*, Vol. XVIII, page 124, shows the plate 1820-1842 which is described as burnished gilt with silver mounts (Fig. 387). This gave way to the design in Fig. 388, 1843-1855; the plate had a matted surface, burnished rim and the design in dead gilt.

66TH

The officers' early oval plate for the 66th had the incised design of '66' within a crowned garter which was inscribed 'Berkshire Regiment'. Other ranks' plates of this period were small oblong brass ones with the design of '66' surmounted by the word 'Berkshire' and below the number the word 'Regiment' incised.

The officers' plate in use 1850 was a gilt burnished oblong plate with silver mounts, according to an article by the late Rev. P. Sumner; its date was 1829-1855. Size 3 × 3¾ inches (Fig. 389).

BUTTONS

49TH

The officers' early bone-backed buttons are reported by the late Mr. Calver, of New York, as having silver fronts with the plain design of '49' (Fig. 390). The other ranks' pewter buttons were of the same design.

In 1768 Colonel Maitland was appointed to command the 49th, and the Regiment, probably in compliment to his Scottish origin, adopted a gilt bone-backed button with the design of '49' below a crown and within a single spray of thistles (Fig. 391). The men's pewter button still had the design of a plain '49' in relief, and another type with '49' within a French scroll and dot.

In 1816 the officers' buttons were flat, single piece, of gilt with the design of '49' within a crowned circle inscribed 'P. Charlotte of Wales' within a Union wreath of single blossoms. This button was worn until 1855. The men's pewter buttons had the same design (Fig. 392).

In 1855 the design was retained, but the wreath made much thicker and had a more even representation of the national flowers.

66TH

The officers' buttons of the 66th were silver until 1830 and had the simple design of the number below a crown within a single-line circle, all in relief, at first on a flat button and later the same design on a convex one. The coatee button down to 1855 had the design of '66' below a crown and within a laurel wreath (Fig. 393). The tunic button had the old design of '66' below a crown within a single-line circle. There were two dies of this button, one having a more ornamented crown than the other. The early pewter buttons worn by the other ranks had the design of '66' in relief. The button had a roped rim.

In 1881 the tunic button had the design of the Chinese dragon on a bar, below which was the title 'Berkshire'; a crown above the dragon superimposed on a circle inscribed 'Charlotte of Wales's'. After 1885 the word 'Berkshire' was replaced by 'R. Berks'.

In 1948 a new design of button was adopted with a silver dragon mounted on a burnished gilt button.

The 1900 Dress Regulations give the cap and mess dress button as having the dragon and crown mounted in gilt. The 1904 Regulations gives the cap button as having 'R. Berks' below the dragon.

387

388

389

390   391

392

393

THE ROYAL MARINES

TITLES

1664-1689 The Lord Admiral's Maritime Regiment.
1694-1697 Several Maritime Regiments raised and disbanded.
1702-1713 Six regiments raised, three of them disbanded, the other three now represented by—
                1st Battalion The East Lancashire Regiment.
                1st Battalion The East Surrey Regiment.
                1st Battalion The Duke of Cornwall's Light Infantry.
            At the same time other regiments were raised for sea service.
1740-1748 Ten Marine Regiments raised and disbanded.
1755-1802 Fifty Companies of Marines permanently established.
1802-1855 Royal Marines.
1855-1923 Royal Marine Light Infantry.
            Royal Marine Artillery. (As companies trace back to 1804; in 1859 became self-contained from the R.M.L.I. Divisions).
1923- Royal Marines. (R.M.L.I. and R.M.A. merged into one Corps).

BADGES

The Royal Crest. An old badge of the Corps.
The Laurel Wreath. Awarded for service at Belle Isle, 1761.
The Globe. Awarded in 1827, but is said to have been borne as early as 1775.
The Motto: *Per Mare Per Terram.*
A Bugle-Horn. 1855.

SHOULDER-BELT PLATES

In Vol. I, page 181, of the *Journal of the Society for Army Historical Research*, the late Colonel Field quoted a divisional order, 12th May, 1773, by which officers were ordered to wear a shoulder sword belt with clasp. In 1784 a divisional order of 17th April directed buckles and slides, and shortly afterwards plates were permitted to be worn instead of buckles.

These, states Colonel Field, appear to have been oval till 6th April, 1797, when it was ordered that "Breast Plates are to be square with the Lion and Crown".

Probably the earliest known officers' shoulder-belt plate is in the collection of Mr. Usher (Fig. 394). The plate is described as thin, silver, die struck, with one hook at the back and two very large studs. The border to the plate is engraved $\frac{1}{16}$ inch broad. The size of the plate is $3\frac{1}{16} \times 2\frac{1}{32}$ inches. The silversmith mark is Jos. Preedy, of London, whose earliest date was 1777 and latest 1798. Mr. Usher dates the plate as being worn between 1782 and 1785.

In "Britain's Sea Soldiers" is reproduced a print of the uniform of 1799;

in this the plate is oval, and in a print of 1796-1799 the plate has the design of an anchor but without any rope.

The "British Military Library", 1799, shows an oblong plate, silver, with the design of a foul anchor.

Almack's book illustrates two oval plates which are attributed to the Marines, but they may have been Royal Navy. Both plates are oval gilt.

(a) A fouled anchor below a crown; round the rim of the plate are a series of dots or 'husks'.

(b) The fouled anchor but displayed inclining to the right within a crowned garter inscribed *Honi soit qui mal y pense*. An ornamental rim similar to Fig. 394.

In the sale of the late Mr. S. M. Milne's collection in 1921 were three oval gilt plates described as follows:

(i) Officers' belt plate, *circa* 1800, $3\frac{1}{8}$ inches, oval, gilt, engraved with crowned anchor within a laurel wreath.

(ii) Early belt plate, oval, gilt, engraved with crowned anchor.

(iii) Oblong, impressed 'Royal Marines' over crown, anchor and laurel.

In the same sale was an oval plate engraved 'British Navy' above an anchor with cartouche charged with two dolphins over trident and palm branch.

Fig. 395 is the officers' shoulder-belt plate worn by the Royal Marine Artillery *circa* 1854, gilt burnished plate, size $3\frac{8}{9} \times 3$ inches.

The officers of the Royal Marine Light Infantry had a similar plate but without a grenade.

According to Vol. I, "Britain's Sea Soldiers", the other ranks' plate, 1802-1823, was oblong with the design of a foul anchor, above which was a crown and a scroll inscribed 'Royal Marines'; below the anchor was a spray of laurel.

Circa 1826-1830 the plate had the design of the Royal crest within a wreath of oak. The plate was matted gilt with the design mounted in gilt. It had very slightly rounded corners. Size $3\frac{4}{5} \times 3$ inches.

BUTTONS

The officers' bone-backed buttons *circa* 1780 had silver faces with the design of a fouled anchor within a wreath; the button's face had a scalloped edge. The other ranks' pewter buttons had the design of a fouled anchor incised.

Circa 1800 the officers' buttons were gilt, flat, with the design in relief as Fig. 396.

The other ranks had a similar design but the wreath was straighter.

The coatee button for officers *circa* 1830-1855 had the same design as above except that the anchor was surmounted by a crown, and in the later issue the anchor was not fouled.

The design on the tunic buttons was the crown and fouled anchor within a circle inscribed 'Royal Marine Light Infantry', with a wreath of laurel round. In the case of the Royal Marine Artillery, on either side of the anchor was a grenade, and in place of a circle was a garter inscribed 'Royal Marine Artillery', otherwise the buttons were the same.

394

395

396

THE QUEEN'S OWN ROYAL WEST KENT REGIMENT

TITLES

1ST BATTALION

1754-1756   The 50th Regiment of Foot. Disbanded.
1755-1782   The 50th. (Raised in 1755 as the 52nd and renumbered 50th Regiment of Foot in 1757.)
1782-1827   The 50th (West Kent) Regiment of Foot.
1827-1831   The 50th (The Duke of Clarence's) Regiment of Foot.
1831-1881   The 50th (or the Queen's Own) Regiment of Foot.

2ND BATTALION

1761-1763   The 97th Regiment of Foot. Disbanded.
1780-1783   The 97th Regiment of Foot. Disbanded.
1794-1795   The 97th (Inverness-shire Highlanders) Regiment of Foot. Disbanded, the Flank Companies going to The Black Watch.
1805-1816   The 97th (Queen's German) Regiment. Renumbered 96th. Disbanded 1818.
1804-1816   The 98th Regiment of Foot renumbered 97th and disbanded.
1824-1826   The 97th Regiment of Foot.
1826-1881   The 97th (Earl of Ulster's) Regiment of Foot.
1881-1920   The Queen's Own (Royal West Kent Regiment).
1920-1921   The Royal West Kent Regiment (Queen's Own).
1921-   The Queen's Own Royal West Kent Regiment.

BADGES

The Royal Crest. An old badge of the 50th.
The White Horse of Kent and the motto *Invicta*. Worn since 1881; had been the badge of the West Kent Militia for a great many years.
Motto: *Quo Fas et Gloria ducunt*. Authorized for the 97th Regiment, 4th October, 1826.
Motto: *Quo Fata Vocant*. Was displayed by the officers of the 1st Battalion '50th' on their shoulder-belt plates and waist-belt plates of field officers *circa* 1810.
The Sphinx superscribed 'Egypt'. Commemorates the services of the 50th in Egypt, 1801. Authorized 6th July, 1802.
Duke of Clarence's Cypher and Coronet. Authorized 7th May, 1828. The 50th had been given the title The Duke of Clarence's in 1827.

BATTLE HONOURS *(Dates authorized from 1802 to 1855)*

50TH
    EGYPT AND THE SPHINX, 6th July, 1802.
    CORUNNA, 20th February, 1812.
    VIMIERA, 14th November, 1812.
    PENINSULA, 6th April, 1815.
    ALMARAZ, * 11th December, 1815.
    VITTORIA, 10th March, 1820.
    PYRENEES, 10th March, 1820.
    NIVE, 10th March, 1820.
    ORTHES, 10th March, 1820.
    PUNNIAR, 22nd June, 1844.
    MOODKEE, 8th June, 1847.
    FEROZESHAH, 8th June, 1847.
    ALIWAL, 8th June, 1847.
    SOBRAON, 8th June, 1847.
    ALMA, 16th October, 1855.
    INKERMAN, 16th October, 1855.
    SEVASTOPOL, 16th October, 1855.

97TH
    SEVASTOPOL, 16th October, 1855.

SHOULDER-BELT PLATES

50TH

The Regimental History states that the shoulder-belt plates for 1770-1775 were an oval silver one for the officers and a brass one for the other ranks.

In 1809 the 1st Battalion officers had a silver plate as shown in Fig. 397, and those of the 2nd Battalion one of the design in Fig. 398. This battalion did not display the motto.

Fig. 399 is of an other ranks' plate worn about 1809.

Fig. 400 is of a silver plate with rounded corners adopted, according to the Regimental History, about 1816. Fig. 401 is also silver and said to have been worn about 1826. It is quite possible that both plates were in use at the same time by different battalions of the regiment. In 1830 the regiment's lace was changed from silver to gold.

The plate in use about 1850 was gilt, oblong, and had a matted ground. The crown and garter were in gilt, the number, the Sphinx and star in silver. The back to the centre was also silver (Fig. 402).

97TH

The officers' shoulder-belt plates of the 97th Inverness-shire Highlanders Regiment of 1794-1795 were gilt, oval, with the design engraved of a crown surmounted by a scroll inscribed 'Inverness-shire Regiment', and beneath the crown '97' within an ornamental oval. Below this a spray of half thistle, half rose. The plate had a scalloped device round the edge. The number '97' was in black.

* At first spelt ALMAREZ, after 1830 ALMARAZ.

BUTTONS

50TH

The design of the buttons of the 50th have had very little change. The officers' bone-backed button *circa* 1780 had silver faces with the design in relief of the number '50' surmounted by a crown, with laurel leaves turned inwards round the edge. This design was also worn on the pewter buttons of the other ranks. Officers' buttons about 1820 were silver, convex, open-backed, and with the design of the Royal crest above the number '50'. The lion was at first displayed looking straight ahead and had no crown (Fig. 403). According to the regiment, the lion was placed above the crown on the buttons about 1810. The officers' gilt buttons after 1831 had the design of '50' within a garter inscribed 'Queens Own', above the garter the Royal crest, the lion now being displayed crowned; round the garter a wreath of laurel (Fig. 404).

The other ranks' pewter buttons up to 1855 had the design of '50' below the Royal crest. The tunic button introduced in 1855 had the same design, the ion being uncrowned.

97TH

The pewter buttons of the other ranks *circa* 1826 had the design of '97' below a crown within a French scroll without a dot at the opening.

The officers' coatee, 1826-1855, had the design of 'XCVII' within a crowned garter inscribed 'The Earl of Ulsters Regt.' Below the garter, resting on a Union wreath, a scroll inscribed *Quo Fas et Gloria ducunt* (Fig. 405).

After 1855 the design was '97' below a crown and within a French scroll.

Since 1881 the design on the tunic button has been the Royal crest. At first most dies showed the lion uncrowned, but since about 1898 it has been crowned.

The 1911 Dress Regulations gives the mess dress button as having the Royal crest mounted in silver.

After 1900 the cap button had the same design die stamped.

397

398

399

400

401

402

403

404

405

246

THE KING'S OWN YORKSHIRE LIGHT INFANTRY

TITLES

1st BATTALION

1754-1756 The 51st (American Provincials) Regiment of Foot. Disbanded.
1755-1757 The 53rd Regiment of Foot renumbered.
1757-1782 The 51st Regiment of Foot.
1782-1809 The 51st (2nd Yorkshire, West Riding) Regiment of Foot.
1809-1821 The 51st (2nd Yorkshire, West Riding) Light Infantry Regiment.
1821-1881 The 51st (2nd Yorkshire, West Riding) or "The King's Own" Light Infantry Regiment.

2ND BATTALION

1761-1763 105th (Queen's Own Royal Highlanders) Regiment. Disbanded.
1782-1783 The 105th (Volunteers of Ireland) Regiment. Disbanded.
1794-1796 The 105th (or Leeds Volunteers) Regiment of Foot. Disbanded.
1839-1858 The H.E.I.C. 2nd Madras (European) Regiment.
1858-1861 The 2nd Madras (European) Regiment.
1861-1881 The 105th (Madras Light Infantry) Regiment.
1881-1887 The King's Own Light Infantry (South Yorkshire Regiment).
1887-1920 The King's Own (Yorkshire Light Infantry).
1920-   The King's Own Yorkshire Light Infantry.

BADGES

The White Rose of York. An old badge of the 51st Regiment.
A French Bugle-horn. The date the design of a French bugle-horn was adopted by the 51st in place of the more ordinary one is not certain. According to tradition, it was adopted by the 51st after the battle of Waterloo to commemorate the Regiment's engagement with a French regiment of Mounted Chasseurs whose badge it was. But this would appear rather doubtful as it was not adopted for some years after.
Motto: *Cede nullis*. The motto of the 2nd Madras Light Infantry.

BATTLE HONOURS (*Dates authorized from 1801 to 1855*)

51ST

MINDEN, 1st January, 1801.
PENINSULA, 6th April, 1815.
WATERLOO, 8th December, 1815.
VITTORIA, 11th December, 1816.
NIVELLE, 11th December, 1816.
CORUNNA, 9th August, 1834.
SALAMANCA, 9th August, 1834.
ORTHES, 9th August, 1834.
PYRENEES, 9th August, 1834.
PEGU, 20th September, 1853.

SHOULDER-BELT PLATES

51ST

According to the Regimental History, the early officers' shoulder-belt plate was an oval silver one with the Royal arms, crown and flags and a scroll below the badge. The plate had a raised rim.

Mr. P. W. Reynolds shows the plate as having below the Royal arms the letters 'Min(G.R.)den' and below this the title '2 York West Riding Regt'.

About 1802-1810 the plate was a gilt oblong one with the design as Fig. 406 mounted in silver.

This plate was followed by a gilt plate with the design as Fig. 407, in silver, of '51' within the cords of a bugle-horn surmounted by a crown, and with a wreath of laurel below which was a scroll inscribed 'Ich Dien'. The plate was 3 inches wide.

About 1828 a gilt plate with a matted surface and a roped border with the design in silver was adopted (Fig. 407). Both these plates had rounded corners. The illustration is from one in the collection of Mr. Tilling.

Fig. 408 is the officers' plate worn prior to 1855; the plate was gilt with the design mounted in silver with a burnished rim.

The brass plate worn by other ranks *circa* 1850 had the design of a bugle-horn within a wreath and crown above; between the cords the number '51'. The design of the bugle-horn was not a French one.

105TH

According to the Regimental History, the shoulder-belt plate, 1839-1847, was a burnished gilt one with the design in silver of the numeral '2' within the curl of a crowned French bugle-horn.

This was replaced by a plate of burnished gilt with the design in frosted gilt of the numeral '2' within the curl of a crowned French bugle-horn, the base of the crown resting on the bugle-horn on a curved scroll below the motto *Cede nullis*.

BUTTONS

51ST

In an Inspection Report of the 51st at Dublin dated 27th August, 1768, it states lace gold, buttons yellow, unnumbered.

The following year the lace is given as silver and the buttons silver, numbered. The silver buttons do not appear to have been worn for long.

The Report on the Regiment when at Exeter in 1771 records buttons yellow, numbered.

The officers' buttons of this period had gilt faces laid on bone backs with the design in relief (Fig. 409).

In 1814 the officers' buttons were flat, gilt, one piece, with the design in relief (Fig. 410). This design was retained on the convex coatee button until replaced by the design of '51' within the curl of a crowned French bugle-horn.

The tunic button, 1855-1881, had the design of '51' within a wreath of leaves with a scalloped edge. There were two designs of this button, one having small numerals, the other large; the design of the wreath also varied.

The other ranks' tunic button, 1855-1871, had the same design with larger numerals.

105TH

There were two designs of tunic buttons worn by the 2nd Battalion when they were the 105th Madras Light Infantry. The first design had 'C.V.' inside the curl of a French bugle-horn surmounted by a crown. The button was rimless. The second had the number '105' within the bugle-horn, with a crown above and the title 'Madras Light Infantry' below.

After 1881 the design on the tunic button for a short time was the white rose within the curl of a crowned French bugle-horn, all within a wreath of leaves. The button had a scalloped edge. After a short time the design was changed to the rose in silver displayed within the curl of a French bugle-horn surmounted by a crown.

The 1904 Dress Regulations gives the mess waistcoat button as having the design mounted of the monogram of the regiment with a crown above. The 1911 Regulations state that the buttons in service dress are entirely of gilding metal, die struck.

406

407

408

409

410

THE KING'S SHROPSHIRE LIGHT INFANTRY

TITLES

1st Battalion

1755-1757   The 53rd Regiment of Foot, renumbered 51st.
1755-1757   The 55th Regiment of Foot, renumbered 53rd.
1757-1782   The 53rd Regiment of Foot.
1782-1881   The 53rd (Shropshire) Regiment of Foot.

2nd Battalion

1759-1763   The 85th (Royal Volunteers Light Infantry) Regiment. Disbanded.
1778-1783   The 85th (Westminster Volunteers) Regiment. Disbanded.
1793-1808   The 85th (Bucks Volunteers) Regiment of Foot.
1808-1815   The 85th (Bucks Volunteers) (Light Infantry) Regiment.
1815-1821   The 85th (Bucks Volunteers) (Duke of York's Own Light Infantry) Regiment.
1821-1827   The 85th (Bucks Volunteers) (The King's Light Infantry) Regiment.
1827-1881   The 85th (The King's Light Infantry) Regiment.
1881-1882   The King's Light Infantry (Shropshire Regiment).
1882-1920   The King's (Shropshire Light Infantry).
1920-   The King's Shropshire Light Infantry.

BADGES

A Bugle-horn with Strings. Adopted by the 85th when constituted Light Infantry in 1808.

Motto: *Aucto splendore resurgo*. Finally authorized 10th May, 1839, but had been originally adopted by the 85th, 3rd August, 1815, but discontinued 16th August, 1827.

The Rose. The badge was given to the regiment in 1881 in common with other regiments which had no particular regimental design. It does not appear to have ever been worn by the regiment in any form of metal. It was changed to the United Red and White Rose in 1888.

BATTLE HONOURS (*Dates authorized from 1815 to 1855*)

53RD

PENINSULA, 6th April, 1815, to the old 2nd Battalion of the 53rd; to 1st Battalion, 28th March, 1829.

SALAMANCA, 9th July, 1816, to the old 2nd Battalion 53rd; to 1st Battalion, 28th March, 1829.

TALAVERA, 8th August, 1818.

VITTORIA, 17th February, 1820.

PYRENEES, 17th February, 1820.
NIVELLE, 17th February, 1820.
TOULOUSE, 17th February, 1820.
NIEUPORT, 10th March, 1825.
TOURNAY, 10th March, 1825.
ST. LUCIA, 10th March, 1825.
ALIWAL, 8th June, 1847.
SOBRAON, 8th June, 1847.
PUNJAUB, 14th December, 1852.
GOOJERAT, 14th December, 1852.

85TH
PENINSULA, 6th April, 1815.
NIVE, 8th July, 1826.
FUENTES D'ONOR, 8th July, 1826.
BLADENSBURG, 26th August, 1826.

SHOULDER-BELT PLATES

53RD

Almack's book gives an illustration of the oval gilt plate with the design of the number '53' below a crown within a spray of leaves. The design was in silver. For the Grenadier Company a silver grenade was placed over the crown, and for the Light Company a bugle-horn took the place of the laurel wreath. In 1820 the plate was a gilt burnished one with the design mounted in silver (Fig. 411). The plate prior to 1855 was a burnished gilt one with the design in silver of '53' within a crowned garter and laurel wreath. The garter inscribed 'Shropshire'.

85TH

In the miniature of an officer of the 85th of the period 1800 the plate is shown as an oval silver one with a gilt rim and the design of '85' within a circle. The 85th plate of about 1815 was an oval silver one (Fig. 412) with the design mounted in the same metal. This was replaced by one of the design shown in Fig. 413. The plate was gilt with the design mounted in silver. Size 3 $\frac{1}{16}$ × 3 inches.

Mr. Hughes has in his collection a gilt burnished oblong plate with the design mounted in gilt of '85' below a bugle-horn, all within a crowned circle inscribed *Aucto splendore resurgo*, a spray of laurel below the circle and below this a scroll inscribed 'The King's Light Infantry'.

Prior to 1855 the design shown in Fig. 414 was worn. The plate was a gilt burnished one with the design mounted in silver. The drawing is from one in the collection of Mr. Tilling.

BUTTONS

53RD

The early pewter buttons had the design of '53' within a French scroll with a dot at the opening. The design was in relief and the button had a raised rim (Fig. 415).

This was followed by one with the design shown in Fig. 416 and then by one of a plain '53' in relief.

The officers' buttons in 1810 had the design of '53' below a crown.

On the introduction of the tunic in 1855 the design for the buttons became '53' within a garter inscribed 'Shropshire' in the centre of an eight-pointed star.

85TH

The officers' silver buttons and the pewter buttons of the other ranks of the 85th in 1800 had the design of '85' within a garter inscribed 'Bucks', all within a star of eight points (Fig. 417).

The officers' buttons in 1815 were silver with the title 'Duke of York's Own' on a crowned circle within which was the number '85', the whole on a star. When in 1821 the title was again changed, the same design was retained but the circle inscribed 'King's Light Infantry'. This design was retained on the gilt coatee button of the officers and on the subsequent tunic buttons.

After 1881 the design was the letters 'K.L.I.' within a crowned circle, at the bottom of which was a spray of laurel leaves.

The 1904 Dress Regulations gives the mess dress button as having the design as for the tunic, but mounted.

411

412

413

414

415

416

417

THE MIDDLESEX REGIMENT
(DUKE OF CAMBRIDGE'S OWN)

TITLES
1st Battalion
1755-1757 The 57th Regiment of Foot, renumbered the 55th.
1755-1757 The 59th Regiment of Foot, renumbered the 57th.
1757-1782 The 57th Regiment of Foot.
1782-1881 The 57th (West Middlesex) Regiment of Foot.

2nd Battalion
1757-1758 The 62nd Regiment of Foot, renumbered 77th.
1758-1763 The 77th (Montgomery's Highlanders) Regiment. Disbanded.
1777-1783 The 77th Athol Highlanders. Disbanded.
1787-1807 The 77th Regiment of Foot.
1807-1876 The 77th (East Middlesex) Regiment of Foot.
1876-1881 The 77th (East Middlesex) (or Duke of Cambridge's Own) Regiment of Foot.
1881-1920 The Duke of Cambridge's Own (Middlesex Regiment).
1920-   The Middlesex Regiment (Duke of Cambridge's Own).

BADGES
The Prince of Wales's Coronet, Plume and motto. Granted to the 77th Regiment, 20th February, 1810.
The Duke of Cambridge's Cypher and Coronet. Authorized as a badge to the 77th in 1876.
A Laurel Wreath and the Honour 'Albuhera'. Commemorates the outstanding gallantry of the 57th Regiment at the battle of that name.
The Arms of the County of Middlesex. Was an old badge of the 57th and of the East Middlesex Militia.

BATTLE HONOURS (*Dates authorized from* 1815 *to* 1855)
57TH
PENINSULA, 6th April, 1815.
ALBUHERA, 1st February, 1816.
VITTORIA, 29th July, 1817.
PYRENEES, 29th July, 1817.
NIVELLE, 29th July, 1817.
NIVE, 29th July, 1817.
INKERMAN, 16th October, 1855.
SEVASTOPOL, 16th October, 1855.

77TH

PENINSULA, 6th April, 1815.
CIUDAD RODRIGO, 4th December, 1817.
BADAJOZ, 4th December, 1817.
SERINGAPATAM, 28th May, 1818.
MYSORE, 28th May, 1818.
ALMA, 16th October, 1855.
INKERMAN, 16th October, 1855.
SEVASTOPOL, 16th October, 1855.

SHOULDER-BELT PLATES

57TH

In Mr. Tilling's collection is an oval gilt burnished plate with the design, also in gilt, of a crowned garter inscribed 'West Middlesex Regiment'; within the garter a shield bearing the arms of the county of Middlesex and the number '57'. Mr. Cattley has in his collection a similar plate which he describes as all gilt, die struck (in deep relief), matt ground.

In Mr. Reynolds' notes is a plate he dates as 1789-1800 period taken from a picture of an officer of the 57th in 1794. The plate is shown as gilt with the design of '57' within a single-line oval.

Soon after 1816 the officers had an oval gilt plate with the design mounted in silver of '57' below a crown and with a spray of laurel below the number; above the crown a scroll inscribed 'Albuhera', and one below the spray inscribed 'Peninsula'.

A plate of the 57th sold at the Day collection is described as silver, oblong, stamped hollow '57' crowned within a laurel wreath; above, 'Albuhera'. The plate was hall-marked 1823. This is probably the plate which came after the oval one and was worn until about 1830. The use of silver is strange as the 57th was a gold-laced regiment.

Fig. 418 is the plate worn by officers *circa* 1836, and Fig. 419 that worn by other ranks in brass at the same period until 1855.

Prior to 1855 the officers' plate was a gilt burnished one with a silver diamond cut star of the Grand Cross of the Order of the Bath complete, with a crown above the cross which was in gilt; the motto of the Order was in gilt letters on a crimson enamel girdle of silver, with three gilt crowns on a white enamel centre. Below the cross, resting on the rays of the star, was a silver label with the number '57'. The rays of the cross are inscribed 'Albuhera', 'Nivelle', 'Nive' 'Vittoria', 'Pyrenees' and 'Peninsula'.

77TH

Fig. 420 is a silver plate of about 1820. The design, also in silver, was mounted and the plate had the rounded corners of the period. Plate shown in Fig. 421 was in use after 1830 and possibly worn until 1855. The plate was burnished gilt with the design mounted in silver. The size of the plate was $3\frac{3}{4} \times 3\frac{1}{16}$ inches.

According to Mr. Reynolds' notes, the other ranks' plate worn prior to 1855 had the design of '77' surmounted by the Prince of Wales's plume.

BUTTONS

57TH

The officers' bone-backed button *circa* 1780 had the design in relief shown in Fig. 422. The men's pewter buttons of the period had the design of '57' in relief, the button having a roped border (Fig. 423). This design of men's buttons was replaced about 1790 by one of '57' within a French scroll with a dot at the opening; the button had a thin raised rim. The officers' coatee buttons *circa* 1810 were slightly convex, with open backs, the design of '57' below a crown. The coatee button, 1830-1855, for both officers and other ranks had the design of '57' below the word 'Albuhera' within a laurel wreath, and with a crown above 'Albuhera'. The same design was retained on the tunic buttons.

77TH

The officers' silver buttons *circa* 1800 were slightly convex with the design in relief of '77' below a crown within a French scroll. About 1810 the crown was replaced by the Prince of Wales's coronet, plume and motto (Fig. 424).

For a short time a silver button with the design of '77' surmounted by the Prince of Wales's coronet, plume and motto and all within a wreath of laurel was worn; and when in 1830 the lace of the regiment was changed from silver to gold, the design was retained on the gilt coatee button worn until 1855 and subsequently on the officers' tunic button until 1881 (Fig. 425).

The pewter button worn by the other ranks was of the same design and was worn on the tunic button until 1871.

After 1881 the buttons had the Prince of Wales's coronet, plume and motto within a laurel wreath, across the bottom of which was a scroll inscribed 'Albuhera'.

The 1900 Dress Regulations gives the cap button as having the design as for the tunic, but mounted in silver.

THE KING'S ROYAL RIFLE CORPS

TITLES

1756-1757	The 60th Regiment of Foot, renumbered as the 58th.
1755-1757	The 62nd (Royal American) Regiment of Foot, renumbered.
1757-1815	The 60th (Royal American) Regiment of Foot.
1815-1824	The 60th (Royal American) Light Infantry.
1824	June: The 60th Royal American Regiment; 1st Battalion Rifle Corps; 2nd Battalion Light Infantry.
1824	July: The 60th (The Duke of York's Own); 1st Battalion Rifle Corps; 2nd Battalion Light Infantry.
1824	August: The 60th (Duke of York's Own Rifle Corps); 1st Battalion Rifle Corps; 2nd Battalion Light Infantry.
1824	September: The 60th Duke of York's Own Rifle Corps.
1830-1881	The 60th King's Royal Rifle Corps.
1881	The King's Royal Rifle Corps.
1920	The King's Royal Rifles.
1921	The King's Royal Rifle Corps.

BADGES

The Maltese Cross with Crown. The Regimental History suggests that the cross was adopted from Hompesch's Regiment, from which the 5th Rifle Battalion of the 60th Royal Americans was largely formed. The cross is said to have been copied from the Bavarian War Medal.

Motto: *Celer et Audax*. According to tradition, given as a reward for the services of the regiment before Quebec. Permission to resume was datep 30th September, 1824.

A Bugle-horn. Was the badge of the old 5th Rifle Battalion. During the 1850 period the design on the head-dress was a French bugle-horn.

BATTLE HONOURS (*Dates authorized from 1815 to 1855*)

PENINSULA, to old 5th (Rifle) Battalion, 6th April, 1815.
MARTINIQUE, to old 3rd Battalion, 28th August, 1817.
ROLEIA, 21st September, 1821.*
VIMIERA, 21st September, 1821.
TALAVERA, 21st September, 1821.
FUENTES D'ONOR, 21st September, 1821.
CIUDAD RODRIGO, 21st September, 1821.
BADAJOZ, 21st September, 1821.
SALAMANCA, 21st September, 1821.
VITTORIA, 21st September, 1821.
NIVELLE, 21st September, 1821.
ORTHES, 21st September, 1821.
TOULOUSE, 21st September, 1821.
ALBUHERA, 12th January, 1825.

---

* Had been granted to old 2nd and 3rd Battalions, 5th June, 1821.

PYRENEES, 12th January, 1825.
NIVE, 12th January, 1825.
To resume motto *Celer et Audax*, 30th September, 1824.
PUNJAUB, 14th December, 1852.
MOOLTAN, 14th December, 1852.
GOOJERAT, 14th December, 1852.

SHOULDER-BELT AND POUCH-BELT PLATES

The Regimental History Appendix on the uniform of the regiment states that in 1770 small silver buckles were worn on the shoulder belt, and that it was between 1776 and 1780 that the silver oval shoulder-belt plates with the design shown in Fig. 426 engraved was adopted. One of these plates is in the Regimental Museum. Officers of the Grenadier Company wore this plate, but had a gilt grenade with the number '60' on the ball in the centre within the garter.

About 1800, according to a miniature of an officer in the Museum, the plate was oblong, silver, with rounded corners, with the design of 'LX', with the word 'Royal' in a straight line above and 'Americans', also in a straight line, below. The plates worn by the other ranks at this period were brass with the design incised.

Fig. 427 is the plate worn by the 1st Battalion. In the case of the 2nd Battalion the plate was oval with the number '2' above '60', probably incised. In the case of the 3rd and 4th Battalions the plates were oval and had the number '60' surmounted by a crown, and the number of the battalion below.

The officers of battalions other than the 5th, in 1812-1818, had silver oblong plates engraved with the design of the Royal cypher 'G.R.', surmounted by a crown, and below the cypher the number '60'. The plates had rounded corners.

According to the Regimental History, the officers of 5th (Rifle) Battalion when raised in 1797 had on their pouch belts the usual whistle and chain and a silver Maltese Cross. The authority for this is a miniature of Captain John Wolff, who served in the 5th Battalion, 1797-1808.

The History gives an illustration of the plate which is apparently based on the miniature, but the uniform shown agrees more with that of Hompesch's Chasseurs, in which Captain Wolff had previously served. Hompesch's Chasseurs had green jackets and breeches with red collars, while the 5th Battalion 60th had green jackets and distinctive blue breeches.

In 1815 the Honour 'Peninsula' was given to the Battalion. The author has seen an open-work scroll inscribed with this Honour and which, as it came from a family connected with the 60th, may well have been worn on the belt.

Hamilton Smith's sketches in the South Kensington Museum show the private riflemen of the 5th Battalion wearing black belts with oval brass shoulder-belt plates with a plain '60'.

In 1815 the regiment was given the title 60th (Royal American) Light Infantry and all battalions were put into green; it is probable that the pouch belt of Rifle Corps was adopted by officers of all battalions, and when in 1821 the Peninsular Honours were awarded the plate shown in Fig. 428 was taken into use.

In June, 1824, the Regiment was comprised of two battalions, the 1st Battalion being Rifles and the 2nd Battalion Light Infantry. The following month the old title of Royal Americans was discarded and they became 60th Duke of York's Own and consisted of the 1st Battalion Rifle Corps, 2nd Battalion Light Infantry. In August the title was again changed and they became 60th (Duke of York's Own Rifle Corps), but the 2nd Battalion continued to be described as Light Infantry until September, when both battalions were Rifles. The plates Figs. 428 and 429 were evidently worn by the two battalions respectively during this period.

From 1828 to 1830 the badge on the pouch belt was a Maltese Cross surmounted by a crown resting on a label inscribed 'Peninsula'; in the centre of the cross the number '60' between the cords of a bugle-horn, the ends of the cords hanging outside the cords, all within a circle inscribed 'Duke of York's Own' 'First Rifle Corps'. The limbs of the cross are inscribed with fifteen Battle Honours (Fig. 430).

After 1830 the same design, but with the change of title on the circle, was worn until 1883, when the label inscribed 'Peninsula' was replaced by one inscribed *Celer et Audax*, the Battle Honours on the limbs of the cross increased to thirty-two and the number '60', removed from between the cords of the bugle-horn to hang down between the cords.

As additional Honours were awarded they were added to those on the limbs of the cross until 1906, when, there being no room for further Honours, the old badge of the Regiment with '60' between the strings of the bugle-horn was adopted for the officers' pouch-belt plate.

BUTTONS

Of the early pewter buttons worn by other ranks there are records of three designs:

(*a*) The number '60' engraved; the button had a roped border (Fig. 431).
(*b*) The number '60' in relief; the button had a roped border.
(*c*) The number '60' within a wreath of leaves, the design in relief (Fig. 432).

The probable order of wearing was as above.

The officers' bone-backed buttons of 1780-1790 had silver faces with the design in relief as worn in 1800 on the flat silver one-piece buttons (Fig. 433), and which was retained on the subsequent convex button.

In the case of the 2nd and 4th Battalions the design was of '2' on '4' below 'LX', within a crowned garter inscribed *Honi soit qui mal y pense*. Whether all battalions wore buttons of this design with their battalion number specified is not certain.

From 1824 to 1830 the officers' silver ball buttons had the letters 'D.Y.O.R.'

Black rifle buttons were taken into wear in 1830. The officers' buttons had the design of '60' within the strings of a bugle-horn, tied with a bow, above which was a crown and with a spray of laurel below. The other ranks' button had, in the case of the 2nd Battalion, the design of a crown above '60' with '2' below. The tunic buttons, 1856-1881, retained the design as worn by the officers on the 1830 buttons. After 1881 the design was the same except for the omission of the regimental number. The ball button is still worn by officers.

262

THE WILTSHIRE REGIMENT
(THE DUKE OF EDINBURGH'S)

TITLES

1ST BATTALION

1755-1757   The 62nd (Royal American) Regiment of Foot, renumbered 60th.

1757-1758   The 62nd (1st Highland Battalion) Regiment of Foot, renumbered 77th (Montgomery's Highlanders).

1756-1758   2nd Battalion the 4th (King's Own) Regiment of Foot. Regimented 62nd.

1758-1782   The 62nd Regiment of Foot.

1782-1881   The 62nd (The Wiltshire) Regiment of Foot.

2ND BATTALION

1761-1763   The 99th Regiment of Foot. Disbanded.

1780-1784   The 99th (Jamaica) Regiment of Foot. Disbanded.

1794-1796   The 99th Regiment of Foot. Disbanded.

1804-1811   The 99th Regiment of Foot.

1811-1816   The 99th or Prince of Wales's Tipperary Regiment of Foot. Renumbered.

1816-1818   The 98th or Prince of Wales's Tipperary Regiment of Foot. Disbanded.

1805-1812   The 100th Regiment of Foot.

1812-1816   The 100th (H.R.H. The Prince Regent's County of Dublin) Regiment of Foot.

1816-1818   The 99th (H.R.H. The Prince Regent's County of Dublin) Regiment of Foot. Disbanded.

1824-1832   The 99th Regiment of Foot.

1832-1874   The 99th (Lanarkshire) Regiment of Foot.

1874-1881   The 99th (The Duke of Edinburgh's) Regiment of Foot.

1881-1920   The Duke of Edinburgh's (Wiltshire Regiment).

1920-   The Wiltshire Regiment (Duke of Edinburgh's).

BADGES

The Duke of Edinburgh's Coronet and Cypher. Authorized to the 99th with title 22nd April, 1874.

A Maltese Cross. An old badge of the 62nd, said to commemorate the services of the 62nd in Sicily in 1806.

BATTLE HONOURS (*Dates authorized from 1829 to 1855*)
62ND

PENINSULA, to the 62nd as a Regiment, 26th May, 1829.
NIVE, 1st February, 1844.
FEROZESHAH, 8th June, 1847.
SOBRAON, 8th June, 1847.
SEVASTOPOL, 16th October, 1855.

SHOULDER-BELT PLATES
62ND

Information concerning the plates worn by the 62nd is scarce.

A feature of the plates of the regiment appears to have always been the cut corners to the plate. The earliest plate worn by the regiment was a small silver engraved plate, oblong in shape, with the corners slightly cut. The design was the Royal arms prior to 1800, and below the arms on a scroll the motto *Dieu et mon droit*. Below the motto the number 'LXII', and below this the title 'Wilts'. The whole within a star of eight points. The size of the plate was $2 \times 2\frac{3}{4}$ inches.

The officers of the Grenadier Company had a similar silver eight-sided plate with the design of '62' and a grenade within a star. A later plate was still oblong with cut corners and had the design engraved of '62' surmounted by a crown, below the number a curved scroll inscribed 'or Wiltshire Regiment', at the foot of the plate a thin spray of laurel leaves. At the top of the plate the letters 'G' and 'R' on either side of the crown respectively. The size of the plate was $3 \times 2\frac{3}{4}$ inches (Fig. 434).

Fig. 435 is from a plate in the collection of Mr. Usher. The plate is burnished gilt with '62' within a wreath on a matted ground, all gilt, in the centre of a Maltese Cross of cut silver with a silver crown. The size of the plate is $3\frac{7}{8} \times 3$ inches.

A plate of similar design, but all silver, is in the Royal United Service Institution collection.

Mr. Hughes has in his collection a silver plate with cut corners and the cross and crown design, but along the top rim of the upper limb of the cross is inscribed 'Peninsula'. The Honour was granted the 62nd in 1829.

The other ranks' brass plate prior to 1855 had the design of '62' within a crowned garter inscribed 'or Wiltshire', all on a star of eight points, the rays having beaded edges; across the bottom of the rays was a scroll inscribed 'Peninsula'.

99TH

The officers' plate of about 1816 was an oblong silver one with cut corners, the design mounted in silver of '99' within a garter inscribed 'Prince of Wales's Tipperary Regt.'; above the garter the Prince of Wales's plume, coronet and motto.

In the late Mr. Reynolds' notes is described a shoulder-belt plate of the 99th in 1839 as gilt with the following design: '99' within a crowned garter and wreath, all in gilt, the garter inscribed *Honi soit qui mal y pense*. The background to the numerals silver, all on a silver cut star of eight points.

BUTTONS

62ND

The early bone-backed officers' button had the design of '62' in relief within a narrow circle of leaves turned inwards, with a wire-bound design similar to that worn at this period by the officers of the 17th. This was replaced after a short time by a design in relief of '62' within a French scroll with a dot at the opening (Fig. 436). The pewter buttons of the other ranks had the same design.

Tradition says that at one time a splash or dent was worn in the men's buttons to commemorate the use of their buttons as bullets in the defence of Carrickfergus, but the author has never seen or heard of any being in existence. It is possible that the dot at the opening of the French scroll gave rise to the tradition.

About 1800 the officers' buttons were flat, single piece, with the design in relief (Fig. 437). These gave place to one with '62' within a crowned garter inscribed 'Peninsula', with a wreath of laurel below, the buttons remaining silver, flat, single piece until 1830, when the same design was worn on the gilt buttons.

On the introduction of the tunic, the earlier design of '62' within a French scroll and dot was reverted to (Fig. 438).

99TH

The buttons of the 99th or Jamaica Regiment of Foot, which was disbanded in 1784, had on them an alligator, the crest of the island.

The officers of the 99th Regiment of 1824 at first for a short time had the simple design of '99' engraved on a gilt convex button.

The coatee button, 1830-1855, had '99' below an ornamental crown; the button had a cut rim.

The tunic buttons of 1855-1874 had the number '99' below a crown and within a French scroll, but no dot at the opening. After 1874, when the title The Duke of Edinburgh's was conferred, the officers' buttons had '99' below a ducal coronet, and below the number a scroll inscribed 'Duke of Edinburgh's Regt'.

After 1881 the design on the buttons was the Duke of Edinburgh's coronet and cypher and the title 'Wiltshire Regiment' below.

The 1900 Dress Regulations gives the cap and mess dress button as having the design mounted in silver as for the tunic, but with the title omitted. The cap button was die struck.

434 435

436 437

438

THE MANCHESTER REGIMENT

TITLES

1st Battalion

1756-1758   2nd Battalion 8th King's Regiment of Foot. Regimented.
1757-1758   The 63rd (or 2nd Highland Battalion) Regiment of Foot. Renumbered 78th.
1758-1782   The 63rd Regiment of Foot.
1782-1881   The 63rd (West Suffolk) Regiment of Foot.

2nd Battalion

1761-1763   The 96th Regiment of Foot. Disbanded.
1780-1783   The 96th (British Musketeers) Regiment. Disbanded.
1793-1795   The 96th (The Queen's Royal Irish) Regiment. Dispersed.
1802-1816   The 96th Regiment of Foot, originally raised as the 2nd Battalion 52nd Regiment and renumbered the 95th in 1816, and as such disbanded in 1818.
1816-1818   The 96th (Queen's Own) Regiment of Foot, raised in 1798 as The Minorca Regiment, became the Queen's Germans in 1801, numbered the 97th in 1805, and renumbered the 96th in 1816. Disbanded in 1818.
1824-1881   The 96th Regiment of Foot.

1881-   The Manchester Regiment.

BADGES

The Arms of the City of Manchester. Adopted with title and worn as a helmet and cap badge, 1881, and as a collar badge in service dress. In the case of the 2nd Battalion it was worn for a short time and then replaced by a crowned star with the Sphinx in the centre.

The Sphinx on a plinth inscribed 'Egypt' was given to the 96th Regiment (raised in 1798) for service in 1801, and was granted to the later 96th Regiment, 16th June, 1874.

Soon after the granting of the badge to the Queen's German Regiment, the Sphinx was displayed with a captured French standard over its left shoulder, commemorating the fighting before Alexandria when a soldier of the regiment, after a single combat, captured and carried to headquarters the standard of a famous French demi-brigade known as the "Invincibles." The standard is said to have previously been taken by The Black Watch, but lost in the severe hand-to-hand fighting which later took place.

The Fleur-de-lis. Authorized as a badge for the regiment, 21st January, 1922. Commemorates the services of the 63rd in the West Indies.

BATTLE HONOURS (*Dates authorized from 1802 to 1855*)

63RD

MARTINIQUE, 1st October, 1819.
GUADALOUPE, 1st October, 1819.
EGMONT-OP-ZEE, 18th June, 1830.
ALMA, 16th October, 1855.
INKERMAN, 16th October, 1855.
SEVASTOPOL, 16th October, 1855.

96TH

The old Honours granted to the 96th, raised in 1798, were authorized to the later regiment on 16th June, 1874. They were EGYPT AND THE SPHINX and PENINSULA, which had been authorized originally on 6th July, 1802, and 6th April, 1815, respectively.

SHOULDER-BELT PLATES

63RD

I am indebted to Mr. H. Y. Usher, who has made a great study of the shoulder-belt plates of the 63rd and 96th, for most of the following details.

In Major Slack's History of the 63rd (West Suffolk) Regiment, published in 1884, it is stated that the fleur-de-lis was worn on the epaulette and was engraved on the regimental plate, but by this is probably meant mess silver.

Colonel Westrop also carried out a lot of research concerning the regiment's shoulder-belt plates, and states: "So far as I have been able to ascertain, the badge never appeared on the officers' breast plates, but showed the badge on the epaulette." Then follows a footnote to the effect that in a miniature of Ambrose William Barcroft "the badge is shown above 63." The present owner of the miniature sent Mr. Usher a rough drawing of the plate, stating that it is not given in great detail.*

Mr. Usher very rightly suggests that what has been given as a fleur-de-lis may be a grenade, denoting the Grenadier Company.

However, Major P. Young has a miniature of Major Johns, 1797-1810, which he states clearly shows the badge. Also in 1918, at Messrs. Glendining, was sold a silver hall-marked 1798 plate, oval, with the design engraved of the fleur-de-lis and '63rd' in Roman characters; a circular garter with 'West Suffolk Regiment'.

Figs. 439 and 440 are early silver shoulder-belt plates.

Fig. 439 is drawn from an actual plate in the collection of Mr. Usher and has hall-mark of 1793.†

---

* A plate sold at Messrs. Glendinings in 1918 had the addition of the fleur-de-lis placed above the number, but this may well have been put on unofficially and privately.

† Actually this date letter is unique in design among all the letters 's' used in any cycle or by any Assay office in the United Kingdom. The 's' on the plate in question has a stroke across the middle.

Fig. 440 is drawn from Almack's book, but as far as I know no actual plate of this shape exists. The late Mr. Milne, in an article he wrote in the *Journal of the R.U.S.I.* in 1902, said that "the plate represents the oldest officers' breast plate of the 63rd." Mr. L. E. Buckell states much more information is now available generally than in Milne's day. He is of opinion that Fig. 440 may have been worn by the 2nd Battalion 63rd (1804-1812). A number of the plates shown in Almack's book are of 2nd Battalions, drawn from Goetze's Bench Book of 1809. Fig. 439 would therefore appear to have been the earliest worn by officers of the 63rd.

About 1822 the plate was silver, oblong, with a burnished rim, and having the design mounted in gilt of '63' below a crown and within a laurel wreath.

When in 1830 the regimental lace was changed to gold, the metal of the plate would have been changed.

This was followed by one of the design in Fig. 441. The plate was burnished gilt with the design mounted in gilt. The numerals have a frosted surface. After the granting in 1830 of the Honour 'Egmont-op-Zee' the same general design was retained, but the Honour was added on a scroll above the crown and there was a slight difference in the wreath.

The other ranks' brass plate 1830 had the design of '63' within a crowned garter, all superimposed on a star with square ends to its rays. Above the crown was a scroll inscribed 'Martinique' and below one inscribed 'Guadaloupe'. Later, about 1844-1855, the Honour 'Egmont-op-Zee' was placed above the star and 'Guadaloupe' below the star, 'Martinique' resting across the lower portion of the star.

96TH

In Mr. Usher's collection is an early silver gilt plate worn 1802-1818, probably by the 96th, which were disbanded as the 95th in 1818. The plate is oblong with the design mounted in silver of '96' below a crown (Fig. 442).

The Minorca Regiment, which became the Queen's German Regiment in 1801, had on their oval shoulder-belt plates the design of the Sphinx within a crowned garter inscribed with the title. When in 1805 they were numbered the 97th, the design was as shown in Fig. 443.

The plate was gilt with a beaded rim; the Sphinx, number and letters, which were pierced, and the garter, were all in gilt on a silver star. Behind the Sphinx and the garter was a bright blue ground.

The Sphinx shown in both these plates did not have the captured French standard over its shoulder.

When in 1816 the regiment was renumbered 96th, the same design as worn before was retained with the necessary alteration of the number (Fig. 444). This was replaced by the design of '96' surmounted by the Sphinx with the flag; a spray of laurel leaves on either side of the central design and a scroll at their point of joining inscribed 'Queen's Own'. This would appear to have been the last shoulder-belt plate worn by the old 96th Queen's Own, disbanded in 1818.

The 96th raised in 1824 had a gilt plate with the design mounted in silver as shown in Fig. 445. The plate was frosted.

BUTTONS

63RD

The officers' bone-backed buttons worn in the 1780 period had silver faces with the design sunk of '63' within a single-line circle in centre of a star of eight points. The other ranks' pewter button had the same design (Fig. 446). This was the design on the buttons until 1881, with various minor changes in the design of the star. About 1800 the rays were short, but later became longer for a time; but on the coatee gilt button about 1830 they once more became smaller. On the tunic button the design was in relief.

96TH

The buttons of the 97th Queen's German Regiment had the design of '97' below a crown within a spray of palm. Below this the title 'Queen's German Regt'. Later changed to one of the same design, but inscribed 'or Queen's Own'.

At the time of disbandment the design was '96' below a Sphinx with flag and within a wreath of laurel. At the top of the button the Honour 'Peninsula' and below the wreath the title 'Queen's Own'. The buttons were gilt, convex, open back, and had the design in relief (Fig. 447).

The officers' gilt coatee buttons and the other ranks' pewter buttons of the 96th raised in 1824 had the design in relief of '96' below a crown and within a French scroll without a dot at the opening.

This gave place soon after 1830 to the design of '96' within a crowned garter inscribed *Honi soit qui mal y pense*. This design was worn on the officers' tunic until 1881.

After 1881 until the present day the design has been of the crowned garter with a Sphinx inscribed 'Egypt' in its centre. The Sphinx is of the usual design and does not display the flag. There is considerable diversity in the way the tail is shown.

The 1904 Dress Regulations gives the mess dress button design as for the tunic, but mounted in silver. In the 1934 Regulations the cap button is given as die struck.

439

440

THE NORTH STAFFORDSHIRE REGIMENT (THE PRINCE OF WALES'S)

TITLES

1ST BATTALION

 1756-1758 The 2nd Battalion 11th Regiment of Foot. Regimented as 64th, 1758.

 1758-1782 The 64th Regiment of Foot.

 1782-1881 The 64th (2nd Staffordshire) Regiment of Foot.

2ND BATTALION

 1761-1763 The 98th Regiment of Foot. Disbanded.

 1780-1785 The 98th Regiment of Foot. Disbanded.

 1794-1798 The 98th (Highland) Regiment of Foot, renumbered 91st.

 1804-1816 The 98th Regiment of Foot. Disbanded in 1818 as the 97th Regiment.

 1804-1818 The 99th (Prince of Wales's Tipperary) Regiment of Foot. Renumbered the 98th in 1816 and disbanded in 1818.

 1824-1876 The 98th Regiment of Foot.

 1876-1881 The 98th (The Prince of Wales's) Regiment of Foot.

 1881-1920 The Prince of Wales's (North Staffordshire Regiment).

 1920- The North Staffordshire Regiment (The Prince of Wales's).

BADGES

The Dragon of China. Commemorates the services of the 98th in the China War of 1842. The badge was authorized 12th January, 1843.

The Prince of Wales's Coronet, Plume and motto. Authorized for the 98th, 17th October, 1876, when the title Prince of Wales's was conferred.

The Stafford Knot. An old badge of the 64th Regiment.

BATTLE HONOURS (*Dates authorized from 1818 to 1855*)

64TH

 ST. LUCIA, 31st January, 1818.

 SURINAM, 31st January, 1818.

98TH

 CHINA, 12th January, 1843.

 PUNJAUB, 14th December, 1854.

 SEVASTOPOL, 16th October, 1855.

SHOULDER-BELT PLATES

64TH

The gilt oval plate *circa* 1800 (Fig. 448) had the design mounted in silver of '64' below a crown within a French scroll and with a dot at the opening.

Mr. Reynolds records two plates: One which was sold in 1916 had a burnished surface with raised ornaments, all gilt, with the design of '64' inside a circle inscribed 'St. Lucia, Surinam', all within a cut star of eight points, the bays very shallow; below the circle the Stafford knot. The other plate, he states, was as worn in the centre of the shako plate, but without a crown. The design was mounted on a silver star with dead gilt '64' on plain silver ground, gilt scrolls, crown, wreath and knot. Other ranks' brass plates, 1820–1830, had the design of 'LXIV' below the Stafford knot. Above the knot was the title '2nd Staffordshire', all this within a wreath of laurel; below the wreath a scroll inscribed 'Surinam' and above at the opening of the wreath a crown resting on a scroll inscribed 'St. Lucia'. The one used prior to the Crimean War had '64' below a crown, with a knot below and a wreath of leaves (Fig. 449).

98TH

Fig. 450 is the shoulder-belt plate probably worn by the 98th (Prince of Wales's Tipperary) Regiment of Foot before 1816 when they were numbered the 99th. The regiment was disbanded as the 98th in 1818.

Fig. 451 is that worn by the 98th Regiment of Foot, raised in 1824. The plate was gilt with a silver star and gilt crown, wreath and numerals. The size was $3\frac{3}{4} \times 3\frac{15}{16}$ inches.

BUTTONS

64TH

The early pewter buttons were of two designs, and it is hard to say which was the earlier; possibly both were worn at the same time but by different battalions of the regiment.

(*a*) Pewter with '64' within a wreath. Mr. Calver placed the date as 1778.

(*b*) Flat pewter with the number '64' in relief with a roped rim.

The officers' bone-backed button had the design in relief of '64' within a wreath of leaves (Fig. 452).

Circa 1800 the officers had flat, gilt, single-piece buttons with the design of '64' in relief; the button had a roped rim. The other ranks' pewter buttons of this period had the same design.

Soon after 1800 the officers' buttons, which were still flat, single piece, had the design of '64' within a wreath of laurel leaves and surmounted by a crown.

This design gave place about 1830 to a convex button with the design in relief of the knot surmounted by the number '64' and a crown, within a wreath of leaves; around the top edge of the button was inscribed '2nd Staffordshire' and at the bottom 'Regiment'. This button was worn until 1855. The other ranks' pewter buttons at this time had the design of '64' below a crown, the button having a raised rim.

On the introduction of the tunic the buttons had plain '64' below a crown.

98TH

A portrait of Major the Honourable Charles Cathcart of the 98th Regiment, disbanded in 1785, shows the buttons with the design of a plain '98'.

The officers' buttons of the 99th H.R.H. Prince Regent's County of Dublin Regiment, disbanded as the 98th in 1818, were gilt, slightly convex, open-backed, and had the design of the Prince of Wales's coronet, plume and motto above the number '99'.*

The officers' buttons *circa* 1824 were flat, gilt, single piece, with the design in relief of '98' below a crown within a single-line circle (Fig. 453). The pewter buttons worn by the other ranks at the same period had the same design. The officers' and other ranks' coatee buttons *circa* 1830-1855 had the same design, but the button had a scalloped rim. The crown in the case of the officers' buttons was of a peculiar design, having a very ornamental arch. This design was retained on the tunic buttons, but in one die at least the crown was of the usual design.

After 1881 the design was the Stafford knot within a circle inscribed 'The North Staffordshire Regiment', above the circle the Prince of Wales's coronet and plume, but without the motto. Below the circle, superimposed on a laurel wreath, a scroll inscribed 'Prince of Wales's'.

The 1900 Dress Regulations gives the cap and mess dress button as having the design as on the tunic, but mounted and with the coronet, plume and knot.

---

* The Inspection Report dated 18th May, 1809, says: "King's Regulations complied with, except in the crest and motto of H.R.H. the Prince of Wales being on some of the appointments."

448   449

450   451

452   453

275

THE YORK AND LANCASTER REGIMENT

TITLES
1ST BATTALION
    1756–1758   The 2nd Battalion 12th Regiment of Foot, renumbered in 1758.
    1758–1782   The 65th Regiment of Foot.
    1782–1881   The 65th (2nd Yorkshire North Riding) Regiment of Foot.

2ND BATTALION
    1758–1763   The 84th Regiment of Foot. Disbanded.
    1775–1779   The Royal Highland Emigrant Corps; soon became known as
    1779–1784   The 84th (Royal Highland Emigrant) Regiment of Foot. Disbanded.
    1794–1809   The 84th Regiment of Foot.
    1809–1881   The 84th York and Lancaster Regiment of Foot.
    1881–   The York and Lancaster Regiment.

BADGES
The Royal Tiger. Commemorates the services of the 65th Regiment in India, 1796-1819.
The badge and Honour 'India' were authorized, 24th February, 1823.
The Union Rose. Authorized as a badge 18th November, 1820. The title 'York and Lancaster' was given to the 84th, 1809.
A Coronet. Worn by the 84th Regiment and would appear to have first been displayed on the shoulder-belt plates about 1811.

BATTLE HONOURS (*Dates authorized from 1815 to 1855*)
65TH
    TIGER AND INDIA, 24th February, 1823.
    ARABIA, 24th February, 1824.

84TH
    PENINSULA, 29th March, 1815 (to the 2nd Battalion).
    PENINSULA, 5th February, 1818 (to the whole Regiment).
    NIVE, 5th February, 1818.
    INDIA, 12th December, 1826.

SHOULDER-BELT PLATES
65TH
Almack's book shows an oval gilt plate with the design of an eight-pointed star engraved and coloured gilt. Superimposed on this was a smaller eight-pointed silver star, in the centre of which on a red backing within a silver

beaded oval the number '65'. This design (Fig. 454) appears to have been worn from about 1780 until 1800 or later.

Mr. L. E. Buckell records it as being shown in the portrait of Colonel St. Leger in Buckingham Palace, painted in 1782 or possibly, according to Armstrong, in 1778. There is also a miniature in the Victoria and Albert Museum of Ensign E. V. Fitzgerald, 1797, showing the badge still in use then.

About 1823 the officers' plate was oblong, gilt, with the design in silver of the tiger below a scroll inscribed 'India', the scroll surmounted by a crown. Below the tiger the number 'LXV', a wreath of laurel leaves around the whole, and below the wreath a scroll inscribed 'Arabia'.

This plate was replaced by one in which the tiger was shown in a crouching position with a scroll inscribed 'India', above which a crown, and with a scroll inscribed 'Arabia' below the tiger.

According to the late Mr. P. W. Reynolds, the plate displayed no number.

84TH

Fig. 455 is probably the plate worn by the 84th Royal Highland Emigrant Regiment of 1779-1784. The later 84th were, when raised in 1794, a silver-laced regiment.

A miniature of Lieutenant A. Bower, who was in the Light Company of the 84th in 1794, shows him wearing an oval gilt plate with the design of '84' below a bugle-horn within a crowned garter.

About 1800, according to Almack's book, the design on the plate was '84' below a crown within a thick French scroll with a dot at the opening.

Soon after 1820 or, according to the late Rev. P. Sumner, 1811, the plate was a silver oblong one with rounded corners. The design, also in silver, was '84' below a rose within a garter inscribed 'York & Lancaster Regiment' and surmounted by a crown (Fig. 456).

The plate in use in 1826 (Fig. 457) appears to have been oblong, silver, with the design of '84' below a rose within a garter inscribed 'York & Lancaster', a wreath of laurel around. Above the garter a scroll inscribed 'India' surmounted by a coronet, at the bottom of the garter a scroll inscribed 'Nive', and below the wreath one inscribed 'Peninsula'. The corners of the plate were slightly rounded. The size of the plate was 2 ⅞ × 3 ⅞ inches.

When after 1830 the colour of the plate was changed to gilt, the same design mounted in silver was retained and worn until 1855.

65TH **BUTTONS**

The early buttons for both officers and other ranks had '65'; the buttons had a roped rim (Fig. 458). Later buttons had the design of '65' within a raised single-line circle (Fig. 459).

The officers' coatee, 1840-1855, had the design of a crown, below which the Royal tiger and below the tiger the number '65', all within a French scroll; on the left, facing, the word 'India' and on the right 'Arabia', both within the circle.

This design was retained on the tunic buttons until 1881.

84TH

The officers' buttons of the 84th Royal Highland Emigrant Regiment of Foot were gilt, bone-backed, with the design shown in Fig. 460. The men's buttons had the design in Fig. 461.

Fig. 462 shows the officers' silver buttons *circa* 1800. They were slightly convex, open back, with the design in relief. After 1809 the design for both officers and other ranks was '84' below a ducal coronet and above a rose, with a laurel wreath around. This design was worn by the officers on silver buttons until 1830 and then on the gilt. It was retained on the tunic buttons until 1881, when the design became a tiger below a coronet and above a rose, at the join of the sprays of laurel. Below this a scroll inscribed 'York and Lancaster Regiment'.

The 1900 Dress Regulations gives the field service cap and mess dress buttons as having the tiger and rose in silver. The cap button was die struck.

454   455

456   457

458   459   460   461   462

T   279

THE DURHAM LIGHT INFANTRY

TITLES

1ST BATTALION
1756-1758   2nd Battalion 23rd Royal Welsh Fusiliers, regimented as 68th.
1756-1782   The 68th Regiment of Foot.
1782-1808   The 68th (Durham) Regiment of Foot.
1808-1881   The 68th (Durham Light Infantry) Regiment.

2ND BATTALION
1760-1763   The 106th (Black Musketeers) Regiment. Disbanded.
1794-1795   The 106th Regiment of Foot or Norfolk Rangers. Drafted.
1826-1858   The H.E.I.C. 2nd Bombay European Light Infantry.
1858-1861   The 2nd Bombay Light Infantry Regiment.
1861-1881   The 106th Bombay Light Infantry Regiment.
1881-   The Durham Light Infantry.

BADGES

A Light Infantry Bugle-horn. Adopted as a badge by the 68th in 1808 when the regiment was made Light Infantry.

A French Bugle-horn. Was worn on the shako star of 1861-1869 by the 106th Bombay Light Infantry and on the glengarry cap badge and buttons until 1881. With the bugle-horn in the case of the shako plate was a wreath of half laurel and half palm.

The Rose. Changed to the United Red and White Rose in 1888. The badge was given to the regiment in 1881 in common with other regiments which had no particular regimental design.

BATTLE HONOURS (*Dates authorized from 1815 to 1855*)

PENINSULA, 6th April, 1815.
SALAMANCA, 20th June, 1823.
PYRENEES, 20th June, 1823.
VITTORIA, 20th June, 1823.
NIVELLE, 20th June, 1823.
ORTHES, 20th June, 1823.
ALMA, 16th October, 1855.
INKERMAN, 16th October, 1855.
SEVASTOPOL, 16th October, 1855.

SHOULDER-BELT PLATES

About 1810 the officers' oval plate was silver with the design of '68' within a crowned girdle, the design mounted. The plate had a raised rim.

Before 1830 the plate was all silver and had slightly rounded corners. The design as shown in Fig. 463 was retained until 1855, but after 1830 the design in silver was mounted on a gilt burnished plate. The size of the plates remained the same for many years. Mr. Hughes has in his collection a copper coloured plate the size of which is 4⅛ × 3⅛ inches. The design is practically the same except that the crown is of the usual design and not of the peculiar design previously worn by the 68th. This plate may have been a warrant officer or N.C.O. plate.

BUTTONS

68TH

The officers' buttons of the 68th in 1800 were flat, silver, with the design in relief of '68' below a crown and resting on a bar, all within a French scroll with a dot at the opening (Fig. 464).

The men's pewter button *circa* 1780-1800 had in relief the design of '68' within a French scroll with a dot at the opening.

After the regiment became Light Infantry the officers' buttons were slightly convex, with the design of '68' within the cords of a Light Infantry bugle-horn suspended from a crown. At first the cords were tied in a bow, but about 1830 they were shown going into the base of the crown (Fig. 465). This design was worn by both officers and other ranks and was retained on the tunic button.

106TH

The coatee buttons, 1826-1855, had the design in relief of the numeral '2' inside the curl of a French bugle-horn surmounted by a crown.

The tunic buttons worn by the 106th from 1862 to 1881 had the design of '106' within the curl of a crowned French bugle-horn (Fig. 466); below the horn the title 'Bombay Light Infantry'.

Since 1881 the buttons have had the design of a Light Infantry bugle-horn suspended from a crown and showing no ends of the strings. The bugle-horn from about 1830 has had a lined surface.

The 1900 Dress Regulations gives the mess jacket button as having the letters 'DLI' in cypher below a crown. The design was mounted in gilt.

463

464 465 466

THE HIGHLAND LIGHT INFANTRY (CITY OF GLASGOW REGIMENT)

TITLES

1st Battalion

1758-1763   The 71st Regiment. Raised as the 2nd Battalion 32nd Regiment of Foot in 1756. Regimented in 1758.
1763-1769   The 71st Invalids. Raised as the 81st Invalids Regiment of Foot in 1758. Renumbered in 1763.
1775-1783   The 71st Highland Regiment of Foot or Fraser's Highlanders. Disbanded.
1777-1786   The 73rd (Highland) Regiment of Foot.
1786-1808   The 71st (Highland) Regiment of Foot.
1808-1809   The 71st (Glasgow, Highland) Regiment of Foot.
1809-1810   The 71st (Glasgow, Highland Light Infantry) Regiment.
1810-1881   The 71st (Highland) (Light Infantry).

2nd Battalion

1758-1763   Raised as 2nd Battalion 36th Regiment of Foot in 1756. Regimented as 74th, 1758. Disbanded.
1762-1769   Formed as the 117th (1762-1763) Invalids, became 74th Invalids, and dispersed as Independent Garrison Companies.
1777-1784   The 74th (Highland) Regiment of Foot, or the Argyll Highlanders. Disbanded.
1787-1816   The 74th (Highland) Regiment of Foot.
1816-1845   The 74th Regiment of Foot.
1845-1881   The 74th (Highlanders) Regiment of Foot.
1881-1923   The Highland Light Infantry.
1923-   The Highland Light Infantry (City of Glasgow Regiment).

BADGES

71ST

A French Bugle-horn. An old badge of the 71st. Appears to have been adopted about 1810.

74TH

The Elephant. As a reward for its services in India, and particularly at the battle of Assaye, the 74th Regiment were presented with a third or honorary Colour which had in its centre an elephant within a wreath of laurel; 15th April, 1817.
An Imperial Crown. As represented in the collar of the Order of the Star of India. Commemorates the long and distinguished services of the 74th in India.
The Star of the Order of the Thistle.

BATTLE HONOURS (*Dates authorized from 1815 to 1855*)

71ST

PENINSULA, 6th April, 1815.
ALMARAZ, 24th November, 1815.
WATERLOO, 8th December, 1815.
VITTORIA, 16th April, 1818.
PYRENEES, 16th April, 1818.
NIVE, 16th April, 1818.
ORTHES, 16th April, 1818.
ROLEIA,* 16th April, 1818.
VIMIERA, 16th April, 1818.
HINDOOSTAN, 23rd May, 1821.
CORUNNA, 11th May, 1835.
FUENTES D'ONOR, 11th May, 1835.
CAPE OF GOOD HOPE, 8th June, 1835.
SEVASTOPOL, 16th October, 1855.

74TH

PENINSULA, 6th April, 1815.
ASSAYE AND ELEPHANT, 15th April, 1817.
BUSACO, 16th June, 1817.
FUENTES D'ONOR, 16th June, 1817.
CIUDAD RODRIGO, 16th June, 1817.
BADAJOZ, 16th June, 1817.
SALAMANCA, 16th June, 1817.
NIVELLE, 16th June, 1817.
VITTORIA, 16th June, 1817.
PYRENEES, 16th June, 1817.
ORTHES, 16th June, 1817.
TOULOUSE, 16th June, 1817.
SERINGAPATAM, 28th May, 1818.

SHOULDER-BELT PLATES

71ST

The 71st were a silver-laced regiment until 1830, when they changed to gold.

An early officers' shoulder-belt plate of the Grenadier Company of the 71st had the design of '71' on the ball of a grenade. The plate was oblong and had a lined edge.

Fig. 467 is of an engraved silver plate worn by Captain H. Mackenzie, 1787-1794; later he became Paymaster of the regiment and served at Waterloo. Placed on half pay, 1824.

---

* An Army Order in 1911 directed the spelling to be "Rolica".

The silver oblong plate worn about 1814-1818 had the design of a bugle-horn which was surmounted by a crown. Below the bugle-horn was the number '71' and a spray of half thistle and half rose, the thistle spray being on the left. The design was engraved and the plate had rounded corners.

After this plate the design in Fig. 468 was worn until 1841. Among the 71st notes in the Campbell collection is a photograph of a 71st plate with the design of '71' within the strings of a Light Infantry bugle-horn, above which is a crown, below and on either side of the bugle-horn a thick spray of thistle. The photograph is unfortunately not very clear, and it is impossible to see if any scrolls figure in the design. Captain Campbell dated the plate as 1818-1832.

After 1841 the plate was of dead gilt with the design in burnished silver of '71' within the curl of a French bugle-horn, and which was worn until 1881.

74TH

The 74th, unlike the 71st, were a gold-laced regiment. Almack's book illustrates the 74th plate of 1800-1815 as having the design of '74' below a thistle with two leaves. The plate was gilt with the design mounted in silver and had a beaded rim.

Another plate of the period had the design of '74' surmounted by a crown, below the number a thistle with two leaves. The plate, which was silver, was oval with a raised rim. Whether this plate was earlier than that shown in Almack's book or whether it was worn by another battalion of the regiment is hard to say.

Fig. 469 is an engraved plate probably worn during the 1817-1820 period. About 1820, after the grant of the Peninsular Honours, a gilt burnished plate with the design (Fig. 470) mounted in silver was adopted.

The plate worn prior to 1881 had the design of '74' in silver on a silver background within a gilt crowned circle inscribed 'Highlanders', a spray of thistle below in silver, and below the spray in gilt metal an elephant on a scroll inscribed 'Assaye'. The whole mounted on a cut silver star of the Order of the Thistle. The rays of the cross are inscribed with twelve Battle Honours. The plate was burnished gilt.

BUTTONS

71ST

The officers' early button of the old 71st Fraser Highlanders had silver faces with the design engraved as shown in Fig. 471. The pewter buttons of the other ranks had the same design.

The officers' single-sheet silver buttons *circa* 1800 had the design of '71' engraved below a crown in low relief. The men's pewter buttons had the same design in relief.

The other ranks' pewter buttons, 1809-1814, had the design in relief of '71' within the strings of a Light Infantry bugle-horn, and below the horn a spray of laurel. The button had been replaced by 1815 by one with '71' below a crown, and soon after one with the design of '71' within the curl of a French bugle-horn with a crown above was adopted. This design was worn by the officers until 1881 and by other ranks until 1871 (Fig. 472).

74TH

The officers' bone-backed buttons *circa* 1780 had gilt faces with the design shown in Fig. 473 in relief. The other ranks' pewter buttons had a similar design.

About 1820 the design was '74' below an elephant, with crown above. Below the number '74' the Honour 'Assaye'. After this the design was changed to one with '74' below an elephant, with a crown above, around this a spray of grass, above the crown the Honour 'Assaye'.

The same design was retained on the officers' buttons until 1881. There were several designs of elephant in the tunic buttons, also in the spray of grass.

The diamond-shaped doublet button of the 74th at first had the design of '74' below a crown. The button had a raised border. The design was later changed to one with '74' below the elephant, with crown above, with 'Assaye' below the number. The button had a burnished rim.

After 1881 the design was as shown in Fig. 474.

The 1900 Dress Regulations gives the mess dress button as having the monogram 'HLI' below a crown, the design mounted in gilt.

467 468

469 470

471 472 473 474

SEAFORTH HIGHLANDERS (ROSS-SHIRE BUFFS, THE DUKE OF ALBANY'S)

TITLES

1ST BATTALION

- 1758-1763   The 72nd Regiment of Foot. Raised as 2nd Battalion 33rd Regiment in 1756. Renumbered in 1758.
- 1763-1769   The 72nd Invalids. Raised as 82nd Invalids in 1758. Renumbered in 1763.
- 1778-1783   The 72nd (Royal Manchester Volunteers) Regiment of Foot.
- 1786-1823   The 72nd (Highland) Regiment of Foot. Raised 1778 as 78th Highlanders or Seaforth Highlanders. Renumbered 72nd in 1786.
- 1823-1881   The 72nd (Duke of Albany's Own Highlanders).

2ND BATTALION

- 1758-1763   The 78th Regiment of Foot (2nd Highland Battalion or Fraser's Highlanders). Raised as 63rd in 1757. Renumbered 78th in 1758.
- 1778-1786   78th Highlanders or Seaforth Highlanders. Renumbered 72nd in 1786.
- 1793-1881   The 78th Highland Regiment of Foot (or Ross-shire Buffs).
- July 1881   Seaforth Highlanders (Ross-shire Buffs).
- Nov. 1881   Seaforth Highlanders (Ross-shire Buffs, The Duke of Albany's).

BADGES

The Stag's Head and the motto *Cuidich'n Righ* (Help to the King). The motto is that of the Mackenzies and is said, with the badge of the stag's head, to have been given to the founder of the clan in recognition of his having saved King Alexander II of Scotland from the attack of a wounded stag. The motto was on the Colours in 1794, but was not officially recognized until 1825. For many years the motto was spelt 'Rhi' and was amended to the correct spelling in 1869.

Motto: *Cabar Feidh* (Antlers of the Deer). The war-cry of the Seaforths.

Motto: *Tulloch Ard* (The High Hill). The war-cry of Kintail, a district of Lochbuich in Ross-shire, the old home of the Mackenzies. The allusion is to the mustering place of the clan.

The Coronet and Cypher of the Duke of Albany. Granted on 21st June, 1824. The title Duke of Albany's Own Highlanders had been given at the end of the year 1823. After the death of the Duke in 1827 the Army List gives it as the coronet and cypher of the late Duke of York.

The Elephant with 'Assaye'. Commemorates the services of the 78th Highlanders. Approved 16th April, 1807.

BATTLE HONOURS (*Dates authorized from* 1807 *to* 1859)

72ND
   HINDOOSTAN, 10th January, 1837.
   CAPE OF GOOD HOPE, 3rd March, 1836.
   SEVASTOPOL, 16th October, 1855.

78TH
   ASSAYE AND BADGE OF ELEPHANT, 16th April, 1807.
   MAIDA, 24th February, 1807.
   JAVA, 28th May, 1818.
   PERSIA, 21st January, 1859.
   KOOSHAB, 21st January, 1859.

SHOULDER-BELT PLATES

72ND

Fig. 475 is the officers' gilt shoulder-belt plate of the 72nd Royal Manchester Volunteers of 1778-1783. The plate was engraved.

The officers' plate of the 72nd Highlanders about 1800 was of silver with the design of '72' below a crowned garter. In the centre of the garter was the Royal cypher 'GR'. The garter was inscribed *Honi soit qui mal y pense*. The late Captain E. A. Campbell was of opinion that this was the first plate worn by the 72nd after being renumbered in 1786 (Fig. 476).

This plate, the late Major I. H. Mackay Scobie states, was followed by another oval one of similar design but larger, and had the 'GR' on a crimson ground.

The officers' plate some four years later had the design of '72' within a crowned circle; the plate was oval and of silver.

Major I. H. Mackay Scobie, in a letter to the author, describes a plate which he ascribes to the 72nd Highlanders *circa* 1810. The plate was silver, oblong, with square-cut corners, and had the design of '72' within the curl of a French scroll, with a crown at the opening; the design was in low relief. The use of the French scroll on breast plates was uncommon.

Fig. 477 is the brass other ranks' plate of 1825-1855. This plate was worn in white metal by N.C.Os.

The officers' plate in use prior to 1881 was of the same design as above, but had the design mounted in silver on a burnished plate.

78TH

Fig. 478 is a silver plate with engraved design, probably dating about 1790 or before, worn by 2nd Battalion 78th. The depth of the plate was $2\frac{1}{4}$ inches. This 2nd Battalion was reduced in 1796. The oval brass other ranks' plate *circa* 1793-1798 had the design incised of the Royal cypher 'GR' and crown. Above the crown the motto *Cuidich'n Rhi* and below the cypher '78th'.

The officers' oval gilt plate *circa* 1797 had the design engraved of '78' below a crown, with the motto *Cuidich'n Rhi* above the crown. The plate had a scalloped edge (Fig. 479).

Fig. 480, a gilt plate with the design in gilt *circa* 1807-1815 or a little later, the elephant is shown with a howdah cloth.

Fig. 481 is a gilt matted plate with burnished edge, the design mounted in silver, probably adopted about 1810.

About 1807 the plate had square-cut corners, but in 1860 it was very similar in arrangement to the one before, but had scrolls inscribed 'Persia' and 'Kooshab' while the design of the elephant and the wreath were changed, the elephant no longer having its trunk raised. The size of the plate was 3 × 3¾ inches.

It remained in use until 1881, when the officers' plate was burnished gilt with the design mounted in silver of the coronet and cypher of H.R.H. the late Duke of York, the elephant, the stag's head, and a scroll inscribed 'Seaforth Highlanders'.

BUTTONS

72ND

The officers' silver buttons of the 72nd were slightly convex with open backs and the design of '72' below a crown within a raised single-line circle (Fig. 482). This design was worn from about 1800 to 1830 by both officers and other ranks on their pewter buttons. After this date the colour of the officers' buttons was changed to gilt; but the same design, only in higher relief, was used and retained on the tunic buttons by the officers until 1881 and by the other ranks until 1871. There were, as usual, differences in the design of the numerals by various firms.

The diamond-shaped doublet button had the design of '72' below a crown. Above the crown a scroll inscribed 'Duke of Albany's'; below the number '72' was a scroll inscribed 'Own Highlanders'. The button was dead gilt with the design in high relief, and had a burnished rim (Fig. 483).

78TH

The officers' buttons of the 78th about 1790 were of silver, flat, with the design in relief as shown in Fig. 484.

In the case of the 2nd Battalion, the number '2' was placed on the left of the number '78', and 'B' on the right. The silver buttons were soon replaced by flat gilt ones, single sheet, with the design of '78' below a crown. The button had a raised rim.

The other ranks' pewter buttons circa 1790 had the design in relief of '78', the button having a lined rim. About 1820 the officers' buttons were gilt, slightly convex, with open backs. The design was '78' below the elephant, with a crown above. Round the top edge of the button was inscribed 'Assaye' and 'Maida', and below the number a spray of laurel leaves. This design was retained on the coatee and tunic buttons with the wording at the top changed to read 'Assaye', 'Maida', 'Java'. There were considerable differences in the shape of the elephant and numerals.

In the case of the button about 1830 the elephant was displayed with very long tusks. The diamond-shaped doublet button had the design of '78' below an elephant with crown above. On the left side was inscribed 'Maida', on the right 'Java', and below the number on a scroll 'Assaye'. The button was dead gilt lined surface with burnished rim (Fig. 485).

After 1881 the tunic button had the design of a stag's head with the letter 'L' between the antlers and the title 'Seaforth Highlanders' on a scroll below.

THE GORDON HIGHLANDERS

TITLES

1st Battalion

1758-1765 Raised in 1756 as 2nd Battalion 37th Regiment. Regimented as 75th in 1758. Disbanded 1765.

1763-1769 In 1762-1763 the 118th Invalids became the 75th Invalids Regiment of Foot. Dispersed for Garrison Service.

1778-1783 The 75th (Prince of Wales's) Regiment of Foot. Disbanded.

1787-1809 The 75th (Highland) Regiment of Foot.

1809-1862 The 75th Regiment of Foot.

1862-1881 The 75th (Stirlingshire) Regiment of Foot.

2nd Battalion

1760-1763 The 92nd Regiment of Foot or Donegal Light Infantry. Disbanded.

1779-1783 The 92nd Regiment of Foot. Disbanded.

1793-1796 The 92nd Regiment of Foot. Disbanded.

1797-1798 The 100th Regiment of Foot.

1798-1861 The 92nd (Highland) Regiment of Foot.

1861-1881 The 92nd (Gordon Highlanders) Regiment of Foot.

1881-   The Gordon Highlanders.

BADGES

The Royal Tiger. Commemorates the services of the 75th Highlanders in India. Authorized 6th July, 1807.

The Sphinx superscribed 'Egypt'. Commemorates the services of the 92nd Highlanders in Egypt, 1801, and was authorized 6th July, 1802.

The Head of a Stag. With antlers of ten tines or branches issuing from a ducal coronet and with a wreath of ivy, the crest of the Marquis of Huntly. The ivy is the badge of the Gordon family.

Motto: *Bydand* (Watchful).

The Star of the Order of the Thistle.

BATTLE HONOURS (*Dates authorized from* 1802 *to* 1855)

75TH

INDIA WITH BADGE OF TIGER, 6th July, 1807.

SERINGAPATAM, 28th May, 1818.

92ND

EGYPT AND THE SPHINX, 6th July, 1802.

BERGEN-OP-ZEE, 15th February, 1813. Changed to Egmont-op-Zee, 31st August, 1814.

MANDORA, 15th February, 1813.

PENINSULA, 6th April, 1815.

WATERLOO, 8th December, 1815.
CORUNNA, 16th February, 1830.
FUENTES D'ONOR, 16th February, 1830.
ALMARAZ, 16th February, 1830.
VITTORIA, 16th February, 1830.
PYRENEES, 16th February, 1830.
NIVE, 16th February, 1830.
ORTHES, 16th February, 1830.

SHOULDER-BELT PLATES

75TH

Fig. 486 is a silver plate with gilt mounts illustrated in the *Journal of the Society for Army Historical Research*, Vol. XXII, page 279. The date is about 1816. The plate had rounded corners.

About 1824 the plate was silver with gilt mounts and had rounded corners, which were later changed to square cut. The design was a roped circle surmounted by a crown; within the circle, the tiger above the number 'LXXV' and a spray of thistle; above the tiger a curved scroll inscribed in script letters 'India', below the circle another scroll inscribed 'Seringapatam'.

Fig. 487 is a gilt plate with silver mounts worn about 1830-1856.

Prior to 1881 a gilt oblong plate had the design mounted in silver of the tiger, above which was a scroll inscribed 'India' surmounted by a crown; below the tiger the number 'LXXV', a spray of thistles and a scroll inscribed 'Seringapatam'.

In Mr. Hughes' collection is a plate of this design, but with the Honour 'Seringapatam' spelt 'Sebingapatam'.

92ND

Fig. 488 is a silver plate worn probably prior to 1800.

The other ranks' oval brass plate *circa* 1800 had the same design incised.

Fig. 489 is a silver plate about 1800-1816 with the design of the crown and thistle in relief. The title was engraved.

In Mr. Tilling's collection is an oblong silver burnished plate with the design in silver of 'XCII' surmounted by a crown and with a spray of thistle below, the thistle having two leaves. This plate is said to have been worn 1816-1829, after which one of the same design but with four leaves to the thistle was adopted and worn until 1835.

Fig. 490 is a gilt plate with silver mounts. The size was $3\frac{3}{4} \times 2\frac{11}{16}$ inches. This plate was worn until 1881.

Since 1881 the plate has been a burnished gilt one with the design mounted in silver of the star of the Order of the Thistle; at the top of the star the Sphinx on a label inscribed 'Egypt', and on the lower part of the star a tiger on a label inscribed 'India'. In the centre of the star the crest of the Marquis of Huntly, above a spray of thistles; above the crest a scroll inscribed 'Gordon Highlanders'. The arms of the star are inscribed with Battle Honours.

BUTTONS

75TH

The other ranks' pewter buttons prior to 1800 had the design in relief of '75' below a crown; round the rim of the button was a design of leaves turned inwards. Officers' buttons were silver with the same design, but with plain rims.

The officers' silver buttons *circa* 1810 were convex with open back and the design in low relief as shown in Fig. 491. This design was retained on the gilt coatee button of 1830-1855 and on the tunic button, and was also worn by other ranks on their pewter button and on their tunic button until 1871.

In the case of the tunic button the wreath was displayed considerably thicker.

92ND

Very little change occurred in the design of the 92nd Highlanders' button. About 1800 the buttons were silver, flat, with the design in relief of '92' within a raised single-line circle (Fig. 492). The same design was worn on the pewter buttons of the other ranks.

For a short time after 1830 the number was surmounted by a crown, but the original design was reverted to for the tunic and remained in use until 1881.

The diamond-shaped doublet button had a lined surface and the design of '92' below a crown; the button had a raised rim (Fig. 493). After 1881 the design of the tunic button was as in Fig. 494.

The 1894 Dress Regulations gives the mess waistcoat as having three small regimental buttons, while the 1904 Regulations state mounted buttons on mess vest. Presumably the design was as on the tunic.

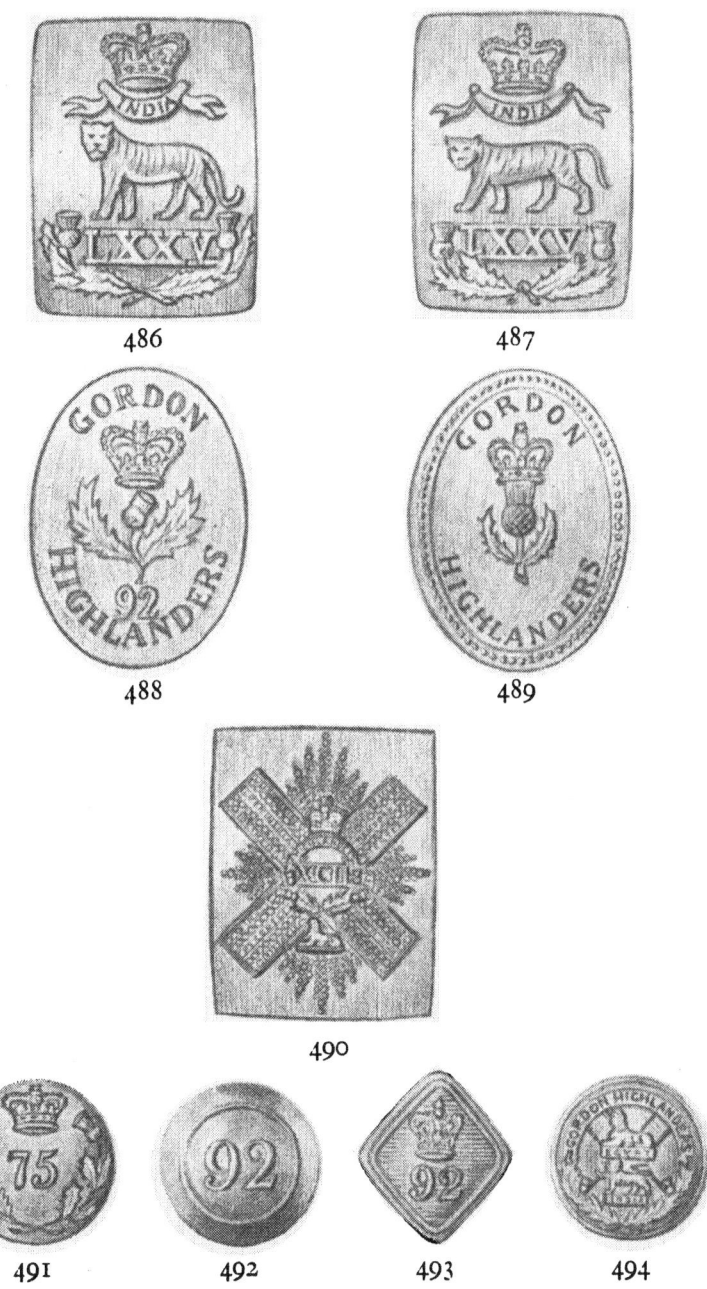

THE QUEEN'S OWN CAMERON HIGHLANDERS

TITLES
1758-1763   The 79th Regiment of Foot and as 64th, 1757-1758.
1778-1784   The 79th (Royal Liverpool Volunteers) Regiment of Foot. (Also as the Liverpool Blues.) Disbanded.
1793-1804   The 79th (Cameronian Volunteers) Regiment.
1804-1873   The 79th (Cameron Highlanders) Regiment of Foot.
1873-1881   The 79th (Queen's Own Cameron Highlanders) Regiment.
1881-   The Queen's Own Cameron Highlanders.

BADGES
The Sphinx superscribed 'Egypt'. Commemorates the services of the 79th in Egypt, 1801. Authorized 6th July, 1802.

The Thistle ensigned with the Imperial Crown. Authorized with the change of title, 12th May, 1873. The design of the thistle surmounted by a crown is the Royal badge of Scotland given by Queen Anne in 1707 at the time of the passing of the Act of Union.

The Cypher of Queen Victoria within the Garter. Appears in the Army List for the first time in September, 1921.

BATTLE HONOURS (*Dates authorized from 1802 to 1855*)
EGYPT AND THE SPHINX, 6th July, 1802.
PENINSULA, 6th April, 1815.
WATERLOO, 8th December, 1815.
TOULOUSE, 9th July, 1816.
FUENTES D'ONOR, 16th April, 1818.
SALAMANCA, 16th April, 1818.
PYRENEES, 16th April, 1818.
NIVELLE, 16th April, 1818.
NIVE, 16th April, 1818.
EGMONT-OP-ZEE, 2nd October, 1818.

SHOULDER-BELT PLATES
Fig. 495 is the officers' oval gilt plate worn 1793-1804. The plate had a deep silver rim, and in its centre a silver crowned garter inscribed 'Cameronian Volunteers', within the garter on a green enamel ground the number '79'. In the case of the Grenadier Company, a white metal grenade with a gilt flame; on the ball of the grenade was engraved the number '79'.

After the change of title in 1804 the plate was as shown in Fig. 496. The same except for the inscription on the garter and being larger in size.

In a MSS. notebook of Lieutenant John Ford in the R.U.S.I., and quoted in the *Journal of the Society for Army Historical Research*, Vol. XXVII, page 133, by Mr. F. H. McGuffie, it is stated that the breast plate in use, 1810-1814, was oval, of copper gilt, with a silver garter or band with a crown over it and '79' in the centre. The figures, the circular band and the outer border were in relief and riveted to the gilt plate; the inner part on which the figures were placed was green enamel; 'Cameron Highlanders' engraved on the circular band.

A few of the privates still retained the breast plate, furnished, I believe, when the regiment was raised, having the words 'Cameronian Volunteers'; all the others have 'Cameron Highlanders'.

Another oval brass plate, possibly worn by other ranks, was engraved with the design of a thistle with two leaves, above which was a crown flanked by 'GIII' and 'R', below the thistle the number 'LXXIX'.

In Mr. G. Pompa's collection a gilt burnished oblong plate with the design in silver of '79' within a spray of thistle, below the number the word 'OR', the whole within a crowned garter inscribed 'Cameron Highlanders'. Mr. Pompa dates the plate as prior to 1820.

Fig. 497 was worn prior to 1840. The plate had the design mounted; in the case of the Light Company the crown was replaced by a bugle-horn.

Fig. 498 is a gilt plate with frosted surface, and the design, mounted in gilt, was worn from 1840 to 1881. The plate had a burnished edge.

From 1881 the officers' plate was gilt, frosted, with a burnished edge. The design was a silver cut St. Andrew's Cross; on the cross a gilt oval collar inscribed 'Queen's Own Cameron Highlanders', surmounted by a crown; within the collar, in silver on a burnished ground, the thistle and crown; below the collar, in silver, the Sphinx over 'Egypt'. Except for the change in the design of the crown after the death of Queen Victoria, the design has remained unchanged.

BUTTONS

Between 1800 and 1881 there was little change in the general design on the buttons of the officers and other ranks of the regiment. The buttons in 1804 were flat, single sheet, with the cypher 'GR', and when in 1830 King William IV came to the throne the cypher was changed to 'WR', on the gilt convex coatee button. Fig. 501 shows the tunic button, 1855-1881.

The other ranks' pewter buttons had the same design as the officers.

After 1881 the design was a crowned thistle with the title 'The Queen's Own Cameron Highlanders' round the edge.

The diamond-shaped doublet button prior to 1881 had two designs:

(a) '79' below a crown in high relief and with a high rim to the edge of the button, which had a lined surface; the number and the edge being burnished (Fig. 500).

(b) '79' within a crowned garter inscribed 'Cameron Highlanders'. The button had a high rim to its edge, a lined surface, and the number, letters and edge burnished.

The 1904 Dress Regulations state on mess vest a plain gilt button with St. Andrew and the Cross mounted in silver.

495 496

497 498

499 500 501

298

THE ROYAL ULSTER RIFLES

TITLES

1ST BATTALION

1758-1763   The 83rd Regiment of Foot. Disbanded.
1778-1783   The 83rd (Royal Glasgow Volunteers) Regiment of Foot. Disbanded.
1793-1859   The 83rd Regiment of Foot.
1859-1881   The 83rd (County of Dublin) Regiment of Foot.

2ND BATTALION

1759-1763   The 86th Regiment of Foot. Disbanded.
1779-1783   The 86th Regiment of Foot. Disbanded.
1793-1809   The 86th Regiment of Foot.
1809-1812   The 86th (or the Leinster) Regiment of Foot.
1812-1881   The 86th (Royal County Down) Regiment of Foot.
1881-1920   The Royal Irish Rifles.
1920-   The Royal Ulster Rifles.

BADGES

The Sphinx superscribed 'Egypt'. Commemorates the services of the 86th Regiment in the campaign of 1801. Authorized 6th July, 1802.
The Harp and Crown and motto *Quis Separabit*. Authorized for the 86th Regiment on 26th March, 1832.
The Bugle-horn.

BATTLE HONOURS (*Dates authorized from 1802 to 1855*)

83RD

PENINSULA, to old 2nd Battalion, 6th April, 1815.
TALAVERA, 4th August, 1819.
FUENTES D'ONOR, 4th August, 1819.
CIUDAD RODRIGO, 4th August, 1819.
BADAJOZ, 4th August, 1819.
SALAMANCA, 4th August, 1819.
VITTORIA, 4th August, 1819.
NIVELLE, 4th August, 1819.
ORTHES, 4th August, 1819.
TOULOUSE, 15th January, 1827.
BUSACO, 10th May, 1827.
CAPE OF GOOD HOPE, 3rd March, 1836.

86TH

EGYPT AND THE SPHINX, 6th July, 1802.
INDIA, 3rd October, 1823.
BOURBON, 3rd October, 1823.

SHOULDER-BELT PLATES

83RD

Fig. 502 is the officers' plate *circa* 1800; it was of dead gilt with a burnished gilt mounted design.

About the same period there was another officers' oval gilt plate with the design mounted in silver of '83' below a crown within a wreath of laurel leaves.

Fig. 503 is a brass plate with the design incised; it was evidently the plate worn by the drum-major about the 1800 period.

Mr. P. W. Reynolds records the plate worn 1816-1836 as gilt, oblong, with silver mounted design of '83' within a crowned wreath; above the crown a scroll inscribed 'Peninsula'.

Fig. 504 is the brass plate worn by other ranks about 1840-1850.

86TH

Fig. 505 is the officers' oval silver plate worn *circa* 1790-1822, the design mounted in silver.

Mr. Reynolds records a gilt plate with a silver star on which is mounted in gilt the design of the Irish harp between the numbers '8' and '6'; the shape of the plate was like that worn by the 7th Fusiliers and 59th Regiment, 1850.

Fig. 506 is the officers' plate worn prior to 1855; the plate was burnished gilt with the design, also in gilt, mounted. The size of the plate was $3\frac{7}{8} \times 3\frac{1}{16}$ inches.

BUTTONS

83RD

The officers' buttons about 1800 were gilt, slightly convex, with open back, and the design in relief of '83' within a French scroll with a dot at the opening (Fig. 507).

The early pewter button had the design of '83' in low relief. About 1810 they had the number in high relief (Fig. 508).

The coatee buttons, 1830-1855, had the design of '83' below a crown and within a laurel wreath. This design was retained on the tunic buttons from 1855 to 1881.

86TH

The officers' silver buttons about 1800 were flat, one piece, with the design in relief of '86' within a French scroll with a dot at the opening, and three dots suspended from within the circle on either side of the opening (Fig. 509).

After 1832 the design on the buttons for officers was a crowned harp with '86' below. The button had a scalloped edge and a frosted surface, with the design in relief in dead gilt. The pewter buttons worn by the other ranks at the same period had the design of the harp within a crowned garter inscribed 'Royal County Down' and with '86' below the garter. The tunic buttons after 1855 had the same design as on the officers' coatee, but on a burnished button.

After 1881, when the regiment had become Rifles, black buttons were worn with the design of harp and crown and motto. Below this design a scroll inscribed 'Royal Irish Rifles', with a spray at each end of the scroll. The buttons retained the scalloped rim of the 86th. One die of buttons had a Light Infantry bugle-horn and harp below the title and omitted the spray of shamrock.

The present button has the same design as before 1920 but with the present title and crown.

301

THE ROYAL IRISH FUSILIERS
(PRINCESS VICTORIA'S)

TITLES
1st Battalion

1759-1763	The 87th (Highland Volunteers) Regiment of Foot; also known as Keiths Highlanders. Disbanded.
1779-1783	The 87th Regiment of Foot. Disbanded.
1793-1811	The 87th (The Prince of Wales's Irish) Regiment of Foot.
1811-1827	The 87th (The Prince of Wales's Own Irish) Regiment of Foot.
1827-1881	The 87th Prince of Wales's Own Irish Fusiliers.
1881-	The 87th (or Royal Irish Fusiliers) Regiment of Foot.

2nd Battalion

1759-1763	The 89th Regiment of Foot. Disbanded.
1779-1783	The 89th Regiment of Foot. Disbanded.
1793-1866	The 89th Regiment of Foot.
1866-1881	The 89th (The Princess Victoria's) Regiment of Foot.
1881-1920	Princess Victoria's (Royal Irish Fusiliers).
1920-	The Royal Irish Fusiliers (Princess Victoria's).

BADGES
The Sphinx superscribed 'Egypt'. Commemorates the services of the 89th in Egypt, 1801. Authorized 6th July, 1802.

The Harp and Crown. An old badge of the 87th.

The Eagle with a Wreath of Laurel. Commemorates the capture by the 87th of the eagle of the 8th French Regiment at the battle of Barrosa, 1811. Authorized 11th April, 1811.

The Prince of Wales's Coronet, Plume and motto. Adopted by the 87th when raised in 1793.

The Cypher and Coronet of Princess Victoria. Granted in 1866 when the 89th received the title 'Princess Victoria's'.

Motto: *Faugh-a-Ballagh*. The old war-cry of the 87th, meaning 'clear the way', officially recognized in Army Order No. 3 of 1910, but which had been the unofficial motto of the 87th for many years. Application for permission to use it in 1877 had been refused.

BATTLE HONOURS (*Dates authorized from 1802 to 1855*)
87th
BARROSA, 11th April, 1811.
TARIFA, 7th October, 1812.
PENINSULA, 6th April, 1815.
MONTE VIDEO, 12th January, 1824.

TALAVERA, 27th January, 1824.
VITTORIA, 27th January, 1824.
NIVELLE, 27th January, 1824.
ORTHES, 27th January, 1824.
TOULOUSE, 27th January, 1824.
AVA, 6th December, 1826.

89TH
EGYPT AND THE SPHINX, 6th July, 1802.
NIAGARA, to old 2nd Battalion, which was disbanded in 1816, 5th May, 1815; and authorized again to the 89th, 29th March, 1831.
JAVA, 28th May, 1818.
AVA, 6th December, 1826.
SEVASTOPOL, 16th October, 1855.

SHOULDER-BELT PLATES
87TH

I am indebted to Lieutenant-Colonel P. M. Marjoribanks-Egerton, M.B.E., for most of the following information concerning the 87th and 89th.

The 87th are particularly lucky in having a great deal of research done concerning their uniforms and badges by General Sir Gerald Templer, the Colonel of the Regiment.

Fig. 510 is a gilt shoulder-belt plate *circa* 1793-1800. This was followed by a gilt plate with the design of the Prince of Wales's coronet, plume and motto in silver above a gilt harp; all above a silver '87'. The plate had a raised gilt rim.

Fig. 511 came into use after the change of title in 1811. The plate illustrated would be that worn by the Light Company.

About 1812-1815 an oblong plate with rounded corners and the design in silver of the eagle surmounted by the Prince of Wales's coronet, plume and motto, and a scroll above inscribed 'Barrosa'. Below the eagle a harp; between the numbers '8' and '7', at the bottom of the plate, a scroll inscribed 'Prince's Own Irish'.

This plate was followed in 1822 by one with a very ornate design which embodied the Prince of Wales's coronet, plume and motto, the eagle, harp, a wreath of rose, shamrock and thistle, and scrolls with the Battle Honours 'Barrosa', 'Tarifa', 'Peninsula'. Lieutenant-Colonel Marjoribanks-Egerton writes of this badge, "the plate may probably be a little before 1822", and states that Milne had three of these plates made up under his instructions for wear in the original production of the Gilbert and Sullivan opera "Ruddigore".

From 1827 to 1855 a gilt plate with a matted surface and burnished rim with the design mounted of a large gilt grenade, on the ball of which was the French eagle. The width of the plate would have varied according to the regulations governing the belt. Prior to 1840 it was 3 inches wide, but after that date increased. Lieutenant-Colonel Marjoribanks-Egerton writes: "As none of the narrower plates have come to light it is possible that the 87th always wore the broad plate."

There were also several variations in the design of this plate. Mr. W. F. Hughes has in his collection one in which the eagle is displayed on a silver grenade. Below the plate was worn an ornamental gilt belt slide.

In the Regimental Museum is a bronze oval plate ascribed to a drummer. It has the design of the Prince of Wales's coronet, plume and motto, but in place of the coronet is a crown, below this the harp, and below the harp '87'.

This plate would have preceded the oblong plate which came in about 1813.

89TH

The officers' gilt plate worn about 1802-1815 had the design mounted in silver of the Sphinx above '89'; the plate had cut corners; the Sphinx was on a base inscribed with Egyptian characters.

In an oil painting of Lieutenant Adam Dunscombe dated 1804, the shoulder-belt plate, although not very clearly shown, appears to have square corners, and the design of the numerals are above the Sphinx, which is not on a tablet.

The other ranks' oval brass plate had the design of '89' within a raised circle which was itself encircled by a raised circle and was in the centre of a crowned star.

Fig. 513 is a gilt plate with matted surface and burnished edges. The design was mounted in silver. The other ranks' plate *circa* 1826 was oblong, brass, with cut corners, and had the design of '89' surmounted by the Sphinx.

Another plate of about the same period had a similar design, but with a more ornamental wreath and the Honour 'Ava' immediately below the wreath and those for 'Java' and 'Niagara' on the small scroll but below; the ends of the scroll being ornamental and with a roped edge. The plate was frosted and had a burnished rim.

BUTTONS

87TH

The officers' buttons *circa* 1800 were gilt, convex, with open backs, and had the design in relief of the Prince of Wales's coronet, plume and motto above a harp, below which was the number '87'.

After 1811 the buttons for a time were flat, single piece, with a similar design, but the eagle added and placed below the coronet and plume, the motto *Ich Dien* being omitted. Round the bottom edge of the button was 'Prince's Own Irish'.

About 1820 the officers' buttons became convex with open backs; the design was the same, but with the title and eagle omitted (Fig. 514). General Sir Gerald Templer states this design was also worn on the other ranks' pewter buttons until 1832.

This design was retained on the later coatee button with closed back until 1855, when the design shown in Fig. 515 was adopted.

The other ranks' buttons prior to 1855 had the same design with scalloped edge.

At first the officers' tunic buttons were flatter and smaller, but after a few years became the same as is still worn by the regiment, with the omission after 1881 of '87'. The button had a scalloped edge, which is still featured.

89TH

The early buttons of the 89th were gilt, flat, with the design of '89' within a star of eight points (Fig. 516).

After 1800 the design on a gilt convex button was of '89' within a French scroll. There were two types of this button for both officers and other ranks, one with a dot at the opening (Fig. 517) and the other without, the latter being probably the earlier. After 1866 the officers' buttons had the coronet of Princess Victoria above the number at the opening of the French scroll. The men's tunic buttons retained the design of '89', the French scroll and dot.

After 1881 the buttons displayed the Barrosa eagle and had a scalloped edge.

In the 1900 Dress Regulations it states that the field cap and mess dress buttons had plain edges, with the eagle and tablet mounted in silver, but in the Regulations for 1911 the button is die struck.

510 511

512 513

514 515 516 517

THE CONNAUGHT RANGERS

TITLES

1ST BATTALION
1760-1763 88th Highland Volunteers; also as Campbell's Highlanders Regiment of Foot. Disbanded.
1779-1783 The 88th Regiment of Foot. Disbanded.
1793-1881 The 88th (Connaught Rangers) Regiment.

2ND BATTALION
1760-1763 The 94th (Royal Welsh Volunteers) Regiment of Foot. Disbanded.
1780-1783 The 94th Regiment of Foot. Disbanded.
1794-1795 The 94th (Irish) Regiment of Foot. Disbanded.
Previous to 1802. The Scotch Brigade. Had been formed in Holland in 1685. Brought into the British Line as 94th in 1802 and were eventually disbanded in 1818.
1823-1881 The 94th Regiment of Foot.
1881-1922 The Connaught Rangers. Disbanded.

BADGES
The Sphinx superscribed 'Egypt'. Commemorates the services of the 88th in Egypt, 1801. Authorized 6th July, 1802.
The Harp and Crown and motto *Quis Separabit*. Was the old badge and motto of the 88th. It was authorized to be retained, 23rd December, 1830.
The Elephant Caparisoned. The badge was originally authorized in 1807 with the Honour 'Seringapatam' to the old 94th of 1802-1818 for service in India. The Honours were given to the later 94th, 18th March, 1874.

BATTLE HONOURS (*Dates authorized from 1802 to 1855*)
88TH
EGYPT AND THE SPHINX, 6th July, 1802.
PENINSULA, 6th April, 1815.
TALAVERA, 28th August, 1817.
BUSACO, 28th August, 1817.
FUENTES D'ONOR, 28th August, 1817.
CIUDAD RODRIGO, 28th August, 1817.
SALAMANCA, 28th August, 1817.
ORTHES, 28th August, 1817.
TOULOUSE, 28th August, 1817.
BADAJOZ, 2nd October, 1818.
VITTORIA, 2nd October, 1818.
NIVELLE, 2nd October, 1818.
ALMA, 16th October, 1855.
INKERMAN, 16th October, 1855.
SEVASTOPOL, 16th October, 1855.

94TH

PENINSULA, 6th April, 1815.
SALAMANCA, 22nd January, 1818.
VITTORIA, 22nd January, 1818.
CIUDAD RODRIGO, 22nd January, 1818.
BADAJOZ, 22nd January, 1818.
NIVELLE, 22nd January, 1818.
ORTHES, 22nd January, 1818.
TOULOUSE, 22nd January, 1818.
SERINGAPATAM, 28th May, 1818.

SHOULDER-BELT PLATES

88TH

Volume II of the Regimental History, by Colonel H. F. N. Jourdain, C.M.G., gives very full details of the changes in the designs worn by the 88th and the 94th.

In the History is the illustration of an oval plate with the design of the harp above the number '88', which is dated 1806.

Almack's book illustrates an oval silver plate with the design in gilt of '88' within a crowned girdle inscribed *Quis Separabit*; below the girdle pendent the Irish harp. The plate had a raised rim. This plate was probably worn until about 1815 or even later, when that in Fig. 518 came into use. This plate was all silver and had rounded corners. The Regimental History dates it as being worn 1817-1822. It was followed by a silver star plate of the same design as worn on the shako of the period, and had the design of '88' within a crowned girdle inscribed 'Peninsula', 'Connaught Rangers', all on a star of twelve points, on the major rays of which were inscribed eleven Battle Honours.

About 1825 the design on a silver plate was of '88' below the harp, above the harp the word 'Peninsula', and below the number the motto *Quis Separabit*, all within a wreath of shamrock with crown above superimposed on a star of twelve rays, inscribed with Honours. Below the wreath a Sphinx over 'Egypt'.

After 1830 the plate became gilt (Fig. 519), with the design in silver.

Between 1835 and 1855 there was little change except that the earlier plate had the harp placed above the Sphinx and the plate worn just prior to 1855 displayed it below (Fig. 520).

94TH

Fig. 521 is the gilt plate with the design in silver worn by the 94th Scotch Brigade prior to 1818. The plate had rounded corners and its size was $3\frac{5}{16} \times 2\frac{11}{16}$ inches. It was replaced by the design shown in Fig. 522; the plate was gilt with silver mounts.

A plate in the *Journal of the Society for Army Historical Research* for the summer of 1952 reproduced a water-colour painting of a colour-sergeant of the 94th *circa* 1824. Mr. L. E. Buckell describes the breast plate as having the elephant with a crown above and the Roman numeral 'XCIV' below. Mr. Buckell suggests that this was the badge worn by the old 94th Scotch Brigade, disbanded in 1818, and that the non-commissioned officer shown in the painting had been in the earlier regiment and retained his breast plate.

Fig. 523 is the gilt plate worn prior to 1855; the design was mounted in silver. In the case of the Light Company of the regiment, the design within the wreath was '94' inside the strings of a Light Infantry bugle-horn.

BUTTONS

88TH

The early design for both officers and other ranks was Fig. 524. It was retained by the latter until 1871. After 1830 the buttons for officers became gilt, but it is not clear from the Regimental History what the design was—it states that from 1854 to 1860 the old design of Fig. 524 was worn, and in 1860 the design was '88' within a crowned circle inscribed 'Connaught Rangers', a wreath of shamrock, at the foot of which the motto *Quis Separabit* and a harp. The button had a scalloped edge.

94TH

The officers' gilt buttons of the 94th Scotch Brigade was as shown in Fig. 525.

From 1832 to 1881 both officers and other ranks of the 94th had the same design of '94' below a crown within a single-line circle.

From 1881 until 1894 the design was the elephant below a harp within a wreath of shamrock. The button had a scalloped rim.

After 1894 the design on the tunic buttons was a harp surmounted by a crown within a wreath of shamrock, a scroll below inscribed *Quis Separabit*. The button had a scalloped edge.

The 1904 Dress Regulations gives the mess waistcoat button as having the letters 'CR' on a lined button with a raised edge. According to the Regimental History this button was worn on the mess waistcoat, which was of special design, 1848-1922. There was also a button of mess dress size with the design of 'CR' in monogram mounted in gilt.

518

520

519

521

522

523

524

525

THE ARGYLL AND SUTHERLAND HIGHLANDERS (PRINCESS LOUISE'S)

TITLES

1ST BATTALION

1760-1763 The 91st Regiment of Foot. Disbanded.
1779-1783 The 91st Regiment of Foot. Disbanded.
1793-1795 The 91st Regiment of Foot. Disbanded.
1794-1798 The 98th Argyllshire Highlanders Regiment of Foot. Renumbered.
1798-1809 The 91st Argyllshire Highlanders Regiment of Foot.
1809-1820 The 91st Regiment of Foot.
1820-1863 The 91st (or Argyllshire) Regiment of Foot.
1863-1872 The 91st (Argyllshire) Highlanders.
1872-1881 The 91st (Princess Louise's Argyllshire) Highlanders.

2ND BATTALION

1760-1763 The 93rd Regiment of Foot.
1779-1783 The 93rd Regiment of Foot.
1793-1796 The 93rd Regiment of Foot.
1800-1861 The 93rd Highlanders, formed chiefly from the Sutherland Fencibles.
1861-1881 The 93rd Sutherland Highlanders.
1881-1882 Princess Louise's (Sutherland and Argyll Highlanders).
1882-1920 Princess Louise's (Argyll and Sutherland Highlanders).
1920-   The Argyll and Sutherland Highlanders (Princess Louise's).

BADGES

The Wild Cat and Butcher's Broom. Is the family cognizance and badge of the Sutherland clan.
The Boar's Head. Is the badge of the Argyll family, and Myrtle is the badge of the Campbell clan. Authorized for the 91st Highlanders, 14th March, 1872.
A Silver Label of Three Points. Is the mark of cadency of the arms of H.R.H. the Princess Louise, Marchioness of Lorne. As in the case of other English princesses, it has a rose in the centre, but has distinguishing billets at each end.
The Coronet of H.R.H. the Princess Louise. Authorized in 1872.
Mottoes: *Ne obliviscaris*, the motto of the Argyll family.
         Sans Peur, the motto of the Sutherland family.

BATTLE HONOURS (*Dates authorized from 1815 to 1855*)

91ST
PENINSULA, 6th April, 1815.
TOULOUSE, 9th July, 1816.
PYRENEES, 17th July, 1818.
NIVELLE, 17th July, 1818.
NIVE, 17th July, 1818.
ORTHES, 17th July, 1818.
CORUNNA, 9th January, 1833.
ROLEIA, 16th January, 1833.
VIMIERA, 16th January, 1833.

93RD
PENINSULA, 6th April, 1815.
TOULOUSE, 9th July, 1816.
CAPE OF GOOD HOPE, 1st December, 1835.
ALMA, 16th October, 1855.
BALACLAVA, 16th October, 1855.
SEVASTOPOL, 16th October, 1855.

SHOULDER-BELT PLATES

91ST

The officers' oval silver shoulder-belt plate *circa* 1798 had the design of '91' engraved within a garter inscribed 'Argyllshire Regiment', set on a St. Andrew's Cross and surmounted by a crown. In the officers' mess is an oblong silver gilt plate with the number 'XCI' surmounted by a grenade and crown and with the word 'Argyllshire' below; this the Regimental History suggests may be the original shoulder-belt plate with the number changed from XCVIII to XCI.

Mr. Reynolds records another plate of similar design, but with slight differences. He writes: "An oval silver plate with '91' within a crowned garter inscribed 'Argyllshire Regiment', mounted on a star of the Order of the Thistle, the '91' in silver in relief, the rest of the design engraved."

The other ranks' brass oval plate *circa* 1800 had the design incised of '91' surmounted by a crown and with the title 'Argyllshire Regt' round the bottom edge of the plate.

According to the late Captain E. A. Campbell, the officers' plate, 1803-1825, was a gilt burnished oblong one with the design of 'XCI' surmounted by a crown and with a scroll inscribed 'Argyllshire' below the number. Mounted in silver. In the case of the Grenadier Company a grenade was placed between the crown and the number, and in the case of the Light Company a bugle-horn.

The Regimental History records that Mrs. Cox has the shoulder-belt plate of Colonel Douglas, 1808-1818. It is oblong, gilt, with '91' in silver within a silver band inscribed 'Argyllshire' in silver on green enamel. At the top of the plate a scroll inscribed 'Toulouse' and at the bottom one inscribed 'Peninsula'. The Regimental History dates the plate as probably being worn 1814, but the Honour 'Toulouse' was not authorized until 1816.

Fig. 526 is a gilt burnished plate and the design mounted in silver. The garter had pierced letters on a green enamel ground. Worn from 1830 to 1864.

From 1864 to 1881 the 91st had a distinctive shoulder-belt plate, an oval one, of silver and enamel; on a girdle in wide lettering the words 'Argyllshire Highlanders XCI'; within the girdle a large St. Andrew's Cross surmounted by a silver and enamel Royal crown, with the letters 'V.R.' below. Intertwined with the cross two green and red enamel thistles on a gilt ground.

93RD

Circa 1800 the officers' plate was a small oblong silver one with the design engraved (Fig. 527).

Mr. P. W. Reynolds records an oval plate with the design of '93' below a grenade shown in a portrait of W. Maxwell. Mr. Reynolds dates the plate circa 1801.

The officers' plate about 1810 was silver with square-cut corners as shown in Fig. 528.

About 1818-1825 it is recorded by the late General Cavendish that officers of the 93rd had oblong plates with the design of '93' within a crowned circle, with a spray of thistle below. The size was $2\frac{1}{2} \times 3$ inches.

Fig. 529 is the gilt plate which came into use about 1837. The design was mounted in silver; the '93' had a frosted background.

Fig. 530 is the plate worn 1864-1881. The plate was gilt with the design in silver. The '93' on a burnished disk.

The other ranks' brass plate circa 1810-1855 had the design of a large '93' surmounted by a crown and with a spray of four thistles below.

After 1881 the plate for officers was of burnished gilt with the design mounted in silver of a myrtle wreath on the left interlaced with one on the right of butcher's broom. Within the myrtle wreath the boar's head on a scroll inscribed *Ne obliviscaris*, and within the butcher's broom the wild cat on a scroll inscribed *Sans Peur*. A label of three points above the boar's head and the cat. The wreath bears scrolls inscribed with the Regiment's Battle Honours. Above the wreath a scroll inscribed 'Princess Louise's'; this surmounted by the Princess's coronet. Below the wreath a scroll inscribed 'Argyll and Sutherland Highlanders'.

BUTTONS

91ST

The officers' buttons about 1830 were gilt, convex, with the design engraved of '91' within a crowned garter inscribed 'Argyllshire'. Soon after, the same design was worn in relief and remained so until 1855. The other ranks' pewter buttons worn prior to 1855 had the design in relief of '91' below a crown, with the title 'Argyllshire Regt' below all within a single-line circle. This design was retained on the tunic button on its introduction in 1855.

In 1863 this button was replaced for the officers by one with the design of St. Andrew and Cross, within a crowned circle inscribed 'Argyllshire Highlanders'; on the bottom of the circle was the number '91'.

The officers' diamond-shaped doublet button was of dead gilt, and had the design of 'XCI' within a garter inscribed 'Argyllshire Highlanders', all imposed on a star of the Order of the Thistle (Fig. 531).

93RD

The officers' buttons of the 93rd were silver, convex, between 1814 and 1830, but in 1826 had closed backs; the design was '93' surmounted by a crown. In 1831 the buttons became gilt, but the same design was retained. According to the Regimental History in 1855 diamond-shaped buttons were worn, but the round one was resumed in 1856. The same design was retained on the tunic button, there being several small differences in the size of the numerals.

The other ranks' pewter buttons and later their tunic buttons until 1871 had the same design as for the officers.

After 1881 the design was as shown in Fig. 532.

526

527

528

529

531

530

532

315

THE PRINCE OF WALES'S LEINSTER REGIMENT (ROYAL CANADIANS)

TITLES
1st Battalion

1760-1763   The 100th (Highland) Regiment of Foot. Campbell's Highlanders. Disbanded.
1780-1784   The 100th Regiment of Foot. Disbanded.
1794-1798   The 100th (Gordon Highlanders) Regiment of Foot. In 1798 renumbered 92nd.
1804-1818   The 100th (H.R.H. The Prince Regent's, County of Dublin) Regiment of Foot, renumbered 99th, 1816. Disbanded 1818.
1816-1818   100th Regiment of Foot, raised in 1789 as New South Wales Corps, later 102nd Regiment of Foot, became 100th Regiment of Foot in 1816. Disbanded 1818.
1858-1881   The 100th (Prince of Wales's Royal Canadian) Regiment of Foot.

2nd Battalion

1761-1763   The 109th Regiment of Foot. Disbanded. For a short time known as the London Volunteers Regiment of Foot.
1794-1795   The 109th (Aberdeenshire) Regiment of Foot. Drafted.
1853-1858   The H.E.I.C. 3rd (Bombay European) Regiment.
1858-1861   The 3rd (Bombay) Regiment.
1861-1881   The 109th (Bombay Infantry) Regiment.

1881-1922   The Prince of Wales's Leinster Regiment (Royal Canadians). Disbanded 1922.

BADGES

The Prince of Wales's Coronet, Plume and motto. The badge of the old 100th Regiment. Disbanded in 1818.

In 1860 the badge of the Prince of Wales's Coronet, Plume and motto, and in 1875 the Honour 'Niagara' awarded to the former 100th, were given to the regiment raised in 1858.

A Maple Leaf. Commemorates the raising in Canada in 1858 of the 100th Prince of Wales's Royal Canadians as an expression of that Dominion's loyalty at the time of the Indian Mutiny.

BATTLE HONOURS (*Dates authorized*)

NIAGARA, 5th May, 1815, to old 100th; to late Regiment, 22nd March, 1875.

SHOULDER-BELT PLATES

100TH

The shoulder-belt plate worn by the other ranks of the 100th (Prince Regent's County of Dublin) Regiment was brass, oblong with rounded corners, and had the design stamped of '100' below a crown.

The officers' shoulder-belt plate prior to 1816 was silver, oblong with rounded corners, and the design mounted in silver of the Prince of Wales's coronet, plume and motto, all within a garter inscribed 'County of Dublin Regt' (Fig. 533).

The plate worn by the other ranks *circa* 1812 still had the design engraved and was oblong with rounded corners; below the crown was the number '100' (Fig. 534).

BUTTONS

100TH

The officers' buttons and the other ranks' pewter buttons *circa* 1810 had the design of the Prince of Wales's plume, coronet and motto; below was the number '100' (Fig. 535).

When in 1858 the new 100th Prince of Wales's Royal Canadian Regiment was raised, the buttons had the same design as their predecessors.

109TH

The design on the tunic button prior to 1881 was '109' surmounted by a crown and with the title 'Bombay Infantry' below.

After 1881 the design was a circle inscribed 'Prince of Wales's Leinster Regiment'. Within the circle the Prince of Wales's coronet, plume and motto.

The 1900 Dress Regulations gives the field cap button and mess dress button as having the design mounted in silver of the Prince of Wales's plume. The 1911 Regulations gives the cap button as die struck, in gilt.

533

534

535

318

THE ROYAL MUNSTER FUSILIERS

TITLES
1st Battalion
- 1761-1763 The 101st Regiment of Foot; also as Johnstone's Highlanders. Disbanded.
- 1781-1783 The 101st Regiment of Foot. Disbanded.
- 1794-1795 The 101st (Irish) Regiment of Foot. Drafted.
- 1806-1817 The 101st (or the Duke of York's Irish) Regiment of Foot. Disbanded.
- 1756-1839 The H.E.I.C. Bengal (European) Regiment.
- 1839-1840 The H.E.I.C. (1st Bengal European) Regiment.
- 1840-1846 The H.E.I.C. 1st Bengal European Regiment (Light Infantry).
- 1846-1858 The H.E.I.C. 1st European Bengal Fusiliers.
- 1858-1861 The 1st Bengal Fusiliers.
- 1861-1881 The 101st (Royal Bengal Fusiliers).

2nd Battalion
- 1761-1763 The 104th (King's Volunteers) Regiment of Foot. Disbanded.
- 1782-1783 The 104th Regiment of Foot. Disbanded.
- 1794-1795 The 104th (Royal Manchester Volunteers) Regiment of Foot. Drafted.
- 1810-1817 The 104th Regiment of Foot. Formerly New Brunswick Fencibles. Numbered 104th in 1810. Disbanded.
- 1839-1850 The H.E.I.C. 2nd Bengal (European) Regiment.
- 1850-1858 The H.E.I.C. 2nd (Bengal European) Fusiliers.
- 1858-1861 The 2nd Bengal Fusiliers.
- 1861-1881 The 104th (Bengal Fusiliers).
- 1881-1922 The Royal Munster Fusiliers. Disbanded 1922.

BADGES
The Royal Tiger. Commemorates the services of the 101st.
A Shamrock.
The Arms of the Province of Munster. Adopted in 1881. Three golden crowns on a field of azure, which was the ancient arms of Ireland.

BATTLE HONOURS (*Awarded prior to 1855*) (The dates of the award of these honours are not available in the War Office Records).

101ST
- PLASSEY
- GUJERAT
- BUXAR
- DEIG

BHURTPORE
AFFGHANISTAN
GHUZNEE
FEROZESHAH
SOBRAON
PEGU

104TH
PUNJAUB
CHILLIANWALLAH
GOOJERAT
PEGU

SHOULDER-BELT PLATES

101ST

A miniature of an officer of the 101st (Irish) Regiment, drafted in 1795, was reproduced in the *Journal of the Society for Army Historical Research*, No. 51, Vol. XXIV. It shows an oval silver plate with the design of '101' below a crown. The other ranks' brass plate of the 101st Duke of York's Irish was oblong with the simple design of '101'. The plate had rounded corners.

In the R.M.A. Sandhurst Museum is an oval silver plate engraved with a star of eight points. In its centre is inscribed '3' over 'Batt', above the star the word 'European' and below the star 'Infantry'; a wreath of leaves below the design. The badge is ascribed to the Royal Dublin Fusiliers as having been worn by the 3rd Battalion Bengal European Regiment *circa* 1796-1798.

Fig. 536 is the plate worn by officers, 1846-1855, of the 1st Bengal European Fusiliers. The plate is described by Mr. Cattley as all gilt except the small crowned garter with the title, the numeral and the small scroll inscribed 'Fusiliers' below the number which are in silver.

104TH

The late Mr. W. L. Calver sent the author a description of the plates of the New Brunswick Fencibles formed in 1806. The first plate of the regiment appears to have had the design of a crown with the words 'New Brunswick' around the top of the plate and 'Fencible Inf.' at the bottom. The officers' plates were silver.

Almack's book illustrates an oval silver plate of the New Brunswick Fencibles, which in 1810 became the 104th and were disbanded in 1817. The plate was engraved with the design of a crown, above which were the words 'New Brunswick' and below the crown 'Fencible Infantry'.

Fig. 537 shows the brass plate worn by the other ranks of the regiment when numbered 104th in 1810. The design was in relief.

The 2nd Bengal European Fusiliers in 1850 had a plate very similar to that worn by the 1st Bengal European Fusiliers, but with the numeral '2' in place of '1' and the wreath having a single scroll at the bottom inscribed 'Punjaub'. The plate was all gilt except for the numeral and the title, which were in silver. The plate was matted gilt with a burnished rim.

BUTTONS

101ST

An Inspection Report of 1781 records the buttons as being of white metal with '101'.

Fig. 538 is of an officers' bone-backed button of the period; the face was gilt with the design in relief. The button had a lined rim.

Fig. 539 is the officers' silver convex button of the 101st Duke of York's Irish. The design was in relief.

The officers' coatee button about 1840 had the design of the numeral '1' within a crowned garter inscribed 'Bengal Eur. Regt.', with an oak wreath round.

Upon becoming Fusiliers, the design was the initials 'BER' on the ball of the grenade, with scroll below inscribed 'Fusiliers'. The button was dead gilt with burnished scalloped edge. The tunic button introduced in 1861 had the design of '101' on the ball of a grenade, with the title 'Royal Bengal Fusiliers' below.

104TH

Fig. 541 is of the other ranks' pewter button of the 104th New Brunswick Regiment, disbanded in 1816.

In Fig. 540 the button is gilt, flat, with the design in relief. The Honour 'Niagara' had been granted to the regiment's Flank Companies, 11th October, 1815.

The gilt coatee button of the 2nd Bengal (European) Regiment, 1839, was convex, with the cypher 'ER' within a garter inscribed 'Bengal'; above the garter the numeral '2', around the garter a wreath of laurel (Fig. 542). The coatee button 1850 had '2' above 'BER' on the ball of a grenade. The button was dead gilt with burnished scalloped edge. After 1861 the design was at first '104' on a grenade, with crown above and a scroll below inscribed 'Bengal Fusiliers'; the button had no rim. Later the design became '104' on the ball of a grenade, and the title 'Royal Bengal Fusiliers' below.

After 1881 until disbanded in 1922 the design was the Royal tiger on the ball of a grenade and the title 'Royal Munster Fusiliers' below.

The 1904 Dress Regulations gives for the mess dress the Royal tiger in silver on a plain button.

536

538 　　　537 　　　540

539 　　　542 　　　54

322

THE ROYAL DUBLIN FUSILIERS

TITLES

1ST BATTALION

1761-1763　The 102nd (Queen's Royal Volunteers) Regiment of Foot. Disbanded.
1781-1785　The 102nd Regiment of Foot. Disbanded.
1808-1816　The New South Wales Corps in 1808 became 102nd Regiment of Foot; in 1816 the 100th Regiment of Foot. Disbanded 1818.
1793-1795　The 102nd (Irish) Regiment of Foot. Drafted.
1746-1830　The H.E.I.C. European Regiment.
1830-1839　The H.E.I.C. Madras (European) Regiment.
1839-1843　The H.E.I.C. 1st Madras (European) Regiment.
1843-1858　The H.E.I.C. 1st Madras (European) Fusiliers.
1858-1861　The 1st Madras Fusiliers.
1861-1881　The 102nd (Royal Madras Fusiliers).

2ND BATTALION

1761-1763　The 103rd (Volunteer Hunters) Regiment of Foot. Disbanded.
1781-1784　The 103rd (King's Irish Infantry) Regiment of Foot. Disbanded.
1794-1796　The 103rd (Loyal Bristol Volunteers) Regiment of Foot. Drafted.
1808-1817　The 103rd Regiment of Foot. Disbanded. Formerly 9th Garrison Battalion.
1662-1668　The Bombay Regiment.
1668-1839　The H.E.I.C. Bombay (European) Regiment.
1839-1843　The H.E.I.C. 1st Bombay (European) Regiment.
1843-1858　The H.E.I.C. 1st Bombay (European) Fusiliers.
1858-1861　The 1st Bombay Fusiliers.
1861-1881　The 103rd (Royal Bombay Fusiliers).
1881-1922　The Royal Dublin Fusiliers. Disbanded 1922.

BADGES

The Elephant. Commemorates the services of the 103rd in India, especially in campaigns in the Carnatic and Mysore. Given 6th November, 1844.
The Royal Tiger. Commemorates the long and distinguished services of the 102nd in India, and especially its part in the capture of Nundy Droog in 1791. The badge was conferred on the 103rd on 6th November, 1844, having previously been awarded to the 1st Madras European Regiment.
The Arms of the City of Dublin. Three silver castles on an azure field. Adopted by the Regular battalions in 1881; had been the badge of the Royal Dublin City Militia, who became the 4th Battalion in 1881.

Motto: *Spectamur Agendo*. Authorized 12th March, 1841, in commemoration of services of the 102nd in India.

An Irish Harp. Added to the badges of the regiment in 1881. In 1874 application was made, but refused, for permission to display the device of "the Lion Rampant bearing an Imperial Crown", the crest of the late East India Company; while a short time after, an application for it to be allowed to have on its Colours some recognition of its "antiquity and honourable traditions" was likewise refused.

BATTLE HONOURS (*Awarded prior to* 1855) (The dates for the award of these honours are not available in the War Office Records).

102ND
- ARCOT
- PLASSEY
- CONDORE
- WYNDEWASH
- SHOLINGUR
- NUNDY DROOG
- AMBOYNA
- TERNATE
- BANDA
- PONDICHERRY
- MAHEIDPORE
- AVA
- PEGU

103RD
- CARNATIC
- MYSORE
- PLASSEY
- BUXAR
- GUZERAT
- SERINGAPATAM
- KIRKEE
- BENI-BOO-ALLY
- ADEN
- PUNJAUB
- MOOLTAN
- GOOJERAT

SHOULDER-BELT PLATES

102ND

The officers' shoulder-belt plate of the 102nd of 1808-1816 was oval, gilt, with the design mounted of '102' within a crowned oval (Fig. 544). Later the plate was changed to silver, but with the same design.

Fig. 543 is the plate worn by the 1st Madras Europeans prior to 1855. The plate was gilt with the design stamped in high relief.

103RD

Fig. 545 is the brass plate worn by other ranks, 1812-1815. The plate had rounded corners; the design was stamped. Its size was $3\frac{1}{16} \times 2\frac{1}{16}$ inches.

BUTTONS

102ND

An Inspection Report dated 1781 states that the buttons were of white metal with '102'.

Fig. 546 is a flat silver button with the design in relief, which was worn *circa* 1816.

In 1830 the buttons of the Madras (European) Regiment were almost flat, single sheet, with the design of the letters 'MER' in script within a crowned garter inscribed 'Maheidpore', and with a wreath round the garter.

The buttons *circa* 1855 had the design of the Royal tiger surmounted by a crown and with the motto *Spectamur Agendo* below. The buttons were frosted and had burnished rims. In 1861 the design was '102' below a tiger and crown, with the title 'Royal Madras Fusiliers' below.

103RD

The other ranks' pewter buttons of the 103rd of 1809 had the design in relief of '103' below a crown within a single-line circle. The officers' button of this period was gilt, single sheet, flat, with the same design in relief (Fig. 547). The tunic button of 1861 had the number '103' on the ball of a grenade and the title 'Royal Bombay Fusiliers' below.

After 1881 the design was an Imperial crown on the ball of a grenade and the title 'Royal Dublin Fusiliers' below.

The Royal Dublin Fusiliers were unique in their mess waistcoat buttons, having two of separate design worn at the same time. The 1904 Dress Regulations gives them as the elephant and tiger mounted in silver.

543

544   545

546   547

THE RIFLE BRIGADE
(PRINCE CONSORT'S OWN)

TITLES

1800-1803   The Rifle Corps.
1803-1816   The 95th or Rifle Regiment.
1816-1862   The Rifle Brigade.
1862-1881   The Prince Consort's Own (Rifle Brigade).
1881-1920   Rifle Brigade (The Prince Consort's Own).

1920-   The Rifle Brigade (Prince Consort's Own).

BADGES

A Bugle-horn and Crown. The original badge of the regiment, now displayed in the centre of the regimental badge.
A French Bugle-horn. The design was worn on the headdress in the 1850's and was on the front of the officers' astrakan cap worn for many years in full dress.
A Naval Crown. Was authorized in 1951 to be associated with 'Copenhagen', which had been granted to the regiment in 1821 to commemorate the services of the Rifle Corps on board the fleet under Lord Nelson.

BATTLE HONOURS (*Dates authorized from 1815 to 1855*)
WATERLOO, 8th December, 1815.
ROLEIA,* 4th January, 1821.
VIMIERA, 4th January, 1821.
BUSACO, 4th January, 1821.
BARROSA, 4th January, 1821.
FUENTES D'ONOR, 4th January, 1821.
CIUDAD RODRIGO, 4th January, 1821.
BADAJOZ, 4th January, 1821.
SALAMANCA, 4th January, 1821.
VITTORIA, 4th January, 1821.
NIVELLE, 4th January, 1821.
NIVE, 4th January, 1821.
ORTHES, 4th January, 1821.
TOULOUSE, 4th January, 1821.
CORUNNA, 1st March, 1821.
COPENHAGEN, 22nd March, 1821.
MONTE VIDEO, 22nd March, 1821.
PENINSULA, 22nd March, 1821.
ALMA, 3rd October, 1855.
INKERMAN, 3rd October, 1855.
SEVASTOPOL, 3rd October, 1855.

---
* An Army Order in 1911 directed the spelling to be "Rolica". The old spelling has been retained on the pouch-belt plate.

THE POUCH-BELT BADGE

Fig. 548 is a silver engraved plate in the Scottish United Services Museum. The size of the plate is 2 1/16 × 2 7/8 inches.

The late Major I. H. MacKay Scobie, the curator when the plate was given to the Museum, suggested that it was the one shown as being worn by an officer of the Rifle Corps in a plate of the uniform of the regiment which appeared in the "British Military Library", but this is very improbable as, in addition to there being little similarity, the fact that it is inscribed '95' makes it later than the book.

In several of the books written by riflemen dealing with fighting in the Peninsular War, mention is made of how the wearing of bright shoulder-belt plates gave away positions, and it is unlikely that any plate would have been worn on the pouch belt, at any rate on active service. Costello, in his book "Adventures of a Soldier", writes: "The dark colour of their uniform, and the total absence of all ornaments gained them the nickname of the sweeps".

Further, in an official manuscript at the War Office entitled "The Clothing of the Infantry, 1767-1802", which gives very full details, no mention is made of such a plate; and in all prints and early miniatures of officers of the regiment which the writer has seen, the belt is only shown as having a whistle and lion's head from which hung the two silver chains which were attached to the whistle head. A miniature of Sir Neil Campbell recently given to the Regimental Museum shows clearly these ornaments. Sir Neil Campbell joined the regiment in September, 1800. It was not until about 1821 that a pouch-belt badge was finally added to the belt, probably in order to display the sixteen newly authorized Peninsular and Waterloo Honours which had been awarded to the Regiment in January of that year.

Fig. 549 is the badge worn for a short time about 1821 by the officers in silver and the staff sergeants in bronze.

The figure of Fame or "an Angel" were evidently copied from the reverse of the then recently issued Waterloo medal, in which battle the regiment was represented by three battalions. It has been stated by the late Colonel W. Verner that he had seen a miniature in which the figure of Fame appeared alone on the belt without the rest of the badge, but unfortunately he left no further details about the picture.

The cross adopted to display the Battle Honours was a copy of that of the Order of the Bath. The Order had been enlarged in 1815, and the first to be made a Grand Commander under the new arrangement was the Duke of Wellington, who had been appointed Colonel-in-Chief of the regiment in 1820. The badge was evidently adopted by the regiment as a compliment to its new Colonel-in-Chief. The badge when first worn was a faithful representation of the Bath cross, having the lions between the limbs of the cross, all facing one way and having knobs on the points of the limbs, while in the centre round the bugle-horn was a circle inscribed with the title of the regiment; all this was within a wreath of laurel, which was again identical with the Bath cross. According to Cope's History of the regiment, the figure of Fame was replaced for a short time by an eagle, but there has never been any actual proof of this; nor has an actual badge with a Royal crown, which Cope also states was worn by officers for a time, come to light, although this was worn in bronze by staff sergeants for some years.

In the paintings of uniforms, 1832, by Drahonet at Windsor Castle, both officer and colour-sergeants are shown wearing a pouch-belt plate with the crown and cross in gilt metal and the wreath in silver. It is doubtful if this is correct.

About 1822-1823 the design of the cross was made more on the lines of that of the Guelphic Order. The wreath in the centre was omitted and the arrangement of the lions changed to that of the Guelphic Order, and an eight-looped crown was adopted (Fig. 550). This crown was peculiar for many years to Light Cavalry and Rifles. In the case of the Rifle Brigade it was retained until 1902. As new Honours were awarded to the regiment they were added to the cross and wreath, except in the case of the three Crimean Honours which when first given were displayed on scrolls below the wreath for a short time.

When in 1926 the question arose as to how to display the Honours for the First World War, owing to the crowded state of the badge, it was decided to only show three, and the opportunity was taken to obtain permission for the original arrangement of the lions to be reverted to. Until about 1870 whistle chains had been two in number; they had become very long and it had become the custom to twist them round the belt. They were then made into three lengths.

The coronet and cypher of H.R.H. Field-Marshal The Duke of Connaught were placed on the buttons, in addition to the bugle-horn in August, 1939, to commemorate the long connection of His Royal Highness with the regiment of which he had been Colonel-in-Chief since 1880, and in which he had previously served as a captain and had commanded the 1st Battalion.

BUTTONS

A manuscript book in the War Office Library entitled "Clothing of the Infantry, 1767-1802" describes the button for the officers' full dress coat as "a flat plated button having the design of a raised Bugle Horn and a Crown over it". The buttons for other ranks are almost certainly to have been of pewter; they are mentioned as being "Small throughout, very much raised with the design engraved". The buttons on the service uniform of the officers appear to have been plain silver ball buttons. Whether in 1803 the number '95' was placed between the cords of the bugle-horn is not certain.

When in 1816 the regiment became the Rifle Brigade the letters 'RB' were placed between the cords on both officers' and other ranks' buttons. In the Regimental Museum is a court dress uniform worn by an officer of the regiment who retired in 1818. The buttons are silver, convex, closed backs, with the design in low relief of the bugle-horn, crown and letters 'RB'. A similar uniform worn by the Duke of Wellington has buttons as shown in Fig. 552; the buttons were almost flat, single sheet, and of silver.

In 1832 the officers' black metal buttons were worn and the strings of the bugle-horn, instead of going into the crown, were finished in a bow, while above the crown was the title 'Rifle Brigade' and below the bugle-horn a spray of laurel. Later the cords of the bugle-horn were again changed and shown with two ends hanging down between the cords. The other ranks' buttons retained the older design for many years (Fig. 553). From 1881 until 1928 a black button was worn by other ranks with the design of a bugle-horn, with a bow between the cords and the crown.

This was replaced in 1928 by a regimental button of the same design, but with the letters 'RB' between the cords.

In 1939 H.R.H. The Duke of Connaught's coronet and cypher was placed on the buttons in conjunction with the bugle-horn (Fig. 554).

331

THE ROYAL ARMY SERVICE CORPS

TITLES

1794-1795	Corps of Royal Waggoners.
1799-1802	Royal Waggon Corps.
1802-1833	Royal Waggon Train.
1851-1857	Land Transport Corps.
1856-1869	The Military Train.
1859-1869	The Commissariat Staff Corps.
1864-1875	The Control Department.
1875-1880	The Commissariat and Transport Department.
1880-1888	The Commissariat and Transport Staff.
1869-1881	The Army Service Corps.
1881-1888	The Commissariat and Transport Corps.
1888-1918	The Army Service Corps.
1918-	The Royal Army Service Corps.

BADGE

A star of eight points, in the centre the initials of the Corps within a garter inscribed with the motto *Honi soit qui mal y pense*, a wreath of laurel leaves around and a crown above. This design was authorized in 1894.

The following information on the badge has been sent to the author by the Curator and Librarian, the R.A.S.C. Museum.

The Corps badge dates back to the formation of the Corps in 1888, its form being quite different from its predecessor, C. & T.C. It was an eight-pointed star surmounted by the Royal crown (Queen's); inset with the Royal cypher 'VR' surrounded by a scroll 'Army Service Corps' and bearing the motto 'For Queen and Country'.

In August, 1892, a commitee representative of all ranks sat under the presidency of Colonel E. Grattan and decided to change the motto to *Nil sine labore.*

In February, 1895, the Royal cypher was deleted and a monogram 'ASC' was put in its place. The scroll 'Army Service Corps' was removed and a garter with *Honi soit qui mal y pense* within a wreath appeared. There was a space between the garter scroll and the wreath.

In April, 1903, the Corps Journal gave the badge and said: "We made official application to the War Office and were informed that the new Officers' Pouch Ornament represents the badge, and, when this was made, special care was taken to make it heraldically correct."

A further change was made in 1918 consequent to the Royal honour, and the 'ASC' monogram was replaced by the Royal cypher, once more 'GR' with a small 'v' between the two letters. The garter scroll had a different kind of clasp, and there was another scroll with the title 'Royal Army Service Corps' on it.

BATTLE HONOURS (*Authorized for the Royal Waggon Train*)
PENINSULA, 6th April, 1815.
WATERLOO, 6th April, 1815.

SHOULDER-BELT PLATES

Fig. 555 is of the shoulder-belt plate worn *circa* 1800. The plate was gilt with the design engraved.

BUTTONS

The officers' silver buttons of the Royal Waggon Train had the design of the Royal cypher below a crown with the title round the edge. The Commissariat Staff buttons were gilt and had the design of a star of eight points, in the centre of which was a crown.

The early ones were single sheet, slightly convex, with open backs; they were replaced by buttons of a similar design, but almost flat and with closed backs and with a rim. The surface of the button was frosted. This design was retained on the tunic button.

The Military Train button was of a simple design, a crown with 'Military' above and 'Train' below; the button had a scalloped rim. The Control, the Commissariat, and the Commissariat and Transport Staff had dead gilt buttons with the design of the Royal crest within a garter inscribed with the title in the case of the first two and with a circle in the case of the Commissariat and Transport Staff. The buttons had burnished scalloped rims.

The Army Service Corps button had the Royal cypher within a crowned circle; the circle had beaded edges and the button no rim.

In 1902 this was replaced by one with the Corps badge design, but in 1948 the older design of the Royal cypher within a crowned circle inscribed with the title was resumed.

555

556   557   558

559   560   561

THE ROYAL ARMY MEDICAL CORPS

TITLES

1873   Army Medical Staff. Before this date Medical officers had been part of the establishment of each regiment. The first regular appointment of medical officers to serve in field and general hospitals appears to have been in the Peninsular War.

1855-1884   The Army Hospital Corps. This corps was merged into the Medical Staff Corps in 1884.

1855-1857   Medical Staff Corps.

1884-1898   Army Medical Department.

1804-1898   Medical Staff Corps.

1898-   Army Medical Staff and Royal Army Medical Corps. Now one corps under the latter title.

BADGES

The Army Hospital Corps had as its badge the Red Cross on a white ground. The Royal Arms above a scroll inscribed with the title.

Within a laurel wreath surmounted by a crown, the Rod of Æsculapius with a Serpent entwined. Authorized in 1898.

BUTTONS

During the period 1830-1837 the Medical Staff button was flat, single sheet, dead gilt, with the Royal cypher 'WR' intertwined and reversed above 'IV' within a crowned garter inscribed 'Medical Staff', all on a cut star; the button had a raised burnished rim. This button was followed by a gilt convex button with closed back and the design of a lined cross within a circle inscribed 'Medical Staff', all within a star of eight points.

After 1837 the button became convex with closed back; the same design was retained but for the change of the Royal cypher and the title being displayed on a circle instead of a garter. The star was much sharper. Later the star became broader and the title was once more shown on a garter. The button of the Army Medical Department, 1883, had the same design but for the title being on a circle.

Gilt, convex, almost flat, with the design of the Royal cypher 'GR' within a crowned circle inscribed 'Hospital Staff', all on a star of eight points. Later this design was on a convex button with a closed back.

The button with the Rod of Æsculapius was taken into use in 1898.

562

563

564

565

THE ROYAL ARMY ORDNANCE CORPS

The history of the Royal Army Ordnance Corps is the most involved of any unit of the British Army; sometimes a Military organization, at other times civil.

The first official entry concerning the Board of Ordnance is in 1418, when John Louth is given as Clerk of the Ordnance.

In 1877 came into existence the Ordnance Store Branch, followed in 1881 by the Ordnance Store Corps, which in 1896 became the Army Ordnance Corps and was formed by an amalgamation of the Store Companies of the A.S.C. and the Ordnance Store Branch.

The title 'Royal' was authorized in 1918.

BADGES

Motto: *Sua tela tonanti* adopted in 1927.

The Ordnance Arms was the original badge of the Corps.

The Royal Crest within a garter inscribed 'Ordnance' was worn for many years on the buttons of the Ordnance Store Department. In 1927 the badge of the Ordnance Arms within a crowned garter inscribed *Honi soit qui mal y pense* was adopted.

This was replaced by one with the Ordnance Arms surmounted by a crown and with the title 'Royal Army Ordnance Corps' round the edge.

Recently another type has been adopted with the Ordnance Arms surmounted by a crown, the title being omitted.

The mess jacket button has the design mounted in silver.

566

APPENDIX
THE STANLEY COMMITTEE
Comd. Number 2793

Colonel Stanley's Committee, 1877, recommended that the connection should be more clearly drawn between the Line Battalions of a Brigade and the Militia Battalions of a Sub-District, and that "We consider that this is best to be effected by their being treated as one regiment, such regiment wearing a Territorial designation; the Line Battalions being the 1st and 2nd; the Militia Battalions the 3rd and 4th, etc., of such Territorial regiment; the Depot being common to all, and being the last battalion of the series."

In February, 1881, the Ellice Committee on the Formation of Territorial Regiments as proposed by Colonel Stanley's Committee made the following suggestions regarding affiliation of regiments and titles, some of which appear in the official Army List for a few months after July of that year.

1	The Lothian Regiment (Royal Scots).
2	The West Surrey Regiment (Queen's Royal).
3	The Kentish Regiment (The Buffs).
4	The Royal Lancaster Regiment (King's Own).
5	The Northumberland Regiment (Fusiliers).
6	The Royal Warwickshire Regiment.
7	The City of London Regiment (Royal Fusiliers).
8	The Liverpool Regiment (The King's).
9	The Norfolk Regiment.
10	The Lincolnshire Regiment.
11	The Devonshire Regiment.
12	The Suffolk and Cambridge Regiment.
13	The Somersetshire Regiment (Prince Albert's Light Infantry).
14	The West Yorkshire Regiment (Prince of Wales' Own).
15	The East Yorkshire Regiment.
16	The Bedfordshire Regiment.
17 and 45	The Leicester and Notts Regiment (Sherwood Foresters).
18	The East Munster Regiment (Royal Irish).
19	North Yorkshire Regiment (Princess of Wales' Own).
20	The East Lancashire Regiment (Fusiliers).
21	The Ayrshire and Border Regiment (Royal Scots Fusiliers).
22	Cheshire Regiment.
23	The North Wales Regiment (Royal Welsh Fusiliers).
24	South Wales Regiment (Borderers).
25	York Regiment (King's Own Borderers).
26 and 74	The Scotch Rifles.
27 and 108	The Inniskilling Regiment.
28 and 61	The Gloucestershire Regiment.
29 and 36	The Worcester and Hereford Regiment.
30 and 59	West Lancashire Regiment.
31 and 70	The East Surrey Regiment.
32 and 46	The Cornwall Regiment (Duke of Cornwall's Light Infantry).
33 and 76	Halifax Regiment (Duke of Wellington's).
34 and 55	The Cumberland and Westmoreland Regiment.
35 and 107	The Royal Sussex Regiment.
37 and 67	The Hampshire Regiment.
38 and 80	The North Staffordshire Regiment.
39 and 75	The Dorsetshire Regiment.
40 and 82	The South Lancashire Regiment (Prince of Wales' Volunteers).
41 and 69	The Welsh Regiment.
42 and 79	The Black Watch and Cameron Royal Highland Regiment (Queen's Own).
43 and 53	The Shropshire Regiment (Light Infantry).
44 and 56	The Essex Regiment.
47 and 81	The North Lancashire Regiment.
48 and 58	The Northampton and Rutland Regiment.
49 and 66	The Berkshire Regiment (Princess Charlotte of Wales).

50 and 97	The Royal West Kent Regiment (Queen's Own).
51 and 105	South Yorkshire Regiment (King's Own Light Infantry).
52 and 85	Oxford and Bucks Regiment (Light Infantry).
54 and 95	The Derbyshire Regiment.
57 and 77	The Middlesex Regiment (The Duke of Cambridge's Own).
60	The King's Royal Rifle Corps.
62 and 99	The Wiltshire Regiment (The Duke of Edinburgh's).
63 and 96	The Manchester Regiment.
64 and 98	The South Staffordshire Regiment.
65 and 84	The Hallamshire Regiment (York and Lancaster).
68 and 106	The Durham Regiment (Light Infantry).
71 and 78	The Inverness and Ross Regiment (Highland Light Infantry).
72 and 91	The Seaforth and Argyle Regiment (Princess Louise's Highlanders).
73 and 90	The Clydesdale Regiment (Light Infantry).
83 and 86	The Royal Irish Rifles.
87 and 88	The Connaught Regiment (Royal Irish Fusiliers).
89 and 94	The Ulster Regiment (Princess Victoria's).
92 and 93	The Gordon and Sutherland Highland Regiment.
100 and 109	The Leinster Regiment (The Prince of Wales's Royal Canadians).
101 and 104	The Royal West Munster Regiment (Fusiliers).
102 and 103	The Royal Dublin Regiment (Fusiliers).
	Rifle Brigade (Prince Consort's Own).

BIBLIOGRAPHY

"Records and Badges of the British Army," by Major H. M. Chichester and Major G. Burges-Short (Aldershot, 1895). 2nd Edition, 1900.

"Regimental Badges Worn in the British Army One Hundred Years Ago," by Edward Almack, F.S.A. (London, 1900).

"A History of the Uniform of the British Army," by C. C. P. Lawson. 2 Vols. (London, 1940).

"The British Military Library." 2 Vols. (London, 1799-1800).

Many Regimental Histories contain details of Belt Plates and Buttons worn in their respective Regiments, and the following are especially helpful:

"The Regimental Records of The Royal Scots," compiled by J. C. Leask and Captain H. M. McCance (Dublin, 1915).

"The King's Own: The Story of a Royal Regiment," by Colonel L. I. Cowper (Oxford, 1939).

"Historical Records of the Royal Fusiliers," by Lieutenant-Colonel P. Groves (Guernsey, 1903).

"History of the 12th (The Suffolk) Regiment, 1685-1913," by Lieutenant-Colonel E. A. H. Webb (London, 1914).

"History of the Somerset Light Infantry (Prince Albert's), 1685-1914," by Major-General Sir H. Everett (London, 1934).

"The Leicestershire Regiment," by Lieutenant-Colonel E. A. H. Webb (London, 1911).

"The Royal Inniskilling Fusiliers from December 1688 to July 1914" (London, 1928).

"The South Staffordshire Regiment," by J. P. Jones (Wolverhampton, 1923).

"A History of the Services of the 41st (The Welch) Regiment," by Lieutenant and Adjutant D. A. N. Lomax (Devonport, 1899).

"History of The Northamptonshire Regiment, 1742-1934," by Lieutenant-Colonel Russell Gurney (Aldershot, 1935).

"The History of the 50th or (The Queen's Own) Regiment," by Colonel Fyler (London, 1895).

"The History of The King's Own Yorkshire Light Infantry," by Colonel H. C. Wylly (London, *n.d.*).

"The Annals of the King's Royal Rifle Corps:" Appendix dealing with Uniform, Armament and Equipment, by S. M. Milne and Major-General Astley Terry (London, 1913).

"History of The Royal Irish Rifles," by Lieutenant-Colonel George Brenton Laurie (Aldershot, 1914).

"The Connaught Rangers," by Lieutenant-Colonel H. F. N. Jourdain and E. Fraser (?), Vol. II (R.U.S.I., 1926).

"Neill's 'Blue Caps' (Royal Dublin Fusiliers)," by Colonel H. C. Wylly, 3 Vols. (Aldershot, *c.* 1922).

"The Predecessors of the Royal Army Service Corps," by Colonel C. H. Massee (Aldershot, 1948).

MSS. Notes by the late Mr. Hastings Irwin at the R.U.S.I.

MSS. Books by the late Mr. P. W. Reynolds in the Victoria and Albert Museum, Kensington.

The *Journal of the Society for Army Historical Research*.

The *Badge Collectors' Quarterly* (The Journal of the Badge Collectors Society). Edited by Major H. P. E. Pereira, E.R.D., F.S.A. (Scots.), F.M.A.

Regimental Journals, Magazines and Chronicles.